THE ADMINISTRATION OF THE MUGHUL EMPIRE

THE ADMINISTRATION OF THE MUGHUL EMPIRE

BY

ISHTIAQ HUSAIN QURESHI

KALPAZ

ISBN: 978-93-5128-809-1(HB)

First Published in 1973
Indian Reprint in 2017

Published by

Kalpaz Publications
C-30, Satyawati Nagar,
Delhi – 110052
E-mail: kalpaz@hotmail.com
Website: kalpazpublications.com
Ph.: +91-9212142040

Cataloging in Publication Data—DK
Courtesy: D.K. Agencies (P) Ltd. <docinfo@dkagencies.com>

Qureshi, Ishtiaq Husain, author.
The administration of the Mughul Empire / by Ishtiaq Husain Qureshi.
Pages cm
"First published in 1973"—Title page verso.
Includes bibliographical references and index.
ISBN 9789351288091

1. Mogul Empire—Politics and government. 2. India—History—1526-1765. I. Title.

DS461.Q7 2017 DDC 954.025 23

PREFACE

THIS BOOK is intended to be a companion volume to my earlier work *The Administration of the Sultanate of Dehli*. Unlike it, however, this is far from being a pioneer effort. There are several full length studies of the Mughul administration. Indeed there are books on some topics which form only chapters in this treatise. I am, therefore, fully conscious of my temerity in writing a new book on this subject. The explanation is that, in all humility, I feel that another book will not be superfluous. A number of controversial problems have been discussed in greater detail and I hope that a more satisfactory interpretation of the available data has been offered. Besides, an attempt has been made to create greater synthesis in the data and to bring out the logical correlation among the different institutions. Thus, I hope, an integrated picture of the administration has emerged.

This study has taken a long time to take shape. It has slowly emerged from lectures given to post-graduate classes in four universities. Several generations of critical students have contributed to my understanding of the subject. Indeed the idea of writing a book on it did not occur to me until I began to feel that I had given so much thought to the various features of the Mughul administration that it would be wasteful not to commit my thoughts and conclusions to writing.

No effort has been made to include all the available details into the study. In view of the extensive nature of the accessible material, this would have been impossible. Besides, it would have marred the general effect and the book would have read like a dictionary of Mughul administrative jargon. However, the availability of these details has helped me in understanding the nature of the institutions. Nevertheless the attempt has been to describe the mansion, not to count its bricks.

This book has taken an inordinately long time to write. The selection of data that should be included is in itself time consuming as there is a natural reluctance to discard information that has taken time to collect. Then long periods of other preoccupations have intervened when the work had to be set aside to find time for more pressing undertakings or duties. It is hoped that the book does not bear scars of long postponements.

I. H. QURESHI

CONTENTS

Page

CONTENTS

Note on Transliteration

The following system has been used:

(i) For Arabic and Persian letters:—

ا	= a	ر	= r	ف	= f
ب	= b	ز	= z	ق	= q
پ	= p	ژ	= zh	ک	= k
ت	= t	س	= s	گ	= g
ث	= th	ش	= sh	ل	= l
ج	= j	ص	= ṣ	م	= m
چ	= ch	ض	= ḍ	ن	= n
ح	= ḥ	ط	= ṭ	و	= w
خ	= kh	ظ	= ẓ	ه	= h
د	= d	ع	= ʿ	ء	= ʾ
ذ	= dh	غ	= gh	ی	= y

Vowel signs :—

Short vowels =a, i, u,

Long vowels =ā, ī, ū, e, o,

diphthongs, in accordance with the pronunciation;

(ii) Hindi words used by Persian chronicles are transliterated in their Persian form *e.g.*, patwarī instead of paṭwarī.

(iii) No attempt has been made to transliterate well-known words like sultan, Hindu, etc.

CHAPTER I

Introductory

THE development of political and administrative institutions during the Muslim rule in the subcontinent of India and Pakistan was undisturbed and continuous. The frequent changes in dynasties were mere ripples on the surface under which the stream of life flowed steadily. Even when the Sultanate was overwhelmed by centrifugal forces and broke into fragments, the administrative institutions were not changed, only the quality of administration was affected. Therefore, we find that with the restoration of the central authority in the northern areas under the Sūrs, the institutions asserted themselves more vigorously. It is now generally conceded that Akbar's administration owed a great deal to Sher Shāh, hence the point need not be laboured any further. It is unnecessary to argue that the administrative institutions of the Mughul Empire were mostly a continuation of the administration of the Sultanate with some alterations and improvements, which form the subject matter of this volume.

The changes began to be introduced by Akbar and therefore the death of his father Humāyūn (1556) has been chosen as the starting date for this study. This is also convenient for the reason that a previous work of the present author deals with the institutions of the Muslim Empire in the subcontinent upto that year. The concluding date has been fixcd at 1707 when 'Ālamgīr I died and the Empire began to decline rapidly. The administrative institutions did not die suddenly. With the increasing weakness of the central authority they gradually lost their vigour and many of them were swept away by the flood of anarchy that engulfed the land destroying the patient work of several centuries. Yet, all was not lost, because at the provincial and local levels wherever some authority continued to exist, many of the old institutions survived. Some of them were taken up by the British who supplanted the Mughuls. It is surprising how many of the administrative institutions of the present day India and Pakistan, after all that has happened during the last two centuries and a half, have their roots in the Muslim past. Nevertheless the death of 'Ālamgīr I marks the end of an epoch and it is convenient to stop there. This has the advantage of studying institutions when they were vigorous and their utility was not marred by decadent incompetence and inefficiency.

This period differs from the Sultanate in one important respect. During these one hundred and fifty one years it was one dynasty that ruled the realm. It is true that the death of a monarch was often a signal for civil war, but the contestants were scions of the same family. And they fought for themselves: they were not puppets in the hands of ambitious nobles. The nobles allied themselves with princes of their choice, in whose service they hoped to attain their own objects, but the nobles themselves were not aspirants to the throne itself. The prestige of the family was so well established that no outsider could dream of questioning its sole right to provide the monarch. Even when, after 1707, the power of the emperor declined and when some princes were merely puppets in the hands of ambitious disruptionists of imperial authority, the right of the dynasty to reign over the realm was not questioned, so much so that when the Marathas and the British usurped imperial authority, they continued to rule in the name of the Great Mughul. It was only after the power of the Muslims had been sufficiently broken that the British decided to do away with the pretence of Mughul sovereignty.

Several factors contributed to the success of the Mughuls in establishing their dynasty so firmly. The Sultanate had existed in stormy times. The Mongol inroads had unsettled the world of Islam. The Sultanate could not afford the luxury of dynastic stability because it needed strong men of action to meet the challenge. When, with the conversion of the Mongols to Islam and their adoption of civilized ways, the challenge seemed to weaken, it did not result in accession to the strength of any dynasty. It only produced disintegration. Provincial dynasties prospered, but Dehlī itself fell a prey to discord and conflict. In any case the feeling that the danger had disappeared was only a delusion. Tīmūr's invasion in 1398 demonstrated the fact that the zeal for conquest had not exhausted itself in central Asia. When the forces of law and order once again began to assert themselves and the Lodīs began to succeed in extending their authority, they were thwarted by Bābur's invasion in 1526. The lesson learnt by the Lodīs was forgotten by the Sūrs, whose lack of cohesion and incapacity to unite gave Humāyūn his second opportunity in 1555.

By the time Akbar established himself firmly, a balance of power emerged in the region. The Mughuls, the Ṣafawīs and the Uzbegs were well established and each one of these was suspicious of the intentions of the other two. The Ṣafawīs had discovered, as the Mughuls were to discover later, that a central Asian adventure was not paying. The Uzbegs had been punished severely by the Ṣafawīs when Shaibānī Khān and Shāh Ismā'īl had tried their strength. The Mughuls had a wholesome respect for the Ṣafawīs as well because of their experience in Qandahār which they finally lost to Iran in 1653. The Mughuls exercised considerable vigilance and were rewarded by the disinclination of their neighbours to undertake an invasion of their territories. The respite from external invasions was a source of great strength to the Mughuls, because all their resources could be diverted to the conquest of the subcontinent and the consolidation of their power.

The establishment of the manṣabdārī system, which gradually eliminated tribal chiefs as nuclei of power and possible intrigue, and its successful working made it possible for the emperor to assert himself more fully. The tribal element was not completely eliminated. For instance the Rajput nobles had a large number of ancestoral adherents and a quasi feudal system to back them. Yet such elements were counter-balanced by others. Through the manṣabdārī system, the habit of looking upon the emperor as the source of all advancement and honour came to be established, which grew into a strong tradition. The Mughuls successfully adopted the strategem of balancing one group against another and making each one dependent upon themselves.

Yet another factor was that under the Sultans the Muslim population, surrounded by danger on all sides, was aware of the need of strong men to defend it from external invasion and local rebellions. It realized the importance of successful generals and was in no mood to tolerate weaklings, even though they might have a better claim to the throne. With the employment of a much larger number of Hindu generals and soldiers under the Mughuls, this reliance upon the Muslim warriors was weakened and its place was taken by a dependence upon the emperor who controlled the warriors and their leaders. It was for this reason that the Muslim masses were lulled into a false sense of security and awoke to the stark reality of the loss of political power when it was too late. It was to deceive them that the Marathas and the British had alike made a pretence of deriving their authority from the emperor.

The good government that the Mughuls gave their empire was no small a factor in winning the affection of the people. As the entire administration was centred in the monarch who looked into every detail himself, his person came to embody the hopes of peaceful existence, justice and prosperity. The Mughul ideals of benevolence, justice and good government secured stability for their dynasty.

The most important factor, however, was the ability of the dynasty to produce, in the course of a century and a half, four capable men who understood the problems of their government and had the energy to enforce their policies. The only period in which the monarch was not able to devote all his attention was when, during his last years, Jahāngīr's health broke down. His ministers, however, maintained their grip on the administration. The dynasty was served by some good ministers. Several names like those of I'timād-u'd-dawlah, Sa'd-u'llah Khān and Mīr Jumlah stand out for their efficiency and wisdom.

It would be useful here to give a brief historical survey of the period so that the background against which the Mughul administrative institutions functioned may be properly understood.

When Humāyūn recovered Dehlī in 1555 after the Sūr interregnum he was by no means the master of his former territories. When he died in 1556, Akbar succeeded to a throne which was insecure. Humāyūn had died when the major part of the Sūr Empire was still unconquered. With a boy of thirteen years as Humāyūn's successor and the chronic disunity in the Mughul camp, the chances of a full restoration of the Mughul authority would have been meagre but for two factors. The first of these was the disunity in the Afghān ranks who were not able to unite their resources. The second was the presence in the Mughul camp of a capable general and statesman, Bairam Khān to whom goes the credit of managing Akbar's affairs in a manner that gave the young monarch a good start in his career of consolidation and conquest.

Akbar spent five momentous years under the tutelage of Bairam Khān, after which he asserted himself. When the emperor took over, his earlier waywardness was replaced by a seriousness of purpose that brought him large gains in territory. He succeeded in extending the frontiers of his empire to include the areas that constitute the present day countries of Afghanistan and Pakistan and the whole of northern and central India with some fringes of the Deccan. A line drawn a little to the north of Ahmadnagar to south of Cuttack from coast to coast roughly defined the southern marches of his empire. This was no mean achievement in itself, but when one thinks of the successful efforts at consolidating and improving the administration of this vast area, one is struck by the greatness of the constructive genius of Akbar. It does not in any way detract from the greatness of the monarch to state that he was helped by the centripetal forces that had been trying to assert themselves for some time. The anarchy following in the wake of the collapse of the Sultanate of Dehlī a little before Fīrūz S͟hāh's death in 1388 and Tīmūr's invasion in 1398 had left the people exhausted and the Lodīs as well as the Sūrs were helped in the establishment of large states by the willingness of the people to give allegiance to anyone who would give them protection. Internal feuds among the rulers and foreign interventions broke the empires of the Lodīs and the Sūrs, but when a capable monarch like Akbar came on the scene, he was able to take advantage of the situation. For this he had to curb his nobles and set up a military machine and an administrative organization that would be completely at his beck and call.

However, Akbar succeeded too well He became so powerful that resistance to his will became impossible. With the growth of the monarch's authority, the power of the Muslim community declined to a degree that the earlier sense of responsibility as the mainstay of the polity was replaced by comparative indifference and, in certain circles, even by political irresponsibility. Akbar's own eclecticism and his lack of philosophic discipline turned him into an active and powerful opponent of orthodoxy. Because of his policies, heterodox and non-Muslim elements of the population gained an ascendancy for which the Muslims had to pay a stupendous penalty. All the waywardness that he had shown in his youth now concentrated itself in his religious beliefs and his own views were so confused and contradictory that they do little credit to him. The public and political results of these views were destructive in the extreme.

In other fields the reign was remarkable because, through the prosperity that good administration brought in its wake, rapid strides were made in the field of culture. Painting, architecture, music, poetry and *belles-lettres* thrived and have left magnificent memorials for posterity.

Akbar was succeeded by his son Salim who assumed the title of Jahāngīr. He had been a little petulant towards the end of Akbar's reign because he had felt that his position as heir apparent should have been recognized by some visible enhancement in his rank and responsibilities. His so called rebellion was more a show of his dissatisfaction with his father's treatment of him rather than revolt and he had no intention of seriously questioning his father's authority. Akbar had shown greater favour to Salīm's son Khusraw, to the extent that a faction had come to support his ambitions to the throne. This ultimately proved the undoing of Khusraw, but during the last days of Akbar's life it proved a real threat to Salīm. He, however, succeeded in securing the support of a sufficiently strong group to ensure his ascent to the throne. In return he had to give an assurance that he would not pursue Akbar's policies which had resulted in weakening the hold of orthodox Islam in the government.

Some later writers have painted Jahāngīr as a besotted drunkard who cared little for the affairs of the state and even less for Islam. This picture is grossly unfair to the monarch. It can be easily proved that he took an active interest in the administration of his empire so long as his health remained sound. It was only during the last few years, when his health broke down, that his active interest decreased and the administration was carried on by others. Similarly in matters of religion, he was a believing Muslim and supported the cause of orthodoxy. His tolerance of other faiths was misunderstood by foreigners like Sir Thomas Roe as unbelief, because in their own lands they were not used to such broadmindedness. They could not understand that a believer need not be intolerant.

Jahāngīr did not forget his own feelings when his father had failed to accord due recognition to his position as the heir apparent. He, therefore, bestowed the title of Shāh Jahān on Prince Khurram and gave him the unprecedented rank of thirty thousand. However, when the government came under the influence of Nūr

Jahān, she created difficulties for Shāh Jahān who was left with no choice but that of rebellion, which was crushed and it seemed that his chances of ever regaining sufficient power to contest the succession had been irretrievably damaged. However, at the crucial time, through the support of his father-in-law, Āṣaf Khān, he succeeded in defeating Nūr Jahān's nominee Shahryār, who had no talent for ruling.

Jahāngīr did not introduce any remarkable reforms in the administration. Efforts to bring about improvement are on record. The monarch's benevolent nature found an expression in trying to secure for the people a just and well run administration. He was a great patron of painting in which he had a refined and cultivated taste. Under him the Mughul school of miniature painting reached the zenith of its progress.

Shāh Jahān's reign has been rightly looked upon as the golden age of the Mughul Empire. Until the beginning of the war of succession, there was peace in the realm. A great wazīr, Sa'd-u'llah Khān, ran the administration with prudence and ability. A number of changes were brought about in the administrative institutions which will find mention later. This brought about a visible increase in general prosperity, which is reflected in the architectural achievements of the reign. Mughul architecture reached the climax of its excellence under Shāh Jahān who gave posterity buildings like the world famous Tāj Maḥal, the Jāmi' Masjid of Dehlī, the exquisite Pearl Mosque of Agra and the romantic pavilions of the palace fortress, Lāl Qil'ah of Dehlī. It is about these buildings that it has been said that the Mughuls built like Titans and finished like jewellers. In this reign red sandstone was replaced by marble and tessellation by *pietra dura.* The same impression of richness is conveyed by the introduction of gold and gold ornamentation in the miniatures and manuscripts. Life was characterized by unparallelled elegance and luxury. The splendour of the imperial and provincial courts under Shāh Jahān dazzled all foreign visitors, whether Asian or European.

When 'Ālamgīr came to the throne, forces of decay began slowly to assert themselves. Indeed the reign of Shāh Jahān gives to the historian the impression of a ripe fruit ready to fall from the tree at the first gust of the wind. It sprang up like a gentle breeze under Ālamgīr I and then developed into a hurricane. The centrifugal forces, always present in the political life of the subcontinent, began to raise their head in the form of rebellions and disorders. In the beginning it was not difficult to deal with them. The Maratha trouble, however, was of a different nature. The Marathas had been employed as hardy and useful soldiers by earlier Muslim rulers, but with the decline in the power of the rulers of Bījāpūr and Golconda they discovered that defiance of authority, after all, was not too difficult.

The ambitious Shīvājī, the son of a trusted noble of the Bījāpūr court, found brigandage and rebellion more profitable than service of the state. This was the beginning of the avalanche that destroyed the Mughul Empire and plunged the subcontinent into anarchy for more than a century. To 'Ālamgīr I goes the credit of fighting the storm with great courage and determination. He almost succeeded in overcoming it. He might have succeeded if he had been supported by his officers more loyally and if his policies had been followed by his successors. But corruption and treachery stalked in his camp and after his death, some selfish nobles made common cause with the Marathas, thus digging the grave of Muslim rule in the subcontinent.

'Ālamgīr showed his administrative acumen while anarchy had yet not drawn him and his forces into its vortex. In spite of the tremendous drain on the resources of the empire and his military preoccupations, he did not permit his administration to fall a prey to disorganization or disintegration. Indeed the prosecution of a prolonged and expensive war would have been impossible but for the proper functioning of the administration. It was not the administration alone that suffered. Both architecture and painting succumed and though some good buildings like the Pādshāhī Mosque at Lahore and scores of paintings of 'Ālamgīr's reign have come down to us, they do not hold a mirror to Shāh Jahān's contribution.

This work deals with the political and administrative institutions of the Mughul Empire, and their development from earlier origins will be discussed in their context. It, would, however, be useful to give a preliminary outline here.

The Mughul Empire was *de jure* as well as *de facto* an independent state. The emperor, styled as pādshāh, was recognized as the caliph within his realm. He, therefore, owned no allegiance to the Ottoman caliphs who claimed to have inherited the mantle from the Abbasid caliphs of Egypt The emperor was vested with the supreme political authority and his writ could be questioned only through rebellion. As legally he was looked upon as caliph as well, rebellion against the monarch was looked upon as sinful by Muslims. Only when he openly transgressed the law of Islam, could rebellion be legally justified. He was subservient to shar', the Muslim law and had no authority to amend or annul it. His actions could be questioned in a court of law. However, because the empire contained a majority of non-Muslims some of whom were powerful, the monarch could ally himself with them and escape retribution for his cold shouldering the law. In addition there were heterodox groups among the Muslims as well who were interes ed in weakening the power of orthodox Islam. Akbar demonstrated how the upholders of orthodoxy could be humiliated. However, even he did not succeed in eliminating the orthodox elements completely from the seats of power and towards the end of the reign they had revived sufficiently to impose their terms on Jahāngir. Thus there were limits beyond which it was impossible for the monarch to go in his disregard for the Muslim law. It so happened that Jahāngir restored the institutions of orthodoxy and Shāh Jahān and 'Ālamgir I were pious and orthodox monarchs.

The highest post in the empire which a subject could hold was theoretically that of the wakil-u's-saltanah. As monarchs were averse to the delegation of much authority, the post first lost its glamour and then fell into disuse. The wazir as the head of the financial administration gained in importance. He came more popularly to be styled as diwān. He had several assistants of ministerial rank under him, whose functions will be discussed later. Another important officer was the bakhshī-i-mumālik, also called the first bakhshī who was in charge of military administration as well as intelligence. It was the first bakhshī who was responsible for the smooth working of the manṣabdārī system. The military and executive servants of the state were grouped into a complex system of grading called the manṣabdārī system in which recruitment and promotion were strictly on the basis of merit. The Imperial Household was separately organized. A number of functions which in reality were of public and administrative importance were also attached to it.

Justice and ḥisbah were organized on traditional orthodox lines. The administration of justice was divided into three categories: siyāsat, maẓālim and qaḍā. The first dealt with military and political offences, the second with cases arising out of the dealings of public servants with the public, and the third with ordinary criminal and civil suits. These courts were differently organized. Qaḍā, ḥisbah and religious affairs were under the ṣadr-u'ṣ-ṣudūr who was also the supreme judge of the empire and in this capacity was called qāḍī-u'l-quḍāt. The mīr 'adl dealt with executive matters relating to justice like the production of litigants in the courts and implementing their orders.

The provincial government was modelled on the lines of the central government. The various departments were reproduced and directly corresponded with their central counterparts under whose general direction they worked. The head of the provincial government was the sipah-sālār who later came to be called ṣūbahdār. The local government was primarily based in the parganah which was a collection of dehs or villages. The parganah was under an 'āmil who was mainly concerned with revenue matters. The organization of the parganah administration underwent considerable change which will be described at the proper place. Between the parganah and the province were interposed sarkārs under fawjdārs whose main duty was the maintenance of peace. The sarkār was for some time an administrative unit as well.

Sri Ram Sharma has given a fairly full description of the source material on this period in his *A Bibliography of Mughal India*. As a matter of fact the material is embarrassingly rich and has not been fully utilized. It is possible to have several detailed studies of the topics discussed in this work. A list of manuscripts and books cited in this book has been given in an appendix. A detailed bibliography of all the material available has not been given because it would be too bulky, and the major part is in any case available elsewhere. Here it would not be out of place to comment briefly on the more important works.

First of all come the works that relate to the events of particular reigns. Of these Abū-'l-Faḍl's *Akbarnāmah* gives a detailed description of the events in Akbar's reign. It is an accurate and true record of events, even though personal references to the monarch are couched in hyperbolic terms. There are veiled and sometimes open references to happenings which a less conscientious writer would have been tempted to ignore or falsify. The student can ignore many of the adjectives used for Akbar but not the events recorded by the historian. After Abū-'l-Faḍl's death the narrative was completed by 'Ināyat-u'llah. The *Akbarnāmah* throws considerable light upon administrative measures, and because of Abū-'l-Faḍl's position at the court, his interest in administrative institutions as evinced by his other work the *Ā'in-i-Akbarī* and his access to all material and documents, it is indispensable to a writer on Mughul government.

The *Tūzuk-i-Jahāngīrī*, being Jahāngīr's memoirs, contains a record of the emperor's impressions and measures. His frankness and regard for truth make the book one of the most interesting essays in autobiography. It has numerous references to the monarch's administrative measures. The *Tūzuk* should not be confused with the spurious memoirs translated by Price. Jahāngīr had to give up writing the book in the seventeenth year of his reign. The work was then entrusted to Mu'tamad Khān who brought the narrative to the beginning of the nineteenth year. Muhammad Hādī brought it down to the emperor's death. Mu'tamad Khān however, wrote *Iqbālnāmah-i-Jahāngīrī* which is a good supplement to the *Tūzuk*.

For Shāh Jahān's reign we have the *Pādshāhnāmah*. Shāh Jahān first entrusted the work to Mirzā Amīnā Qazwīnī who covered the emperor's life as a prince and the first ten years of the reign. Then 'Abd-u'l-Hamīd Lāhūrī was summoned from Patna where he was living in retirement and entrusted with the work. He wrote about twenty years of the reign in detail in the *Pādshāhnāmah*. 'Abd-u'l-Ḥamīd died in 1065 A.H./1653 A.C. of old age. His pupil Muḥammad Wārith was asked to complete the work and brought the narrative to the thirtieth year of the reign. Another important work is by Muḥammad Ṣāliḥ Kanbū, the '*Amal-i-Ṣāliḥ* which has drawn amply on the earlier work, the *Pādshāhnāmah*. The work, however, is of considerable merit because it brings new facts to our knowledge.

Chandra Bhān Brahman's work *Chahār Chaman* throws interesting light on the working of the administration in the reign of Shāh Jahān. He was posted in the office of the chief dīwān of the empire and knew the great Sa'd-u'llah Khān personally. He served under four dīwāns in several capacities. For some time he was in charge of the department for drafting farmāns and thus had direct access to the emperor. His book, therefore, is of considerable use to the student of Mughul administration. His comments, coming from an eminent Hindu scholar and public servant, give an indication of the esteem in which Mughul rule was held by the Hindus. He calls himself a Brahman of orthodox beliefs.

Munshī Muḥammad Kāẓim describes in his '*Ālamgīrnāmah* the events of the first ten years of 'Ālamgīr I's reign. The emperor, in keeping with his character, did not like the idea of an officially sponsored history of the reign, hence he asked Muḥammad Kāẓim to discontinue the work. Muḥammad Sāqī Musta'id Khān wrote his *Ma'āthir-i-'Ālamgīrī* after the death of the monarch in which he deals with the rest of the reign.

Now we turn to books on general history which, however, throw special light on certain reigns. The first of these, Khwājah Niẓām-u'd-dīn Aḥmad's *Ṭabaqāt-i-Akbarī* is reliable but it does not interest itself in religious, social or administrative matters. On the other hand 'Abd-u'l-Qādir al-Badā'ūnī's *Muntakhab-u't-tawārīkh* is rich in reference to Akbar's religious policy and administrative measures. He wrote his book with the set purpose of placing on record Akbar's aberrations from orthodox Islam, He has taken the main events from Khwājah Niẓām-u'd-dīn Aḥmad which he has used as pegs on which he has hung his disapproval of the monarch's errors. His criticism of certain measures is a useful corrective to Abū-'l-Faḍl, because it shows that all reforms were not successful and, therefore, those which failed had to be discarded or amended. A work of considerable importance is Muḥammad Hāshim Khān's *Muntakhab-u'l-lubāb* which throws welcome light on 'Ālamgīr I's reign. Muḥammad Hāshim Khān is better known as Khawāfī Khān and imiginative historians have woven a fable around him. Generally spelt as *Khāfī*, the name is supposed to have been derived from *khafā*, secrecy, hence it has been assumed that the writer laboured on his book in secrecy so that 'Ālamgīr should not discover that he had been guilty of maligning him by writing about his reign. The story falls to the ground because of its own premises. The book is a fair evaluation of the reign and is nowhere defamatory, malicious or too critical. It is not even disrespectful. Ni'mat Khān 'Ālī's *Waqā'i'* is a continuous satire, in places not even in good taste, and there are reasons to believe that it was in secret circulation during 'Ālamgīr's reign. If no harm befell 'Ālī, none could have come to Khawāfī Khān. Of course, the book would have been somewhat different if it had been written as an official history with 'Ālamgīr's full knowledge. The word Khawāfī comes from Khawāf, a town, from which the family had migrated. The *Muntakhab-u'l-lubāb* is rich in giving details of administrative measures and is of considerable value.

In addition to the above there are a number of other general histories which add little to our knowledge. For instance Nūr-u'l-Ḥaqq al-Mashriqī's *Zubdat-u't-tawārīkh* and 'Abd-u'l-Ḥaqq's *Tārīkh-i-Ḥaqqī* contain little that cannot be culled from primary sources. Indeed they are more in the nature of redactions than independent or original works. Muhammad Qāsim Hindū Shāh Firishtah's *Gulshan-i-Ibrāhīmī* has been widely used by European writers. He is not too helpful to a student of Mughul administration and in certain places he misunderstands earlier writers and places glosses which are misleading.

There is so much material available that it is not necessary to cull details regarding administrative institutions from purely literary works. Books like Ni'mat Khān 'Ālī's *Jangnāmah* and *Waqā'i'* belong as much to historical literature as to *belles-lettres*. The latter, however, conveys little apart from the general impression that the author's sole purpose was to heap ridicule on the head of 'Ālamgīr I. The reason seems to have been the fact that the author was peeved at the Mughul efforts to conquer the fast disintegrating Shī'ah sultanates of the Deccan because the author himself belonged to that sect. The works of the main poets would yield little information, except occasional flashes like the lines written by the buffoon poet Ja'far Zatalli on the death of 'Ālamgīr I, which bear the stamp of genuine grief at the passing away of a great and God fearing monarch whose death, it was obvious, would herald the onslaught of anarchy and consequent suffering and misery.

There is considerable source material on administration itself. The place of pride is held by Abū-'l-Faḍl's *Ā'īn-i-Akbarī* which the author intended to form a supplement to his *Akbarnāmah*. The *Ā'īn* is the fundamental text not only for a writer on Mughul administration but a large number of cognate subjects. It is almost an encyclopaedia of Akbar's reign, covering philosophy, religion, geography, administrative institutions, agricultural and industrial products and a host of miscellaneous data. It is more than a gazetteer of the empire. The information contained in it has only been partially utilized. It needs much more detailed study than has hitherto been made. It has not been properly edited, because the figures need checking and rechecking. In places the punctuation is wrong because ignorant copyists did not understand the real significance of the text and editors were not well versed in all the subjects with which the book deals. Its statistical data is so formidable that, upto now, it has defied proper interpretation and utilization. It has been written in a terse and simple style, but the simplicity is deceptive, because of the complexity of the contents and their technical nature. In places the language becomes technical jargon, which has to be carefully interpreted if it has to yield sense. Besides, the author has used words mostly of Persian origin and discarded the more familiar vocabulary derived from Arabic which makes the style even more difficult. The availability of official records and returns to the author makes the *Ā'īn* one of the most reliable documents of history in any language. Another work of great interest to the student of Mughul administration is *Mir'at-i-Ahmadī* by Mirzā Muḥammad Ḥasan *alias* 'Alī Muḥammad Khān Bahādur. The author has added a supplement to his work which describes the administration of Gujrat in detail and gives valuable statistical data. He was the dīwān of Gujrat in the reign of Muhammad Shāh and, therefore, was familiar with the working of the provincial government. There is indirect evidence in the book itself to show that there had been little change in the administration since the days of 'Ālamgīr I. It reproduces some farmāns of 'Ālamgīr's reign which are of primary importance in understanding the nature of the agrarian administration.

There are other treatises on various aspects of the Mughul administration. Some of these are called *dastūr-u'l-'amals*, or manuals of administration, others give statistical data, and yet others describe either certain institutions or the functions of some central, provincial, sarkar, parganah and village officials. There is hardly an aspect of administration that is not covered by this literature. These are scattered in various libraries and collections but there is a representative collection in the India Office Library of London and the British Museum. The importance of this literature cannot be overemphasised. It would be cumbersome to describe all of these tracts and treatises, but a few important ones may be brought to the notice of the reader. The *Dawābiṭ-i-'Ālamgīrī* (anonymous), *Ḥaqīqathā'i-Hindustān* by Lachhmī Narāyan Shafīq, *Kaifiyat-i-Ṣūbajāt-i-mumālik-i-maḥrūsah-i-Hindustān*, Chhatar Mal's *Dīwān Pasand*, Rājah Rūp's (who claims to be a disciple of the famous Todar Mal) *Dastūr-u'l-'amal*, another treatise by Khwājah Yāsīn and Najaf 'Alī's *Risālah-i-manāsib* have been found useful by this writer.

Of equal importance are the various collections of letters and documents. Of these most conspicuous are the letters of 'Ālamgīr I which throw a flood of light on the history of the period. Apart from the well known *Ruqqa'āt-i-'Ālamgīrī* of which there are several lithographed editions, there is Saiyid Najib As͟hraf Nadwi's *Ruqqa āt-i-'Ālamgīr* to which is appended a detailed introduction containing a good discussion of source materials as well as Prince Awrangzīb's character and relations with his father and brothers. Another collection is Muhammad Sādiq Ambālwī's *Ādāb-i-'Ālamgīrī*. The compiler was secretary to 'Ālamgīr's son Prince Akbar. These letters were written for Awrangzīb by his secretary Qābil K͟hān There are two collections by 'Ināyat-u'llah K͟hān, *Aḥkām-i-'Ālamgīrī* and *Kalimāt-i-ṭayyibāt*. *Raqā'im-i-ḳarā'im* was compiled by Saiyid As͟hraf K͟hān Mīr Muhammad al-Ḥusainī. These letters were written to the compiler's father Mīr 'Abd-u'l-Karīm. The *Dastūr-u'l-'amal-i-āgāhī* was compiled on the order of Rājā Ayā Mal, dīwān of Rājah Siwā'ī Jai Singh of Jaipūr. This is by no means an exhaustive list of the collections of 'Ālamgīr's letters because there are several anonymous collections scattered in various libraries of the world.

Then there are a large number of documents like farmāns, sanads, and other certificates scattered in museums, libraries and private collections. Many families who were beneficiaries of grants of one kind or another have preserved such documents or their copies. A fair number has been preserved in *ins͟hās* as models of elegant writing or of official correspondence. Of these a few deserve mention. *Ins͟hā-i-Mādho Rām* and *Muns͟hi'āt-i-Tāhir Waḥid* were at one time known to every school boy. *Ruqqa'āt-i-Muns͟hī* and *Majma'-u'l-afkār* are preserved in Khuda Bakhsh Public Library of Patna. Izad Bak͟hs͟h Rasā's *Riyāḍ u'l-widād* is fairly common. *Haft Anjuman* by Tāli'yār and *Ins͟hā-i-rūs͟han kalām* by Bhopat Rā'i are collections by Hindu officials. There are also a few anonymous collections which contain much useful material.

The state archives of Jaipur contain a large number of letters of S͟hāh Jahān and 'Ālamgīr I as well as newsletters regarding important events.

A number of European travellers came to the empire whose writings have been published. Some of them have left voluminous descriptions of what they heard and saw These accounts are of little use as source material for history, even though their importance has been exaggerated by European writers. In the first place most of these travellers share the common human weakness of magnifying the dangers which they faced while travelling in strange lands. Then they had poor access to records or news. They relied mainly upon bazar gossip which might or might not contain some little core of hard truth. They were complete strangers to the general spirit of religious tolerance that they found in the Mughul Empire, because in their own lands at that time it was unthinkable that a true believer could also be tolerant of other faiths. Therefore, they considered tolerance to be a hall mark of disbelief or at least deviation from the norms of faith. They came from feudal lands and were not able to understand the nature or the working of the Mughul bureaucracy. They assumed that the manṣabdārs were feudal barons and therefore they ought to have had the same hereditary rights. Those writers on history who have given much weight to the writings of European travellers have often been led into errors. For instance, for quite a long time, it was fashionable to talk of escheat as a fundamental of Mughul policy because it was held that the emperor was the heir of his "nobles" Instances of similar errors can be multiplied. Whatever might have been their other aptitudes, these travellers were certainly not students of administrative institutions. It needs a trained mind to understand the functions of institutions to which one is a complete stranger. The Mughul structure of government was quite complex and then reforms were introduced from time to time. When the British first tried their hand at agrarian administration, in spite of their having been familiar with conditions in the subcontinent for more than a century, they completely misunderstood the theory and spirit of agrarian administration and some theories propounded by them have not only persisted despite scientific investigation leading to the conclusion that they were wrong but have also done considerable injury to the social structure of the subcontinent. For instance it was firmly believed that the state was the owner of the peasant's holding. The economic and social repercussions of such theories, when implemented over long periods, can well be understood. If this is true of those whose business it was to study administrative institutions and who had ample opportunities of doing so, what reliance can be placed on travellers whose statements could not but have been perfunctory, based as they were on superficial contacts and observation?

As a matter of fact when the British were faced with difficulties created by a faulty understanding of the agrarian system, they made an effort to understand it and one comes across certain studies made for them, but quite a few of these suffer from a persistence of preconceived notions and, therefore, they have not proved of much use.

In the presence of an embarrassingly large quantity of original recorded source material, it is not necessary to rummage through epigraphy for an occasional ray of light. The use of numismatics and epigraphy is not denied, but in view of ample records it has not been necessary to base any important conclusions upon these. R.B. Whitehead's work on Mughal numismatics will always remain a classic. Another significant contribution is by Hodivala.

The Mughul period has attracted comparatively more attention than the Sultanate and there are a number of modern works available to the student. Apart from general works like the *Cambridge History of India* (Volume IV), there are monographs on each reign. For the period covered by this book, there is Vincent Smith's *Akbar*, Beni Prasad's *Jahangir*, Banarsi Prasad Saksena's *Shah Jahan* and Faruki's *Aurangzib and His Times*. Then there is Jadunath Sarkar's voluminous *History of Aurangzib*. Vincent Smith's *Akbar* is a comprehensive work, but it suffers from serious drawbacks. It was written almost half a century ago and a good deal of research has taken place since then. His preference for European sources has led him quite often to conclusions which have been proved to be wrong. In the matter of administration, because he has relied heavily on translations, too many errors have crept into his statements. Beni Prasad's *Jahangir* also was written many years ago, but it is more sound and has stood the test of time better. The discussion on institutions is out of date and suffers from the fact that the study is based on a single reign. Banarsi Prasad Saksena's *Shah Jahan* is comparatively more recent and it gives a readable account of the reign. Faruki has brought in new material but his book is amateurish and lacks confidence. It is apologetic which mars its value. Jadunath Sarkar's reputation was built on his book on 'Ālamgīr I and it has considerable material. It is old fashioned and rather disappointing because he finds himself out of sympathy with his subject and the spirit of the reign has eluded him. He quite unnecessarily says uncharitable things about Islam which mars the quality of his work because it betrays a deep seated prejudice.

A good deal has also been written on the Mughul administration and some of its particular branches. Jadunath Sarkar was the first in the field so far as a monograph on the administration as a whole is concerned. It has a good deal of stray information mostly based on eighteenth century materials, but the book's main fault is that it lacks synthesis and fails to give the reader any insight into the logic of the administrative organization. It describes, as if it were, bricks rather than the building. He is also handicapped by his lack of knowledge of Persian because he relied mostly on translations or the renderings of his munshīs. Ibn Hasan's *The Central Structure of the Mughul Empire* set a new standard in writings on the history of the Mughul administration and its study is profitable even now. Parmatma Saran's *Provincial Government of the Mughuls* gives a good picture but it does not give a correct interpretation of the details. S. A. Q. Husaini's *Administration under the Mughuls* is well written and has the additional advantage of relating Mughul institutions to their Muslim origins. Sri Ram Sharma's *Mughal Government and Administration* is the latest book on the subject in the field. It is a competent study. The conclusions in the main are sound but there are important details in which it is necessary to differ from the author. There are certain institutions which might have been discussed in greater detail. It does not limit itself to the institutions but gives interesting sidelights on the social and economic conditions of the period.

There are certain works on some particular problems. Abdul Aziz has one study of the treasures etc. of the Mughuls and another of the mansabdārī system. Both of these are helpful and reliable. Irvine has a book on the Mughul army which is mostly based on eighteenth century in details. Irvine's understanding of the mansabdārī system is defective. Moreland's *The Agrarian System of Moslem India* is an excellent book and has removed many cobwebs of misunderstanding. However, the book was written more than quarter of a century ago and our understanding of the system has gained through further research. Moreland's two other books *India at the Death of Akbar* and *From Akbar to Aurangzib* are in a different category, because they are disappointing. There is not the same scientific probing and there are many erroneous assumptions on which other assumptions have been piled up and thus a totally misleading picture has been built up. Irfan Habib has collected a good deal of detailed informations in his *Agrarian System of Mughal India.*

It will not be out of place to mention here that incalculable harm has been done to the history of the period by an uncritical dependence on translations, some of which are far from reliable. Those who have put total reliance upon Elliot and Dowson have built on faulty foundations. Hodivala has rendered a great service by commenting upon some of the errors, but nothing can fully remedy the errors both of commission and omission which mar the utility of the work. These remarks also apply to several other translations, in particular to Blochmann and Jarrett's translation of the *Ā'īn-i-Akbarī.* For the scrupulous student there is no alternative to the original texts.

CHAPTER II

The Monarch

ISLAM takes a comprehensive view of life and does not separate politics from religion. It was confronted early with the necessity of organizing a state. When Muḥammad migrated to Medina, he was accepted by the believers not only as their preceptor in religion but also as the head of their community, which had to be organized not only for prayers and devotion but also for ordering its mundane affairs and for defending itself from the hostility of its neighbours who saw in the rise of the new faith a danger to their own beliefs and customs. This organized community of believers was the nucleus of the Islamic state which grew in size as well as authority with the spread of Islam. Its progress was helped by the environment in which the Prophet and his early followers found themselves. There was no political power higher than tribal authority in Arabia at that time which could protect the believers from the persecution of their opponents, and because tribal authority was incapable of establishing general peace, there had been a state of chronic anarchy and warfare for such a long time before the birth of the Prophet that the tribes had almost lost the conception of general peace enduring for more than the agreed period of one or two months every year. In this environment the Muslims had to fend for themselves; therefore they were forced to integrate all believers into an organized community. The teachings of Islam laid great emphasis upon unity and brotherhood and inculcated discipline and loyalty to the community if it did not engage itself in activities which were palpably un-Islamic.[1] As priesthood was forbidden, there could be no church to look after the spiritual welfare of the Muslims or their religious needs, and only the organized community could be the guardian of the Faith. To prevent the community from straying away from the tenets of Islam it was laid down that it would seek guidance from the Qur'ān in all its activities and would not transgress its injunctions in any manner.[2] During the lifetime of the Prophet, there could be no danger of deviation, yet he laid it down that his opinions were valid only so far as they did not come into conflict with the letter or the spirit of the Qur'ān.

By the time of the Prophet's death, the Muslim state was already strong and well consolidated. In its essence it was the organized Muslim community functioning as a religious entity to preserve and propagate its beliefs and to provide the facilities to practise them, confronted with social, economic and political needs to sustain its life as an independent society, hence organized into a state without which its prime object of maintaining its Islamic character could be jeopardized. This need could be felt by any religious group, but in Islam religion was not merely a matter of prayer and belief but it also embraced the external behaviour of man to a degree that such a conception of the Islamic community was inevitable. The Muslim thinkers have mostly upheld this conception of the Islamic state. Their legal thinking also has been affected by this belief; indeed this conception is so deeply immersed

[1] *Qur'ān*, III, 102, V.2; I.H. Qureshi, *The Administration of the Sultanate of Dehli*, p. 50.

[2] This is implicit in the doctrine of the infallibility of the *Qur'ān*, II, 1.

in the Islamic doctrine that it would be difficult to separate it from religious thought. It was this fact which led Ibn Khaldūn to lay it down that the khilāfat—the form which the Islamic state assumed immediately after the death of the Prophet—was a canonical necessity.[3]

The completion of the Qur'ān and therefore of the fundamental religious doctrine of Islam had been proclaimed on the occasion of the Prophet's last pilgrimage to Mecca some time before his death; it was understood that the Prophetic mission had come to an end.[4] Therefore, when the Prophet died, the community was concerned with the question of finding a new head who would conduct their affairs. These affairs, necessarily, were both religious and political and the khalifah, the successor of the Prophet, had combined in his office, both religious and political functions. This fact has led to misconceptions regarding the nature of the caliphate; some have seen in it the combination of spiritual and temporal authority, having in their minds the Papacy and the Holy Roman Empire. The parallel is misleading because the caliph is not the head of a church, there being no priesthood or church in Islam; nor has he any religious or spiritual authority, such authority not being vested in any person or organization; he has no overriding power of interpretation or issuing rulings on religious matters. It is necessary to understand the Islamic conception of religion to be able to grasp the nature of the caliphate. The Muslim believes that it is impossible to divorce religion from all human activity, because all actions must be motivated by man's innermost convictions and externally they should interpret his ideals; hence religion and other aspects of life cannot be separated. The organized Muslim community is, therefore, essentially religious, but it is not a church; its organization is political and non-ecclesiastical; it is a polity organized for the purpose of enabling Muslims to live in accordance with Islam, not a church to interpret continuously the doctrines of the Faith for its followers; the interpretation is necessary for the application of the principles to

[3] Ibn Khaldūn, *Muqaddimah*, (Urdu translation), pp. 155, 156.

[4] *Qur'ān*, V. 3.

the ever growing and increasing complexities of life; but Islam leaves this work ultimately to the enlightened conscience of the community. The caliph is the head of this community and its chief executive.[5]

In such a community, which did not possess a church, the purity of the doctrine and conformity with the principles could be insured only by laying the greatest emphasis upon the inviolability of the fundamentals; fissiparous tendencies could be prevented by some compromise between freedom and conformity. It was only a corollary of the Islamic belief in the infallibility of the Qur'ān that it should form the immutable basis of law; yet its application to the diversity of human life would need interpretation and deduction. The best interpretation of the Qur'ān was considered to be the Prophet's sunnah, his attitudes, actions and sayings relating to general or specific problems. Hence there grew up a vast literature of ḥadīth, searched, sifted and compiled by competent, careful and diligent scholars, largely authentic, but lacking the finality of total certainty in all its details; by the application of critical methods, the degree of the authenticity of each tradition could be determined with varying success. Where it was not possible to find a clear ruling from either of these sources, ijtihād, or the method of rational deduction was to be used; conclusions so reached achieved general validity only after their acceptance by concensus of competent opinion, technically called ijmā'. The body of law so built up during the ages came to be called shar'.[6] Those who are acquainted with the vast literature of ḥadīth and the work of the great jurists of Islam know that the principles of criticism as well as deduction adopted by the scholars were sound and extremely cautious. Thus the shar' based upon an immutable source is yet mutable in the matters of detail; like all legal systems, it tends to be conservative, yet it lends itself to adjustments to growing needs, if they can be made without violating fundamentals. In the absence of a church, this could be the only guarantee of cohesion and viability of the Muslim community. In view of the belief in

[5] Faḍl bin Rūzbahān, f 209 b.

[6] Khudā Bakhsh, *Essays, Indian and Islamic*, p. 51.

the divine origin of the Qur'ān and its immutable nature, the Muslims recognized no authority higher than that of the shar'. The sovereignty of the shar' became the cornerstone of an Islamic polity.[7]

The caliph was the highest executive and 'the commander of the Faithful,' but he was one of the believers. Hence he was as much under the authority of the shar' as the other Faithful. He could not alter or overrule the shar'; he could only enforce it.[8] He had a limited authority of adding to the law executive decrees which were not part of shar', but were valid as the orders of the executive authority for such period as the authority did not discard them; but if they came into conflict with the shar', they were invalid and it was the duty of a Muslim to disobey them. He also had a limited authority of choosing one interpretation in preference to another if the jurists happened to differ on any point, because the executive must enforce the law and if there is ambiguity on any issue, it must have the right to decide for itself. The legal position of the caliph thus came to be defined fairly early in the history of Islam. The duties assigned to the caliph by the Muslim jurists can be divided into certain broad categories. He was to defend the frontiers of the territories of Islam, maintain peace and order, enforce the shar', and thus act as the arbiter in disputes among the people, and take necessary steps to ensure the happiness and prosperity of his people.[9] It is the duty of every Muslim to obey him in all matters which are lawful; in case he transcends the limits of the shar', disobedience becomes a duty.

The election of the first caliph, Abū Bakr, has provided the jurists with the precedent on which they base their rulings regarding the succession to the office. The caliph should legally be nominated by some electors and accepted by the community.[10] The jurists, however, did not lay down any specific qualifications for the electors who were to make the nomination nor did they pre-

[7] *Ibid;* also *Tadhkirat-u'l-ukhulafā fī tawṣīyat-i'l-mulūk wa'l-umarā*, f 12.

[8] Faḍl bin Rūzbahān, f. 19a.

[9] *Ibid;* also a'n-Nuwairī, p. 5.

[10] Von Kraemer, p. 9; I.H. Qureshi, *The Administration of the Sultanate of Dehlī*, p. 150.

scribe any quorum for such electors. Abū Bakr's election was a spontaneous action; the assembled elders chose him and their choice was accepted by the community. It established precedents only in principle which lacked the definite characteristics of law. Nor did any definiteness come into the procedure during the reigns of the next three caliphs which forms the period of the Republic and is looked upon by the orthodox as the days of "the rightly guided caliphate," and to which the jurists turn for precedents if they do not find any clear ruling in the Qur'ān or the sunnah.

The principles of nomination by the leaders of public opinion and the acceptance by the community could have worked well if selfish power politics had not crept into Muslim polity after the end of the Republic. In the hands of politicians, the indefinite nature of the rulings of the jurists became a potent instrument for ignoring public opinion and precedents alike. The fear of anarchy further led the jurists to whittle down the conditions of a proper election; they ruled in favour of the recognition of caliphs who seize power by force. Election, therefore, became an empty formality; and the democratic spirit of Islam was shut out from the sphere of politics by the failure of its jurists to preserve the reality of election by going further than the outward forms of the precedents. The Muslim respect for the shar' is demonstrated by the fact that the forms of election were maintained for several centuries. In India the Sultans preserved them, though sometimes the succession was in reality decided by the sword.[11] The acceptance by the community was represented by the bai'at, by which the citizen bound himself in obedience to the caliph. The jurists differ whether a person having thus bound himself once could release himself from the obligation. Some think that a bai'at is inviolable, but the consensus of opinion is that the incapacity of a caliph to discharge his functions imposed by a mental or physical disability like blindness or lunacy or loss of the power of judgment renders the bai'at invalid; also where the caliph transgresses the shar' in giving an order, he should not be obeyed. Physical or mental disability also provide justification for the deposition of a caliph; some jurists

[11] *Ibid.*, pp. 53, 55.

think that tyranny and injustice also are sufficient reasons for his removal.[12]

The Sultans of Dehlī recognized the authority of a caliph, sometimes by vague references on their coins or in the khuṭbah to a commander of the Faithful, sometimes by definite acts of allegiance. The only certain exception is Quṭb-u'd-dīn Mubārak Shāh Khaljī, who called himself the caliph. The position, however, changed under the Mughuls who considered themselves the caliphs within their own territories. Abū Bakr had established the principle of the indivisibility of the Muslim community and had taken grave risks in enforcing it. This doctrine, however, received a set back when the Umayyid caliphate was established in the West after the rise of the Abbasid power. In the East, the weakening of its effective political strength did not weaken the legal myth of the supremacy of the Abbasid caliphate. Even the sack of Baghdad and the execution of Musta'sim-bi'llah in 1258 did not kill the idea of an Abbasid caliphate and it was revived in Egypt in 1261. The transfer of the caliphate to the Ottomans was, however, a different matter. Even before this a school of thought had grown up which believed that independent sovereigns were caliphs within their own territories.[13] This doctrine was accepted by the Timurids; the hostility between the Ottomans and the Timurids would in any case have prevented the recognition of the Ottoman caliphate by the Timurids. The Mughul emperors, therefore, claimed to be caliphs within their empire and their claim was accepted by their orthodox subjects. This, however, did not make any fundamental difference in their legal duties and obligations and those of their predecessors on the throne of Dehlī. The Sultans had, as *de facto* independent monarchs, all the legal authority which was assigned to the caliphs by the jurists; their dependence upon the Abbasid caliphs had been purely formal. The jurists had taken cognizance of the rise of virtually independent states within the Caliphate and had transferred the legal authority and obligations to the sultans in their respective territories and, in course of time, this paved the way for the legal

[12] Von Kraemer, pp. 248, 264, 267, 268.

[13] For a fuller discussion, see I. H. Qureshi, *The Administration of the Sultanate of Dehlī*, pp. 22-39.

recognition of independent caliphates. The Mughul claim to the caliphate, therefore, did not raise any legal difficulties; nor did their Muslim subjects find the transition from the recognition of a distant and almost mythical caliph to the acceptance of their own emperor as the caliph inconsistent with their beliefs or sentiments. The assumption of the caliphate by the Mughuls and the continuance of the title should have emphasized the Islamic nature of the Mughul state, but many factors crept into the situation which worked in a different direction.

Turkish traditions had affected the institution of monarchy in the Sultanate of Dehlī, but they had not undermined the essential loyalty to the shar‘ as it was expounded by the jurists. The reason was that the sultans were guided in all legal matters by the ‘ulamā, and, in particular, by the ṣadr-u'ṣ-ṣudūr.[14] The state had shown tolerance to the non-Muslims without losing its Islamic nature; if, at times, intolerance crept into some actions of a few monarchs, for most of the period Hindus were treated liberally. They were employed by the state in large numbers, indeed some departments of the government like Revenue and Finance were almost their monopoly; the army also had Hindus in considerable numbers, both in the ranks and among the officers; socially and economically they were well-off and prosperous. All this was achieved without infringing the laws of Islam and without endangering the Muslim hold upon the state.[15] With the Mughuls, however, a profound change came over the polity; for a time the dominant Muslim tone of the government was endangered. So many factors contributed to this change that it is not possible to discuss all of them in detail.

It should be remembered that the ancestors of the Mughul emperors were, comparatively, much later converts to Islam; whereas, the Turkish and Afghan dynasties of Dehlī had owned their rise to Islam, Chingīz Khān had conquered the lands of Islam as a heathen. When his descendants were converted, they were already mighty monarchs, and their belief in the political efficacy of their ancestor's yāsā or institutes was still strong. They

[14] For a fuller discussion, see *Ibid.*, pp. 41-50, 219-20.

[15] For a fuller discussion see *Ibid.*, pp. 219-20.

had a political code divorced from Islam, which code gradually sank into a secondary place, limited mostly to matters of protocol and the Imperial Household, yet which existed in its own right. Humāyūn's expulsion from his empire and his visit to the Ṣafawid court established contacts between the Mug͟hul court and Iran which led to a stream of Irani migrants to India in search of employment. The Mug͟hul court, under the circumstances, could not remain a stronghold of orthodoxy, because the Irani immigrants were mostly S͟hī'ah. With the establishment of matrimonial alliances with the Rajputs and the growth of their influence at the court, the decline of the power of the orthodox ṣadr-u'ṣ-ṣudūr was but a question of time. The position of orthodoxy had been challenged in the country by several movements of great proportions. Mahdawism had not been a weak adversary and the growth of the Bhaktī Movement had softened the Muslim antipathy for the beliefs of the Hindus.[16] By its acceptance of the Sufic approach to religion and turning it in favour of its own doctrine of all religions being the same in essence, it had created laxity and indifference among the Muslim masses, whose enthusiastic support could be the mainstay of the influence of orthodoxy at the court.

Naturally all the opponents of orthodoxy combined themselves in their efforts to dethrone it. S͟haik͟h Mubārak's family had suffered at the hands of the orthodox 'ulamā at the court, and he and his sons Abū-'l-Faḍl and Faiḍī worked skillfully to avenge themselves.[17] They found many allies in this effort; the historian Badā'ūnī who was such a critic of Akbar's heterodoxy was himself deeply tinged with Mahdawism and was no friend of the orthodox 'ulamā at the court.[18] Indeed he was looked upon in the beginning as a likely instrument for overthrowing them. He did not prove useful because, like so many heresies in Islam, Mahdawism was itself exceedingly puritanical and fundamentalist

[16] For Mahdawism, Erskine, ii. p. 476-82; Tara Chand gives an excellent account of the Bhaktī Movement. For a fuller discussion of heterodoxy under Akbar, see I.H. Qureshi, *The Muslim Community of the Indo-Pakistan Subcontinent*, chapter vi.

[17] Blochmann, Biography of Abū-'l-Fadl in his translation of the *Ā'īn-i-Akbarī*.

[18] *Ibid*, p. ix, fn.

in its beliefs and outlook. However, Abū-'l-Faḍl found many allies among the non-Muslim and the non-Sunni Muslim courtiers and turned Akbar into an antagonist of orthodoxy.[19] Those who accuse Akbar of abjuring Islam go too far; their conclusions are not based upon sound evidence and they overlook many important facts which point in a different direction.[20] However, there can be little doubt about Akbar's feelings towards Makhdūm-u'l-mulk and 'Abd-u'n-Nabī and the school of thought represented by them. Even when allowance is made for Abū-'l-Faḍl's animosity and Badā'ūnī's prejudice, the two theologians do not seem to be worthy representatives of the orthodox 'ulamā nor qualified by their learning to hold their own against the brilliant attacks of more learned adversaries.[21] It would, however, be misleading to attach too much importance to personal factors; though the role played by the leading men was not negligible, yet they were merely agents of the forces at work in the subcontinent, where the contacts between Islam and Hinduism, in particular the great interest in the mystic aspects of religion both among the Hindus and the Muslims created by the Sufis and then by the Bhaktas, had created an indifference towards the orthodox forms. Akbar was not the sole claimant of being a religious preceptor who could guide people to spiritual awakening irrespective of their religious affiliations, nor was he the greatest of those who had a following among diverse religious groups, but his position as a monarch and the atmosphere in his court produced political and administrative changes of considerable importance.[22]

The ostensible legal break from the past was a document drawn up by Shaikh Mubārak which was based upon a universally accepted principle.[23] In case the learned jurists differed and offered

[19] Badā'ūnī is full of references to their leaders.

[20] e. g., Abū-'l-Faḍl, *Akbararnāmah*, iii, pp. 498, 499; where Akbar protests strongly that it is a calumny that he has abjured Islam.

[21] Badā'ūnī's descriptions of the debates in the 'Ibādatkhānah leave this impression: it would take too much space to give a description of their inability to defend orthodox doctrines. Later Shaikh Aḥmad of Sarhind demonstrated how orthodoxy could be defended.

[22] Kabīr, Kamāl and Dādū are only a few of numerous spiritual guides who attracted men of diverse religions.

[23] For the text vide Badā'ūnī, II. pp. 270-2.

varying interpretations of the sacred text, the just monarch, technically described as imām-i-'ādil could choose any one of the interpretations offered. It is obvious that if there is no agreement or ijmā' on a point, and if the monarch's bonafides cannot be questioned and if he is capable of judging the merit of one interpretation against another, he must choose before he can enforce or apply a particular interpretation. There was nothing revolutionary in this principle, because it had always been accepted.

The document was signed by several theologians, by some against their will, and was in the form of a statement by those assembled and present, hence it was called a maḥḍar. It was not because of the principle which was enunciated that the maḥḍar encountered opposition; it was considered a dishonest document because Akbar was mentioned as imām-i-'ādil, the just 'leader' or ruler, who was invested with the authority to choose between several interpretations. According to Muslim jurisprudence, a monarch to be technically 'ādil' for this purpose should have sufficient knowledge of the law to be able to judge the merits of the different interpretations. Akbar had no such qualifications. Besides, Shaikh Mubārak's intention was to undermine orthodoxy. Akbar had shown too great a predilection in favour of heterodoxy to leave any doubt about his choice. Monarchs who were not learned jurists had delegated the authority mentioned in the maḥdar to their ṣadrs. With the signing of this maḥḍar, the orthodox 'ulamā of the court sealed their fate. However, such a document was made possible by the decline in the influence of orthodoxy in the court and the realm. Though it is wrong to characterize the document as 'the Decree of Infallibility' as has been done by some European scholars, it did vest the monarch with considerable power if his intentions were to uproot orthodox influence from the court. The maḥḍar limited the monarch's authority within the basic limits of the Muslim Law, the Qur'ān and the agreed interpretations, which shows the limits up to which the opponents of orthodoxy could venture safely. The investment of an orthodox monarch with these powers would not have aroused such opposition. The document, however, remained a dead letter. It was never utilized. Akbar preferred to use the device of appointing men of pliable conscience as ṣadrs and judges to carry out his behests.

It is not possible to discuss here in detail the extent of Akbar's deviation from orthodoxy. It is now generally accepted that Akbar did not abjure Islam; he built upon the foundations of his Sufic and pantheistic notions, which he does not seem to have understood fully, a structure of eclectic notions and even fantasies without showing a uniform insight into their nature; but the question of abjuring Islam never arose in his mind. He seems to have thought honestly that he understood Islam better than his orthodox opponents; he claimed that his policies had expanded the power of Islam much further than the policies of his more orthodox predecessors; in the beginning this policy had the approval of persons whose loyalty to Islam cannot be questioned.[24] He was only the victim of a widespread confusion in the public mind regarding the validity of the exclusive claims of any religion to hold all the truth; if other religions did contain some truth, as was generally accepted by most Muslims, Akbar saw no harm in finding out the truth which other religions claimed to possess.[25] Whereas the orthodox would accept only such features of other religions as did not come into conflict with Islam, Akbar did not respect these limits. However, from the political point of view there can be little doubt that Akbar went too far: it would have been wiser to gain popularity and greater support among his non-Muslim officers and subjects without earning any opprobrium among the orthodox, who after all were the mainstay of the Mughul power. Akbar and his supporters could have achieved much more if they had been more moderate. The empire might have been saved many an acute tension which ultimately brought about its downfall.

The reaction against Akbar's policy found a leader in Shaikh Aḥmad of Sarhind, who is, because of his efforts and success, popularly known as the Mujaddid-i-alf-i-thānī, or the Reviver (of

[24] Abū-'l-Faḍl, *Akbarnāmah*, III. p. 498, 499. Also, vide Badā'ūnī, (ii, p. 233) who quotes a poem by a Muslim poet Mulla Sherī containing the famous line:

که هندو می زند شمشیر اسلام

[25] Nūr-u'l-Ḥaqq, ff. 202 b, 203; Khawāfī Khān, I, p. 196.

Islam) for the Second Millennium (of the Hijri era). This title shows not only the importance of the Mujaddid's work in the eyes of the orthodox, but also their estimation of the injury that had been inflicted upon the body politic of Islam. He fought against some of the beliefs which had found currency among the Muslims to create a healthier attitude towards the doctrine of Islam; to save the polity, he had to reform the Muslims. His political endeavour, however, is no less important, because he continuously canvassed the politically important classes among the orthodox, especially the government officials and dignitaries, for restoring orthodoxy to its previous position in the councils and policies of the empire.[26] He was successful, because he voiced the feelings of the majority of the Muslims. Even before he came to the forefront, we find Akbar taking much less interest in religious experiments and speculation towards the end of his reign and, indeed, he is reported to have repented before his death.[27] Jāhāngir had to promise before his succession that he would restore and maintain those Islamic traditions which had been discarded by his father.[28] Shāh Jahān, a deeply religious man, went further in reimposing the laws of Islam.[29] This shows that in spite of the growth of the power of the non-Muslims and the dissenting sects of Islam, it was not easy for the emperor to deviate flagrantly in his public policies from orthodox Islam, and even his personal conduct and behaviour had to conform with prevailing religious opinion.)

26 The collection of his letters, *Maktūbāt-i-Imām-i-Rabbānī*, has too many epistles of this nature to be quoted.

27 Blochmann notices in his translation of the *Ā'īn-i-Akbarī*, (I, p. 212) that Badā'ūnī's "remarks on Akbar's religion become more and more sparing towards the end." This is significant, because Badā'ūnī's main purpose in writing his history seems to have been the discussion of Akbar's religious views; the rest of the book is mainly a redaction of Niẓām-u'd-dīn's *Ṭabaqāt-i-Akbarī*. Badā'ūnī died ten years before Akbar's death. The story of Akbar's repentance appears in the spurious memoris of Jahāngīr translated by Price. The book was not written by Jahāngīr, because we possess his memoirs which were edited by Sir Syed Ahmed Khan; yet all the facts in the book are not fictitious. Blochmann's reasons for dismissing the story are not conclusive. Jahāngīr and his successors were anxious to hide Akbar's vagaries in religion and any emphasis upon his repentence would defeat this purpose. Repentance at the time of death is universal among Muslims, and Akbar also seems to have followed the custom, perhaps, a little more significantly.

28 *Cambridge History of India*, iv, p. 152.

29 'Abd-u'l-Ḥamīd, i, p. 110.

It was, however, equally impossible to ignore the feelings of the non-Muslims and the Shī'ahs. They held important offices and the emperors needed their cooperation. Jāhāngir and Shāh Jahān reconciled orthodoxy, but in doing so, they did not offend others. It was understood that the dominant partners in the empire were the orthodox Muslims and also that the emperor belonged to the same group. A certain amount of preference to them was, therefore, not resented, if this did not result in the withdrawal of any privilege which the others enjoyed. The non-Muslims and the dissenters often made common cause and cooperated with one another. It was, therefore, in their interests to have a less orthodox emperor on the throne. One can discern the formation of two parties on these lines since the later part of Akbar's reign, but Jāhāngir and Shāh Jahān succeeded in maintaining a balance between the two. By his partiality for Dārā Shikūh, Shāh Jāhān, towards the end of his reign, upset this balance, for the favoured prince was the cynosure of the eyes of the non-Muslims, because he promised to be another Akbar.[30] 'Ālamgīr, both by temperament and necessity, had to rely on the support of the orthodox, and he failed to get the fullest cooperation of the non-Muslims and the Shī'ahs. The reasons were complex. The conflict between the Mughuls and the Ṣafawids regarding Qandahār had put the loyalty of the Shī'ahs to some strain even under the previous two monarchs; the war against the Shi'ah Sultanates of the Deccan, howsoever necessary, was not popular with them.[31] The Hindus were not entirely unaffected by the Maratha slogans of Hindūpad pādshāhī and a crusade against the slayers of the cow. If the Marathas had abstained from looting and plundering fellow Hindus, they would have been more successful. Under these circumstances 'Ālamgīr's decision to re-impose jiziyah and enforce some of the discarded regulations against the Hindus created dissatisfaction. He, therefore, did not get the same cooperation as his predecessors had been able to secure from their Hindu and Shi'ah officers. The extent of

[30] Ḥasrat gives a good insight into his religious beliefs.

[31] Ni'mat Khān 'Ālī, *Waqā'i'* is an index to Shī'ah feelings.

this lack of cooperation has been exaggerated by many writers, but its existence cannot be doubted. Hindu and Shī'ah officers continued to serve and some of them rendered creditable assistance, but there were many whose hearts were not in their work.[32] 'Ālamgīr's difficulties cannot be assigned only to this factor, but its existence shows how sensitive the empire was to the degree of affection in which the emperor was held not only by his own sect, but by the entire people.

It would be clear from this discussion that the Mughul emperors were dependent for the success of their policies upon the cooperation of the politically active classes. In turn, these classes could not be isolated from the opinions and feelings of the people in general, in so far as they were articulate. The orthodox Muslims being the dominant political section of the population, their sentiments were of the utmost importance and could not be neglected too long with safety; hence the Islamic concept of the monarch being subservient to the shar' and its servant was politically effective and valid in the empire, yet its validity was limited to some extent by the feelings of the non-Muslims and the dissident sects of Islam in so far as the application of the shar' to them was concerned. This limitation had crept into the polity because of the immigration of influential Iranis into the Mughul Empire and the advancement of these immigrants and the Hindus in considerable numbers to key positions in the government. When this limit was transgressed, it created grave difficulties for the emperor.

Abū-'l-Faḍl in his crusade against the orthodox 'ulamā at the court, does not seem to be unconscious of the fact that the empire needed a philosophy and a political theory to sustain it. If he had relied upon the Islamic concepts for this purpose, he might have been forced to accept the claims of orthodoxy. Akbar's claim to be the caliph, which was never given up, could be sustained only by the Sunni schools of jurisprudence; this did not suit Abū-'l-Faḍl. No school of Islam could really serve his purpose; therefore, he put forward a theory which he thought would satisfy all.

32 'Ālamgir I found it difficult to enforce many of his measures successfully for this reason; hence a flow of orders to the subordinates, *e.g.*, Khawāfi Khān, II, p. 212, 213.

According to him, "royalty is a light emanating from God," which "is communicated by God to kings without the intermediate assistance of any one;" and "no dignity is higher in the eyes of God than royalty."[33] The inspiration for this theory seems to have come from the Shi'ah theory of the imāmate, which, of course, Abū-'l-Faḍl could not adopt in its entirety, because of Akbar not belonging to the line of the hereditary imāms. According to Abū-'l-Faḍl it is only the true king who is the recipient of divine distinction, not the selfish ruler, who may nevertheless possess all the outward requisites of monarchy. Success is the criterion of true kingship, because the selfish rulers soon lose their power and possessions.[34]

In addition, the king's devotion to duty and the higher virtues provides a proof of his being a true monarch. The real function of a monarch is to provide stability and safeguard property by maintaining peace and order. "If royalty did not exist, the storm of strife would never subside, nor selfish ambition disappear. Mankind, being under the burden of lawlessness and lust, would sink into the pit of destruction; this world, this great market place, would lose its prosperity and the whole earth become a barren waste. But by the light of imperial justice, some follow with cheerfullness the road of obedience, whilst others abstain from violence through fear of punishment."[35]

This is the argument, so familiar to Eastern thinkers, of the need of a ruler to save the people from the horrors of anarchy.[36] Abū-'l-Faḍl, however, goes further and expects the king to be the spiritual guide of his people as well, because "the light emanating from God," which is the true mark of "royalty" is also "the ray of Divine wisdom, which banishes from his heart everything that is conflicting." Sitting "on the throne of distinction," he is "equally removed from joy or sorrow." Such an ideal monarch would naturally be the most suitable spiri-

[33] Blochmann, i, pp. ii, iii (Abū-'l-Faḍl's Introduction).

[34] *Ibid.*, p. iii.

[35] *Ibid.*, p. ii.

[36] Vide I. H. Qureshi, *The Administration of the Sultanate of Dehli*, chapter III, pp. 39-41.

tual preceptor of the people. According to Abū-'l-Faḍl, Akbar was such an ideal monarch, but then he was born with a spiritual and temporal destiny, because "men versed in foretelling the future knew this when His Majesty was born, and together with all others that were cognizant of the secret, they have since been waiting in joyful expectation" for Akbar to open "the gate that leads to the right path, and satisfies the thirst of all that wander about panting for truth."[37] In plain language this means that Akbar's spiritual destiny was not shared by all monarchs. Even in the mundane sphere, they might not possess "the ray of Divine wisdom"; therefore, Abū-'l-Faḍl's theory of kingship is not universally applicable. It was invented to extol Akbar and to justify his spiritual claims.

Weaning Akbar away from orthodoxy needed first of all building up his confidence, and the best way of doing so was to convince him that he had spiritual powers which could guide others, hence he need not rely upon the opinions of others, howsoever learned they might be. The next need was to find him supporters to replace those whom he would lose by breaking away from the orthodox. For this purpose the *Akbarnāmah* and its supplement the *Ā'īn-i-Akbarī* did not begin with the usual bismi'llah and the eulogy to the Prophet and adopted some conceptions foreign to the orthodox belief but known to others. The reference to the predictions of "men versed in foretelling the future" would strongly appeal to the astrologically minded Hindus and the superstitious among the Muslims. Besides, one of the virtues of the ideal monarch was that because of his love for his subjects, "sectarian differences do not raise the dust of strife."[38] To reinforce the claims of spiritual achievements, alleged miracles are pressed into service. This curious mixture of philosophy, superstition and political acumen is also characteristic of Akbar's character; besides, it cannot be dismissed easily because it had serious political repercussions. It had some popular appeal as well; because whereas the legal position of the monarchy was known only to the learned, the superstitious appeal penetrated the

[37] Blochmann, i, p. 163.

[38] *Ibid.*, p. iii (Abū-'l-Faḍl's Introduction).

masses. Akbar's religious idiosyncrasies died with him; his policy towards the non-Muslims could not be discarded easily; such legal institutions as had been discarded by Akbar and were considered necessary by the orthodox like jiziyah could be revived by 'Ālamgīr I only with difficulty; the halo created around the office of the emperor lived until the end. The Mughul soldiers fought with greater confidence against the Satnāmīs who were reputed to be sorcerers when they were supplied with charms by 'Ālamgīr,[39] and the faineant emperor Bahādur Shāh II was revered for his sanctity, when all semblance of power had deserted the Mughul throne at Dehlī.

The Islamic ideas of monarchy were revived after Akbar's death. Even the maḥḍar vesting Akbar with the authority to choose between different interpretations of the shar' was a compromise with Islamic legalism, because it was clothed in its language and based upon its principles. Akbar did not invoke it; Jahāngīr never mentioned it; Shāh Jahān's motives in respect of orthodoxy could not be questioned; 'Ālamgīr I was a learned jurist himself. These monarchs looked upon themselves as Muslim emperors and did not come into conflict with the shar'. They increasingly, and to the extent they thought it politic, brought the polity into conformity with the dictates of the law; they were religious minded people who were sincere in their desire to serve Islam.[40] Even 'Ālamgīr I was not unmindful of the difficulties in his way, nor of the necessity of being politic.

[39] *Cambridge History of India*, iv, pp. 230-318.

[40] Jahāngīr has generally been painted by modern historians as almost completely devoid of Islamic feelings and indifferent to religion. This is not correct. His own memoirs and contemporary works leave a different impression. He had an 'ibādatkhānah, not for religious controversies, but, as literally indicated by the name, for worship and contemplation (Mu'tamad Khān, p. 193); he spent Thursday nights, which according to Muslim calculation form part of the Muslim day of congregational worship, Friday, in the company of the learned and the pious (Jahāngīr, p. 9); he asked them to make for him a rosary of the more easily remembered names of God which he might repeat (*ibid.*); he kept awake to spend part of the night in meditation and worship (*ibid.*, p. 232); and even engaged in polemics with Hindu pandits (*ibid.*, p. 14).

Shāh Jahān was depicted as being the man of destiny who would restore the glory of Islam in his realm ('Abd-u'l-Ḥamīd, i, p. 134).

It is needless to emphasize 'Ālamgīr's religious zeal.

The Mughul emperors assumed the title of pādshāh. Abū'l-Faḍl explains the etymology by saying that pād signifies stability and possession and shāh means origin and lord; thus pādshāh is a lord or a king who is so powerful that he cannot be ousted by anyone. It was, however, used for a superior king, an emperor.[41] The Turkish imperial title of 'sultan' was degraded by the Mughuls and awarded to princes; some of whom, like Shāh Jahān and Bahādur Shāh I were given the title of shāh before they succeeded to the throne. The Mughul government was highly centralized, and the emperor was the real pivot of the government. No important administrative decision was taken without his full cognizance; many matters of detail and, by modern standards, trivial were regularly brought to his notice. There was no branch of the administration which did not receive his attention; there was very little delegation of power. He very often commanded armies in person; if expeditions were entrusted to others, he kept in close touch with the progress of the campaigns and would intervene when he thought it necessary. The affairs of the household, of finance, of matters relating to the provincial administration and the safety of the communications, the condition of the peasants, prices, trade, industry, the promotion of learning and the patronage of the talented, in short, all governmental activity received his closest scrutiny. His officers were all his servants depending upon him for advancement, and even for holding the ranks which were assigned to them; the only permanent aristocracy consisted of the Rājpūt and other Hindu chiefs who were hereditary rulers of their states which varied in size. Many of them served as Mughul officers and held their states, in theory at least, as assignments; others were recognized to hold authority in their territories, but dependent upon the emperor. They, however, did not form a well-knit class to challenge the authority of the emperor. In theory, the only limitation of his authority was provided by the shar', and Akbar demonstrated that he could transgress these limits to some extent with the help and cooperation of the non-Muslims and the dissident sections of Muslims themselves.

41 Blochmann, i, p. ii (Abū-'l-Faḍl's Introduction); also, Nūr-u'l-Ḥaqq, f. 5.

Though much more absolute than their predecessors, the Sultans of Dehlī, in their power, the Mughuls were yet no exception to the political doctrine that no power is without its limitations. Akbar's experience itself shows that the orthodox Muslims could be alienated only up to a point, and it was dangerous to provoke them into opposition. Some of the historians writing in or near Akbar's reign did not consider his lapses to be serious, yet they led to discontent and rebellion, and quite early a strong movement came into existence which restored orthodoxy to its former position. Besides, the old harmony in the ranks of the governing classes was replaced by such acute struggle that ultimately the empire succumbed to it. The Mughul Empire built up a prestige for itself which was the outcome of its respect for the needs and welfare of the people; if it had not followed an enlightened policy of keeping the people contented and happy, it would have succumbed earlier to its inner tensions. 'Ālamgīr realized that it was difficult to impose the injunctions of the shar' again once they had been discarded, and howsoever great might be orthodox support, it was not sufficient to enable him to pursue smoothly the policy of reconverting the empire to the position of pre-Akbar days when orthodox Islam was supreme.[42] The Rajputs and other Hindu chiefs could have created difficulties, as the Marathas did later, if they had made common cause, and it was not too difficult to provoke them to that extent by wrong policies. 'Ālamgīr is held up by modern writers as a paragon of intolerance against the Hindus but he did not go beyond the imposition of jiziyah, the demolition of temples built or repaired without sanction, and the suppression of certain spectacular and festive institutions, some of which, like Holi, caused annoyance and inconvenience to others. These measures were provocative; some of them were new and others created resentment because they had been discarded in the previous reigns. As against these measures, there are many documents still in the possession of Brahmin families which record grants of land to temples and their priests, the lists of Hindu officers holding high

[42] *e.g.*, 'Ālamgīr I himself mentions how difficult it was for him to reimpose the jiziyah, Khawāfī Khān, ii, p. 378.

ranks, letters praising Hindu servants of the state for duties well performed and rewarding them for their loyalty and efficiency, of rebuking Muslim officers who sought preference over non-Muslim servants because of their religion. It was because of such acts that he still was served loyally by many non-Muslims; yet his measures which were disliked by the non-Muslims weakened the empire and involved him in difficulties.[43] It is, thus, obvious that the same political factors as impose limitations upon the power of other absolute governments were active in the Mughul Empire.

As the shar' does not envisage hereditary monarchy, it provides no law of succession for monarchical dynasties. The law held on tenaciously to the principle of election, but it was generally believed that there was no bar to the succession of a son to the throne of his father. This was a compromise with the position created by the establishment of dynasties in the Muslim world. There were several precedents among the Mughuls when territories were virtually divided among several sons; sometimes princes went on contending for power and thrones, the fact of rebellion being treated rather lightly. Bābur had to fight for his heritage from a very early age; Humāyūn was faced with the opposition of all his brothers at one time or another. Only too often did he forgive his brothers and ultimately Kāmrān, the arch rebel, was blinded and exiled, which, judging by his long record of rebellion and fighting against his brother was not such an extreme measure, because his life was spared. The other brothers who also had rebelled and proclaimed themselves emperors on various occasions, were leniently treated. Akbar's brother, Ḥakim, who had marched against the emperor at a critical time in his reign to contest the imperial throne was forgiven. Salīm's rebellion was not serious; it was petulant behaviour to draw Akbar's attention to the fact that the prince had grown into a mature man which needed some recognition. At the time of his father's death, Salīm had a serious

[43]References to Hindu officials employed by 'Ālamgir I are too numerous and well known to be quoted; some Brahmin families hold documents of grants of land made by 'Ālamgīr I to temples, *e.g.*, Indian Historical Records Commission Proceedings, 1946. Also Jnan Chandra, "Aurangzib and Hindu Temples", *Journal of the Pakistan Historical Society*, October 1957, pp. 241, 242.

competitor for the throne in his son Khusraw who could not reconcile himself, even after Salīm's accession, to have to wait for the crown. Khurram's way to the throne also was littered with difficulties which had been created by Nūr Jahān and her party. The War of Succession which led to Awrangzīb's enthronement involved almost the entire empire in war and led to considerable weakening of the administrative machinery. When he was able to establish his power Awrangzīb, now 'Ālamgīr, had to take special measures to restore the economic life of the empire and its administrative efficiency.[44] The climax, however, came after 'Ālamgīr I's death. His sons had prepared too long and the result would be more a matter of resources than personal character. 'Ālamgīr I was fully aware of the consequences of such a war and he tried to persuade his sons to agree to a division of the empire.[45] They did not agree. The empire, bled by the long war in the Deccan, with anarchy still threatening to swallow it up, was subjected to another war of succession. Gradually the empire lost all power, but it never lost, up to its final extinction, the tradition of rivalry among the princes for the throne. Nothing contributed so much to its final dissolution as the absence of any recognized principles of succession.

The Mughul Empire provided a real need in filling up the vacuum in political power after the weakening of the Sultanate of Dehlī. It started on its career of glory under Akbar and fell to pieces soon after 'Ālamgīr I. Bābur's initial victories had shown the military decadence of the Sultanate; Humāyūn's easy conquests of Gujrat and Mālwah had demonstrated further that the other kingdoms of the subcontinent also were no better. It was Sher Shāh's military and political genius which took advantage of the divisions in the Mughul camp and succeeded in turning out the Mughuls; but after his death the chronic divisions among the Afghāns recrudesced until Humāyūn was able to come back. Then began the historic mission of the Mughul Empire to give peace and good government to the subcontinent which had been torn

[44] Kāẓim, p. 438.

[45] Ashraf Khān, f. 7 b.

with internecine warfare. The Mughuls created confidence and by following their ideal of benevolent and paternal government won the respect of the people. The empire achieved almost a sanctity. Even when the forces of anarchy succeeded in depriving the emperor of all his power, they took considerable time to reduce his prestige. Sindhīyā held the Emperor Shāh 'Ālam as a puppet and granted him so meagre an allowance that the court was almost starving and in tatters; and yet his master the Peshwā received the imperial grant of appointing him the vicegerent of the Empire with great ceremony attended with public rejoicing and Sindhiyā himself was proud of having been appointed the deputy vicegerent. The British officers signed themselves as "servants of the Emperor Shāh 'Ālam" although the company would not pay him a pie out of the revenues of the land which they ostensibly administered for him. The need to hide the political reality under a legal myth arose from the fact that the empire was too deeply enshrined in popular affection to make it good policy to proclaim that its authority had been usurped. To the Muslims, the emperor was a symbol of their sovereignty; to the non-Muslims, of ordered and benevolent government. It is not surprising that the myth propounded by Abū-'l-Faḍl that royalty was a ray of Divine Light, though un-Islamic in spirit and transgressing the Hindu ideas of exclusiveness, found a place in popular belief.

CHAPTER III

The Imperial Court and Household

THE Mughul Emperor was the pivot of the government. The centralization was so great that many a matter of detail was referred to him for orders. Foreign travellers and local observers were alike impressed with the diligent and painstaking habits of the monarchs during the days of the greatness of the empire.[1] Their lives had, therefore, to be strictly regulated, and their schedule of work well defined. The ceremonial, as well as the methods of work, needed a rigid and exacting time table to enable the machine to function smoothly. The people and the servants of the emperor alike had to know when a particular category of business was to come up for disposal or discussion before the emperor to prevent confusion. The nature of business also determined the number of people attending the audience, and, therefore, various

1 *e.g.*, Bernier, pp. 129, 130.
Ni'mat Khān 'Āli, *Waqā'i'*. a work full of hostile satire on the Emperor 'Ālamgīr has several references to his hard work and paucity of rest and sleep.

institutions grew up which, through convention and necessity, became the media of the transaction of the business of the state. This laid restrictions upon the time of the monarch to an extent that he was no longer the master of his daily routine. The conduct of all state business was so dependent upon his attention that he could not neglect his onerous duties without dislocating the administration. He had also to conquer the disabilities imposed by indisposition, as long as his strength permitted, to prevent the circulation of rumours regarding his safety or health which might set into motion forces which could result in serious consequences.[2] When Shāh Jahān's illness prevented him from showing himself to the people, the consequences were that the emperor lost his throne and his freedom and his favourite son the chances of succeeding to the throne and his life.

We have authentic accounts of the daily routine of work of Shāh Jahān and 'Ālamgīr I. Akbar, also, worked hard and, in addition, spent considerable time in meditation and discussion of religious problems.[3] Jahāngīr, until his declining health prevented him from attending to strenuous duties, was conscientious in the transaction of public business and, contrary to popular notions, was interested in religious discussions as well as devotional exercises. The impression created by certain writers that he was a besotted drunkard is not true.[4] Even when he was unwell, he did not abstain from attending the jharokah-i-darshan, the dīwān-i-'ām or the dīwān-i-khāṣ.[5] When the emperors did find themselves unequal to such an arduous life, the empire lost its vitality, because, among the medley of causes, the character and calibre of the later emperors played an important role in the decline of the empire.

A study of Shāh Jahān's daily schedule will illustrate the rigour of a Mughul emperor's life. He got up before the first streak of the light of the dawn, made his morning ablutions and went from his sleeping quarters, the khwābgāh, to the royal mosque in the palace. There he offered his prayers in congregation and then

[2] *e.g.*, Jahāngīr, p. 130.

[3] Abū-'l-Faḍl, *Ā'īn-i-Akbarī*, i, Ā'īn 72.

[4] Jahāngīr, p. 9, p. 232; Mu'tamad Khān, p. 129.

[5] Jahāngīr, p. 130.

remained busy in reading the Qur'ān and worship and meditation until the Sun had risen fully. Then he went to the jharokah-i-darshan, where he spent two or three gharīs. At about four gharīs after dawn he held the dīwān-i-'ām. Then he moved to the dīwān-i-khāṣ. This was followed by the transaction of confidential business in Shāh Burj.

At noon he retired to his private apartments, where he had luncheon with the empress and other ladies of the court. The empress or the chief stewardess of the palace brought to the notice of the emperor the cases of deserving women who needed help, and the monarch was pleased to make suitable grants. Then the emperor had a short siesta and came out after offering the afternoon prayers. He then went to the dīwān-i-'ām and inspected the guard who displayed the royal standards. If there was any outstanding business, it was executed.

By now the dīwān-i-khāṣ had been lit, and the emperor went there. First the sunset prayers were offered; then for about four or five gharīs official business was transacted, after which the emperor rose for the evening prayers. This was followed by another session in the Shāh Burj.

At midnight he retired to his sleeping apartments, the khwābgāh.[6]

Other emperors made minor variations in the strict schedule in accordance with their predilections or necessity, but during the period when the empire was vigorous, all devoted themselves to their duties in an exemplary manner. It was only towards the end when the emperors became degenerate and lost grip over he affairs of the state that they wasted their time in pleasure or idle pursuits.

Each one of the institutions mentioned above had its functions and utility. It would be correct to say that the emperor's time was spent mostly in the transaction of public business.

The jharokah-i-darshan was the balcony from which the emperor showed himself to the populace. In the fortress palaces of

[6] Ashraf Khān, ff. 34, 35; 'Abd-u'l-Ḥamīd, i. pp. 146-153.

A gharī=24 minutes; a day=60 gharīs, *ibid*, ii, p. 339; for 'Ālamgīr I, vide Kāẓim, pp. 1097-1106. There are naturally minor variations in his schedule.

Agra, Delhi and Lahore, there was provided a balcony overlooking the open space lying between the moat and the river, where a large concourse of men could collect without let or hindrance. Akbar was the originator of this idea.[7] A sect, called the Darshaniyahs, grew up among the Hindus, who considered it auspicious and an act of worship to behold the face of the emperor before transacting any business; they neither ate nor drank until they had seen the emperor.[8] Any person who had any plaint to make to the emperor or sought redress of some grievance could raise his hand and men attached to the department of maẓālim would collect these petitions and escort the petitioners into the emperor's presence in the dīwān-i-'ām or, sometimes, dīwān-i-khāṣ.[9] Sometimes elephant fights were held here and occasionally troops were reviewed. 'Ālamgīr I did not like the adulation of the emperor by the Darshaniyahs, which smacked to him of man worship; therefore he abolished the institution.[10] Besides it was Shāh Jahān's absence from the jharokah-i-darshan which started the rumours which ultimately cost him his throne. This could not have been the main reason in 'Ālamgīr's mind, because the emperor's illness could not be kept a secret anyhow. The beneficial nature of the jharokah-i-darshan must have been known to 'Ālamgīr I because it had kept the monarch in close touch with his people, who, in this way, had direct access to him. 'Ālamgīr I tried to remedy this situation by devoting to the dispensation of justice the time which had been given to jharokah-i-darshan by the previous emperors.[11] Care must have been taken to see that all who sought the emperor's intervention were escorted to his presence; but even this was not an adequate alternative.

The hall of public audience was called dawlat-khānah-i-'ām wa khāṣ or, more briefly, dīwān-i-'ām.[12] All business of a formal

7 Abū-'l-Faḍl, *Ā'īn-i-Akbarī*, i, Ā'īn 73.

8 Khawāfī Khān, i, p. 213; Ashraf Khān, f. 34 b.

9 'Abd-u'l-Ḥamīd, i, p. 144.

10 Khawāfī Khān, i, p. 213.

11 Kāẓim, pp. 1097, 1098.

12 'Abd-u'l-Ḥamīd, i, p. 146. Popularly the building is even now called dīwān-i-'ām; Ashraf Khān uses the terms dīwān-i-'ām and dīwan-i-khāṣ f. 34.

nature was mostly transacted here. The dīwān-i-a'lā or the chief dīwān, the first bakhshī, the royal princes, the higher officials of the state and the manṣabdārs were in attendance.

The princes stood on the right and the left, and, sometimes when permission was granted, they sat in their appointed places. The high officials stood near the throne, which was raised, and made reports about political and financial matters. The petitions of the manṣabdārs were presented by the bakhshī; some of the manṣabdārs received orders for promotion or assignment of new duties; those who came from the provinces and the remote parts of the empire paid their respects; those who were posted away from the capital were given leave to depart. It was here that the ahadīs were presented through their bakhshī and the mīr ātish brought the mounted musketeers for review. Matters regarding the khāliṣah and the buyātāt were reported by the dīwān and mīr sāmān. The petitions of the princes and governors of provinces were presented here; the emperor read the important applications himself, while those from officials of lower grades were read out to him by the officers. The ṣadr presented the applications of the provincial ṣadrs and made recommendations regarding the stipends and grants for the learned and the pious. The emperor reviewed the beasts belonging to the imperial stables. The officer in charge of 'arḍ-i-mukarrar received confirmation of the previous orders.

The official name of the dīwān-i-khāṣ was dawlat-khānah-i-khāṣ. It was popularly called the ghuslkhānah, because earlier, there was a building between the harem and the offices of the dīwān which had contained the imperial bath. In a section of this building Akbar, after his bath, received some of the important officers. Later a separate building was put up for this purpose, but it continued to be called the ghuslkhānah. The name of dawlat-khānah-i-khās was conferred upon it by Shāh Jahān; this building also came to be called dīwān-i-khāṣ in course of time.[13] Only the highest officials were admitted to this hall. Here the emperor

[13] 'Abd-u'l-Ḥamīd, i, p. 148. The building came to be known popularly as dīwān-i-khās.

sometimes wrote the replies of important communications in his own handwriting; drafts prepared by the secretariat were approved and signed; instructions for the preparation of drafts of orders on petitions or of replies to various communications were given here. The dīwān, the bakhshī and the ṣadr obtained orders on such matters as were not considered fit for being dealt with in the dīwān-i-'ām. The reports of the various newswriters stationed in the provinces were considered by the emperor. Craftsmen who had produced something worthy of royal interest were permitted to display their wares; architects presented the plans of new buildings; sometimes the emperor inspected his hunting falcons and leopards; occasionally horses of exceptional quality were also inspected in the court of the dīwān-i-khāṣ. The audience in Shāh Burj was meant for even more exclusive meetings to which only the royal princes and a few high officials were admitted.[14] Matters of state which needed secret consultation with the wazīr or with a few of the highest officials were brought up here.

The privy chamber, or the khalwat-kadah-i-khāṣ was intended to give the emperor an opportunity of cultivating the company of the learned and the accomplished.[15] It was here that the monarch listened to music, or poetry composed by poets either employed by the court or outsiders. Historians described the events of the previous reigns and ages; religious leaders discussed matters of theology; mystics explained the recorded experiences of those who had gone before; philosophers expounded the theories of their schools; in short this was the time when the monarch found relaxation from the daily routine of business in cultural, artistic and intellectual pursuits.

Such an elaborate system could work smoothly only with a large staff trained to arrange large functions efficiently and silently; because the Mughul emperors were aware of the need of maintaining a high standard of splendour and pageantry; besides nothing which could compromise the dignity of the imperial audiences

14 'Abd-u'l-Ḥamīd, i, p. 153. Ashraf Khān mentions Asad Burj in place of Shāh Burj, f. 35b; *Ruqqa'āt-i-'Ālamgīrī* (p.6) has also Asad Burj.

15 Ashraf Khān, f. 35b; 'Abd-u'l-Hamīd simply calls it mushkawā-i-dawlat

could be tolerated. The mechanism was perfected over a number of years and became, in course of time, almost sanctified even in matters of detail.

Though theoretically it was recognized by the Mughuls that the Imperial Household was a distinct branch, yet this distinction was blurred and the Imperial Household was integrated with the general administrative organs to a larger degree than it had been formerly.[16] The Sultans had an officer called wakīl-i-dar who was the head of the administration of the imperial household. Humāyūn had a corresponding officer called wakīl-i-dar-i-khānah but this office seems to have fallen into disuse quite early.[17] Akbar was fond of integrating various services into monolithic organizations; in the field of religion as well, his philosophy was to create some kind of unity out of diversity; the same spirit seems to have been at work in the reorganization of the Imperial Household. It was recognized under the Sultans as well that the Imperial Household occupied an important place in the administration of the empire; but its organization was kept separate; under the Mughuls, however, high officials of the government were assigned household duties. The wakīl, who corresponded to the malik nā'ib of the Sultanate and was lord lieutenant of the realm, was also the head of the Imperial Household.[18] A large number of important household duties were performed by mīr sāmān, whose importance was recognized later by the award of the more dignified nomenclature of khān sāmān, but he was subordinate in some respects to the dīwān and many of his functions related to public administration.[19] The fact of the matter is that the Mughuls did not draw a firm line between the household and public functions; the monarch was the state so far as the Mughuls

[16] The distinction was not completely obliterated, as Abū-'l-Faḍl refers to the Household directly as well as indirectly; *Ā' īn-i-Akbarī,* i. Ā' In 1, 73 etc.

[17] I. H. Qureshi, *The Administration of the Sultanate of Dehlī*, pp. 59, 60.

[18] Abū-'l-Faḍl's Preface in *Ā'īn-i-Akbarī*, under wakīl, p. 4.

[19] One incumbent of the office under Jahāngīr was called khān-i-sāmān; under 'Ālamgīr I the higher title was officially adopted, *Ḍawābiṭ-i-' Ālamgīrī* lists him as khān-i- sāmān, *f.* 21. Abū-'l-Faḍl, *Ā'īn-i-Akbarī*, ii, Ā'īn 11, also mentions khān-i-sāmān; the title, therefore, had come into use under Akbar.

were concerned; their personal needs and the needs of the state were all mixed up and were alike looked after by public officers.

Indeed, Abū 'l-Faḍl seems to imply that it was only in the sphere of purely domestic matters that the functions of the Imperial Household could be separated from public business, because he classifies merely the monarch's companions and "the servants who at court perform the duties about the king" separately from the public servants.[20] The more important officials, who in accordance with the classical Muslim practice would have been considered to be Household officers, have been classified by Abū 'l Faḍl as public officials.[21] The confusion has become worse because Abū 'l-Faḍl has followed the classical Muslim fashion of describing many of the departments held by these officers under the broad classification of the Household.[22] It may be argued that the imperial court and its various institutions through which the emperor transacted business were media of public business and should be treated as such; this view may have considerable justification; but even then there is no other category except that of the Household to which several officers and many of the functions of certain other officers can be assigned. It is for this reason that the wakīl has been called the emperor's lieutenant in matters relating to the realm and the Household.[23] Under him among the officers of the Household, were the mīr māl, the muhrdār, the bārbegī, the qūrbegī, the mīr tuzuk, the mīr manzil, the k͟hwānsālār, the mun͟shī, the qū͟shbegī, and the āk͟htahbegī.[24] The mīr māl was, as the title implies, the emperor's private treasurer; the muhrdār was the keeper of the royal seals, though sometimes the main seal, the uzuk muhr, was kept in the custody of the

[20] Vide Abū-'l-Fadl's Preface to *Ā'in-i-Akbarī* where the monarch's assistants and servants are divided into four classes: (i) the nobles of the state, (ii) the assistants of victory, (iii) the companions of the monarch and (iv) the servants. Of these the last two obviously come under the category of the Household, pp. 4,5.

[21] All the officers whose functions have been described in this chapter fall under the first two categories mentioned in 20.

[22] Book i of Abū-'l-Fadl's *Ā'in-i-Akbari* deals with the departments of the Household.

[23] *Ibid.*, Preface, p. 4.

[24] *Ibid.*

empress.[25] The bārbegī controlled the admission to the various audiences; the qūrbegī was the keeper of the royal arms and insignia; the mīr tuzuk was the master of ceremonies at the court and organized the various audiences. The mīr manzil was the quartermaster of the court; it was an onerous assignment because the court travelled frequently and, for considerable parts of the year, lived in camps which were really cities of tents often pitched only for a single night. The khwānsālār was in charge of the kitchen and the table. The qūshbegī looked after the aviaries, which consisted of pigeons, hawks, falcons and other birds. Akbar was very fond of pigeons, and liked to watch their performances and acrobatics. The hawks and falcons were used in hunts.[26] The ākhtahbegī was an important officer and looked after the royal stables which also raised horses for the army. His importance was based on the fact that the cavalry was the most important arm in the Mughul military organization.[27] The wazīr, or dīwān as he was often called, also played an important role in the affairs of the household.[28] A large section of Household affairs was under the mīr sāmān. Abū-'l-Faḍl places him among the subordinates of the wazīr. The wazīr's jurisdiction extended to all matters of a financial nature in the realm as well as the Household.[29]

The mīr sāmān had charge of all government property, all sequestration of other property, arrangements made on the occasions of the weddings of the members of the royal family, the general supervision of the buyūtāt and the certification of the salaries of the palace servants.[30] He was assisted in the management of the buyūtāt by the dīwān-i-buyūtāt, who was almost independent of him in financial matters.[31] Later an officer called

[25] 'Abd-u'l-Ḥamīd, i, p. 148.

[26] Abū-'l-Faḍl, *Ā'īn-i-Akbarī*,ii, Ā'īn 29.

[27] *Ibid.*, i, Ā'īn 53.

[28] *Ibid.*, Abū-'l-Faḍl's Preface, pp. 4,5.

[29] *Ibid.*

[30] *Ḍawābiṭ-i-'Ālamgīrī*, ff. 22b, 23a.

[31] 'Abd-u'l-Ḥamīd, i, pp. 146, 147, mentions that the mīr sāmān and the dīwān-i-buyūtāt were in attendance upon the monarch in the dīwān-i-'ām and made various statements; *Ḍawābiṭ-i-'Ālamgīrī* says that the dīwān-i-buyūtāt functioned in cooperation with khān-i-sāmān (باتناق); ff. 22, 23.

nāẓir-i-buyūtāt was added.[32]

The titles and the functions of these officials throw some light upon the organization of the Household and its administration and needs. Abū-'l-Faḍl mentions that the affairs of the Household received the personal attention of the monarch, which was natural in view of its importance in the affairs of the state.[33] Though many of the servants of the Household received their salaries from the general payroll, yet in the year 1595, a sum of 309,186,795 dāms was disbursed as salaries in the Household.[34] Abū-'l-Fadl mentions that there were more than one hundred offices and workshops attached to the Household at that time.[35] Many of these, however, did not fall exactly under the category of merely Household departments and were, in fact, institutions of public administration. For instance, the imperial treasuries were really the treasure houses of the empire; the mints performed no household function; some of the departments had a dual capacity, catering for the needs of the Household as well as the state.[36]

For historical reasons three cities had come to be looked upon as imperial cities. The earlier Mughuls had preferred Agra to Delhi. Akbar built the famous Fatḥpūr Sīkrī, which, however, was deserted after a brief occupation. Agra expanded greatly under the fostering care of Akbar and came to be called Akbar-ābād for that reason. The need for vigilance on the northwest frontier led to long sojourns of the court at Lahore. Shāh Jahān built the city of Shāhjahānābād near Sher Shāh's Dehlī. All these cities had palace fortresses for the emperor; their layout shows how much the system of the various audiences had been standardized; because the halls for the various ceremonies were provided in all of them and to some extent were imitated elsewhere as well, especially at Amber, the seat of the Kachhwāhahs. Unlike the arks of the Persian cities, these fortresses were not in the centre of

32 The nāẓir-i-buyūtāt had come into existence under Akbar, Abū-'l-Faḍl *Ā'īn-i-Akbarī*, i, p. 4.

33 Abū-'l-Faḍl, *Ā'īn-i-Akbarī*, i, Ā'īn 1

34 *Ibid.* There were 40 dams to a rupee.

35 *Ibid.*

36 *e.g.*, the arsenal, the imperial stables.

the township, but were placed on one side near the river, so that the palace might have a good view of the river as the Mughuls were fond of running water. In this way a good and constant supply of water could also be insured. Such a location also provided plenty of room for the review of troops and sports, as well as the concourse of the people who came to see the emperor when he sat in the jharokah-i-darshan.

The palace was roughly divided into three sections, the outmost was open to all officers and subjects who had any business in the palace. The next was earmarked for the more exclusive audiences.[37] In the Red Fort at Dehlī, in the later days, there was a red curtain at one end of the enclosure of the dīwān-i-'ām; only those specially privileged were admitted beyond it.[38] A little farther from the various buildings, where the monarch held council or transacted business, was the harem. In Muslim lands the quarters reserved for women are called ḥaram, or a sanctuary; it is the same word which is used for the holiest places in the world of Islam. The word signifies the respect shown to women and to the sanctity of domestic life.

The Mughul harem consisted of the royal espouses, the emperor's mother, sisters, daughters and other female relations who were permitted to live there. There was an army of servants, guards and officials; the ladies of rank had their own apartments; and the harem consisted of several palaces and pavilions, assigned to the ladies in accordance with their ranks.[39] The ladies were paid allowances either in cash or in the form of assignments, called barg bahā.[40] The harem had a financial officer attached to it for the purpose of drawing up the estimates of the expenditure and supervising all disbursements.[41] Under him there were dāroghahs

[37] Vide the plans and descriptions of the various fortress palaces in the Archaeological Survey Reports of India; *Cambridge History of India* iv, plate XXXIX has a good plan of the citadel of Shāhjahānābād.

[38] Syed Ahmed Khan, *Āthār-u'ṣ-ṣanādid*, Chapter II, p. 42. In later days those privileged to go beyond the curtain were called Lāl Parda'ī.

[39] Abū-'l-Faḍl, *Ā'īn-i-Akbarī*, i, Ā'īn 15.

[40] *Ibid.*, p. 40. The allowance came to be called barg bahā, price of leaves, *i.e.*, the money for pān, betel leaves, Mukhliṣ, *Mir'at-u'l-iṣṭilāḥ*, f. 26 a.

[41] Abū-'l-Faḍl, *Ā'īn-i-Akbarī*. Ā'īn 15.

or superintendents, all of them women, who supervised various departments connected with the administration of the seraglio.[42] The inside of the harem was guarded by armed women guards; the most trustworthy of them were placed near the emperor's sleeping apartments. Beyond them was a guard of eunuchs; then there were male guards, mostly faithful Rajputs. Then there were the usual porters and beyond them was the military guard.[43]

Those troops which were easily available, not having been posted at long distances, were divided into eighty-four divisions for the purpose of mounting guard at the imperial residence. Seven of these were brought up every month to mount guard, so that each one was on duty once a week for a month. They were under the command of a manşabdār. Every evening the royal arms, standards and insignia were brought out and displayed; the contingents who were to be on duty for the next twenty-four hours were drawn up on the right in front of the dīwān-i-'ām, those who were being relieved were drawn up on the left. The emperor generally inspected the guards himself and took their salute; if, for some reason the emperor was not able to come, he invariably asked a prince to officiate for him.[44]

The Household maintained armed personnel for special needs as well. For instance, the qūrchīs were in charge of the royal insignia; the silaḥdārs were the custodians of the royal arms; they acted as the royal bodyguard in all public audiences as well as in royal processions. Contingents of archers and mounted musketeers were also in attendance. Mace bearers, yasāwals with encrusted gold and silver batons, khidmatiyahs and other footmen maintained order on these occasions. The mace bearers and the yasāwals were also used to carry the royal orders to public officials and were sometimes asked to ensure compliance.[45] An important officer of the Household was the mīr 'arḍ; it was he through whom all the petitions were sent to the emperor. All

[42] *Ibid.*

[43] *Ibid.*

[44] *Ibid.*, ii, Ā'īn 9 , called kishik from Turki kishik, also chaukī, Abū-'l-Faḍl, *Akbarnāmah*, iii, p. 146.

[45] Brahman. *Qawā'id-i-salṭanat-i-Shāh Jahān*, p. 51.

orders of the emperor which were issued directly from the palace were communicated through the mīr 'ard to the commander of the guards, who took steps to see that they were delivered to the parties concerned.[46]

When the court was travelling, it spent the nights, and in cases of sojourns at some spot, days as well, in well-planned camps.[47] The Mughuls were exceedingly partial to camp life and, therefore, a good deal of time was spent in travel.[48] The Mughul camp was like a moving city.[49] The imperial tents were in the centre. The harem, the dīwān-i-'ām, the dīwān-i-khās and other buildings of public importance had their counterparts in the camp. The larger tents were made of timber and in fact were portable buildings which could be taken apart and reassembled; some of these were two storeys high. These tents were all in duplicate; when the court moved from one site, the tents and all the equipment and furniture was moved two stages ahead, and erected there; in this way, there was always a fully constructed camp available for sojourn when the court reached a new spot. This was possible because the tents travelled twice the distance which was covered by the court in one day. The mīr manzils went ahead and selected suitable sites for camps; for each of these two camps were employed a thousand farrāshes, five hundred pioneers, one hundred water carriers, fifty carpenters, tent makers, torch bearers, thirty workers in leather and one hundred sweepers. In addition, were those who constituted the staff of the manṣabdārs. When the entourage moved in, they knew exactly where they would find their quarters; because the internal plan of this mobile city was never altered. The location for the humblest shopkeeper and camp follower was defined to prevent any confusion. In the middle was planted the ākās diyā, the lamp of the sky, so called because of its height. Its main purpose was to show to stragglers and wayfarers where the

[46] Abū-'l-Fadl, *Akbarnāmah*, iii, p. 147; also Abū-'l-Faḍl, *Ā'in-i-Akbari*. ii, Ā'in 9.

[47] *Ibid.*, Ā'ins 16, 17.

[48] It is surprising how little time was spent by the court at the capital; if military campaigns or political needs did not take the emperor to a distant province for some time, the court moved to Kashmir for the summer.

[49] Abū-'l-Fadl, *Ā'in-i-Akbari*, i, Ā'ins. 16, 17.

imperial camp was situated. Behind it was the naqqārkhānah, where the royal band played music, and, farther away, was the dīwān-i-'ām. The tents and the furnishings needed one hundred elephants, four hundred carts and one hundred porters for transportation. When the entourage was moving, water carriers ran in front sprinkling the road to prevent the dust from rising.[50]

The first insignia of royalty was the inclusion of the monarch's name in khutbah, which is a formal sermon delivered on the occasion of the congregational prayers of Friday and the two 'Ids.[51] It included a prayer for the welfare of the Muslim community and, as its head, for the reigning monarch. The next in importance was that the coins of the realm bore the emperor's name, though a departure in this respect was made by Jahāngīr, who struck some pieces in which his name was coupled with that of his beloved empress Nūr Jahān.[52] He had also struck some coins at Allahabad when he was still a prince and sent a few to his father; in these coins his own name appeared along with the name of his father. Akbar was displeased at this action.[53] The throne, the chatr, the sāi'bān and the kawkabah were meant exclusively for the emperor. The chatr was an umbrella adorned with precious jewels; the sā'ibān, also called āftābgīr, was an oval umbrella encrusted with jewels to be held over the monarch like the chatr. The kawkabahs were hung up in the assembly halls; a kawkabah consisted of two globes. Under Akbar the shamsah also was considered to be an important emblem; it resembled, as its names shows, the sun and was affixed to the walls or gates of the imperial palace. Abū-'l-Faḍl gives it the first place among the royal insignia because of the veneration in which his royal master held that luminary. Various kinds of flags and standards also were included among imperial insignia, as was the right to play the band in front of the imperial residence; but these privileges were conferred upon

[50] *Ibid.*, Ā'īns. 16, 17.

[51] This was universally recognised in the world of Islam; compare I. H. Qureshi, *The Administration of the Sultanate of Dehli*, p. 74.

[52] *Cambridge History of India*, iv, 180.

[53] *Ibid.*, p. 149.

distinguished subjects as well.[54] Sometimes the emperors conferred title of shāh or king upon some favoured prince and then he was permitted to use some of the insignia usually associated with royalty.[55]

Mention has already been made of the buyūtāt or the kārkhānāhs. The former term was used by the Mughuls; it is a double plural of the Arabic word bait, a house; hence the association of the buyūtāt with the Household in the mind of the Mughul administrators is quite obvious. The more ancient and popular kārkhānah, however, persisted. The kārkhānahs played an important role not only in the sphere of the Household, but also in the military and fiscal setup of the empire; besides they had considerable impact upon the industrial progress of the territories. For this reason, the entire organization was under the general supervision of the dīwān.[56] The internal finance were looked after the the dīwān-i-buyūtāt who was assisted by the wazīr. These officers were under the mīr sāmān, who was responsible to the dīwān. Traditionally there were thirty six buyūtāt or kārkhānahs; the following are mentioned in the Ā'īn: the treasuries, the mint, the farrāshkhānah, illumination and lights, the qūrkhānah, the workshop for making the royal seals, the ābdārkhānah, the kitchen, the fruitery, the perfumery, the wardrobe and the bedding and mattresses, the pīlkhānah, the stables for horses, the camel stables, the cow stables, the mule stables, buildings, the library, the arsenal, the workshops for the manufacture of shawls and textiles.[57] Other authorities mention many more; Sir Jadunath Sarkar has collected more than seventy names from various sources.[58] It seems more probable that the number thirty-six was traditional, having come down from the days of the Sultanate when it had some

[54] Abū-'l-Fadl, *Ā'īn-i-Akbarī*, i, Ā'īn 19. "Khusraw (of Iran)......... made two globes of steel and called it a kawkabah," Najaf 'Ah, f. 31a.

[55] *e.g.*, Shāh Jahān, vide Jahāngir, p. 195.

[56] Abū-'l-Fadl, *Āin-i-Akbari*, i, p. 4.

[57] For the traditional number of 36, vide *e.g.*, Shākir Khān, f. 13b. Farrāshkhānah = the store for carpets etc., qūrkhānah = store of insignia, banners, flags, etc., ābdārkhānah = water and drinks, pīlkhānah = elephant stables.

[58] Sarkar, *Mughal Administration*, pp. 170-175.

relevance.[59] In those days, the classification was logical and defined. Under the Mughuls the number of the various stores, factories, workshops and stables grew in view of new needs; some of the older ones had to be split into independent organizations; it was not considered necessary to confine the number to the traditional thirty-six or to make out lists of a strictly logical nature. Every need which was felt had to be fulfilled, and a store or a workshop was added to the existing establishments. The staff of every kārkhānah varied in accordance with the needs; for instance the matbakh or the kitchen would have chefs and cooks whereas the library would employ calligraphists and painters.[60] At the head of every kārkhānah, however, there was a dāroghah or a superintendent, assisted by clerks and accountants.[61]

The main function of the kārkhānahs was to keep the palace and some branches of the government supplied with the commodities which they needed. These varied from the food served on the monarch's table to the pieces of artillery required by the imperial forces. The buyūtāt included the public treasury, because the final trustee of the public funds was the monarch himself and he had unquestioned authority over the disposal of the resources of the government; the mint was included because the minting of the coins of the realm was an imperial responsibility, given up only when the emperors were no longer able to control the provincial governments. The artillery, once again, was attached to the household, because it was considered imprudent to leave it in the hands of the mansabdārs. Parks of artillery were placed under their command, but they did not have artillery as part of their routine equipment. The emperor gave away thousands of robes of honour to his officers and others, and it was considered economical to get the cloth manufactured and the robes tailored directly in the imperial workshops. Precious stones were cut, pearls pierced, ornaments made and encrusted in the kārkhānahs not only for the use of the monarch but also for presents; horses,

59 I.H. Qureshi, *The Administration of the Sultanate of Dehli*, pp. 69, 70.

60 Abū-'l-Fadl, *Ā'in-i-Akbarī*, i, Ā'ins 23, 34.

61 *Dastūr-u'l-'amal-i-āgāhī*, f. 36 a; etc.

elephants, camels and mules were bred and trained for various duties; animals and birds were tamed and taught to help the monarch in the hunt; in short all the needs of the monarch and the court were met through these institutions. It is, therefore, not surprising that they should have multiplied with the growth of luxury in the court and the extent of the empire. Their close connection with the administration can also be seen from the nature of their functions. The Treasury, the mint, the arsenal have an obvious relationship; but even some of those related more closely to the person of the monarch played some direct or indirect part of the business of the state.

Their impact upon the economic life of the people was by no means negligible. The imperial workshops created standards of excellence in production which were sought to be imitated; thus the skills of the artisans were improved. The craftsmen employed in the imperial workshops were at pains to produce articles which would bring rewards and promotion. The excellence of their products can be gauged from the scattered specimens in the museums of the world. The handicrafts practised in the subcontinent which earn the admiration of connoisseurs everywhere in the world are but shadows of what was achieved under the Mughuls. They improved the standards attained under the Sultans by continuing their traditions of patronage; contacts with the world had widened; the wealth of the empire had multiplied; peaceful progress in the neighbouring lands, especially in Iran, and the conquest of Kashmir had given greater impetus to industries and skilled immigrants were encouraged. The standards reached in gold and silver work, in copper utensils, in textiles, in carpets, in papier-mâché and ivory work, to mention only a few, have never been surpassed; indeed many a craft has died out; the secret of manufacturing the gossamer muslins of Dacca and the light shawls of Kashmir has been lost; only the scarce remnants of the Mughul days can reveal the beauty of these articles. Anarchy followed by a period of foreign rule all but destroyed the traditions by changing the economic pattern of life in which lack of encouragement and unfair competition from abroad played the vital role.[62] In the days of the Mughuls, however, these handicrafts were of great importance in the economy of the land and the workshops attached to the Imperial Household contributed greatly in sustaining them. Even in unsuspected areas, the kārkhānahs had a beneficial impact. The royal fruitery encouraged the cultivation of improved varieties of fruit; the royal gardens were constantly busy in raising the quality of the local fruits and importing new varieties; the imperial library employed the best calligraphists and painters and thus created patterns of excellence in these arts and in the art of bookbinding.[63]

The empress was not formally a partner in sovereignty; she was not enthroned or crowned. Her influence in the affairs of the state was personal. Nūr Jahān took an active part in the politics of the realm and became quite powerful; her influence was felt even in the administration.[64] Generally, however, the empresses interested themselves in relieving distress among poor women and in other charitable deeds.[65] They were treated with the utmost respect, as were all the ladies of the court; sometimes their intercession saved delicate political situations. When Salīm annoyed Akbar by displaying insubordination, the ladies interceded for him and brought about reconciliation.[66] Nūr Jahān worked against the interests of Shāh Jahān in the lifetime of Jahāngīr and after his death raised Shahryār to the throne. If a man had done it, he would have paid the last penalty and been executed, but Nūr Jahān was given a handsome pension and treated with consideration. She also had the good sense of retiring completely from the political arena.[67] Shāh Jahān's daughter Jahānārā intrigued in favour of Dārā Shikūh, but 'Ālamgīr I handled her with respect. No brother could get away so easily.[68] The ladies, whether royal consorts or princesses, were provided with ample means to lead a life of dignity and

62 Vide *History of Freedom Movement*, ii, Part II, Chapter XIII.

63 Abū-'l-Faḍl, *Ā'īn-i-Akbarī*, i, Ā'īns 28, 34; Khawāfī Khān, i, p. 757.

64 *Cambridge History of India*, iv, p. 163.

65 *e.g.*, 'Abd-u'l-Ḥamīd, i, pp. 151, 152.

66 Smith, p. 231.

67 *Cambridge History of India*, iv, pp. 183, 184.

68 Tavernier, i, p. 275.

luxury; out of their own funds they entertained lavishly and when they invited the emperor formally, made him large and valuable gifts.[69] The princesses were highly educated and cultured. Some of them wrote excellent poetry; 'Ālamgīr I had a daughter, Zib-u'n-nisā who bore the *nom de plume* of Makhfī and whose poems are read by lovers of Indo-Persian poetry even today with delight; Nūr Jahān and Mumtāz Mahal are also credited with writing poetry. Humāyūn's sister Gulbadan Begam has left an account of her brother's activities which is elegant and full of useful information. 'Ālamgīr I mentions his wife again and again in his writings with extreme fondness; Jahāngīr's devotion to Nūr Jahān is well known; the most beautiful monument to a woman in the world is the Tāj Maḥal, which was built by Shāh Jahān to enshrine his love for Mumtāz Maḥal.

The princes were given a good general education. The Mughuls were cultured monarchs. Bābur is famous for his memoirs and is called the prince of diarists; through his work he stands revealed as a man of deep culture and artistic tastes. At no other occasion Humāyūn seems to have expressed the pleasure which he did when, in the course of his wanderings after the defeat inflicted upon him by Sher Shāh, he was able to recover the camels which were carrying some of his books and which were lost owing to some mishap. Similarly, after he had been promised help by Shāh Tahmāsp, instead of going back to Qandahār, he wandered on towards Tabrīz, because he could not resist the temptation of visiting some of the famous calligraphists and painters of that city.[70] He had actually to be hustled out of the country by his royal host, or he might have spent a little more time in making contacts with other artists and literati. Akbar is considered to be illiterate; but this does not seem to be correct, because there is definite record of tutors having been appointed to teach him. He certainly could write his name; but what he missed in formal education, he made up subsequently through his association with men of learning, though his thinking always displayed a lack of discipline and consistency,

[69] For the affluence of the ladies see Manucci, ii, pp. 339-342, 345, 346, 353 etc.

[70] Percy Brown, pp. 52-54.

which perhaps was due to the neglect of formal education.[71] In any case, his father was not responsible for his neglect of studies. He himself gave sound education to his son Salīm, the future Jahāngīr, whose memoirs show an urbanity and culture which could come from good education alone. They do not rise to the heights of Bābur's memoirs, but this is due to the fact that Jahāngīr did not have so exciting a story to tell. Besides, his originality was marred by the lack of that ruggedness of spirit which Bābur had possessed. Shāh Jahān had scholarly tastes; he also was proficient in calligraphy.[72] 'Ālamgīr I was a theologian and jurist of no mean order; he had a succinct style in Persian prose; his letters are treated as classics by the Persian scholars of the Indo-Pakistan subcontinent.[73] All of his sons knew the Qur'ān by heart; they had been given a good grounding in the contemporary disciplines; and, like their father, were at home in the use of several languages.[74] Even in the days of decadence, Shāh 'Ālam II, Akbar Shāh II and Bahādūr Shāh II were well educated and good poets.[75] Indeed the last emperor is considered to be one of the best classical poets of Urdu. Among the princes who did not succeed in capturing the throne, Dārā Shikūh was pre-eminent as a scholar and thinker. He has to his credit solid works on sufism and Hindu religious thought.[76]

The education of the princes was not limited to academic subjects, though these were considered important. They were trained to be soldiers and administrators. They were taught skills like horsemanship, swordsmanship, marksmanship and the use of the arms of the period; very early in life they were put in com-

71 Smith, pp. 16, 17.

72 Brahman, *Qawā'id-i-salṭanat-i-Shāh Jahān*, p. 54.

73 This is apparent from his writings where (in his letters) he occasionally discusses points of theology and law *e.g.*, Ashraf Khān, f. 12a. Also vide Kāzim, pp. 1086-1087, 1091 ff

74 *Ibid.*, p. 1096.

75 Shāh'Ālam's ode on his captivity and misery under 'Abd-u'l-Qādir Rohilla is well known; *Dehlī Akhbār* and other contemporary newspapers of Delhi published poems by Akbar Shāh II; Bahādur Shāh II has left a dīwān (collection of poems) which is one of the classics of Urdu poetry. He used the *nom de plume* of Zafar.

76 For a discussion of his works see Hasrat.

mand of troops and sent to fight battles under the supervision of experienced generals so that they might learn the arts of good generalship and strategy. They were also given provinces to administer; in the beginning they had an experienced officer associated with them, who trained them to deal with administrative affairs, but as soon as the training was complete, they were given independent charge.[77] They were promoted to large viceroyalties in accordance with their ability and talent for administrative work. In the palmy days of the empire, the record of the princes as soldiers and administrators was quite creditable. Shāh Jahān and 'Ālamgīr I both won their spurs when they were viceroys of the troublesome Deccan. The princes were given elaborate instructions when they were sent as generals in charge of campaigns or as governors of provinces; 'Ālamgīr I had an elaborate manual drawn up which he handed over to his sons on such occasions and which contained detailed instructions not only regarding their duties but also about the etiquette and protocol to be observed in all ceremonies and processions.[78] Special emphasis was laid upon the treatment of the nobles and the officials. Bernier mentions an interview between 'Ālamgīr I and his erstwhile teacher in which the emperor is reported to have rebuked the scholar for giving him so theoretical and unrealistic an education, because it took no account of the future probability of the prince having to fight for the throne and even for his life.[79] This anecdote is highly improbable because Awrangzīb, of all princes, could not complain that his training had been entirely theoretical; nor for that matter was it this tutor's responsibility to go beyond the scope of academic teaching, in which he was so eminently successful, because 'Ālamgīr I was a well educated monarch.

The lack of a proper law of succession to the throne vitiated the relations between the princes, who looked upon their brothers and close male relations as rivals. This created

[77] *e.g.*, in the 20th year of his reign, Akbar gave some duties to the princes, each one of whom had officers associated with him, Abū-'l-Faḍl, *Akbarnāmah*, iii, p. 405. Also *Letters of 'Ālamgīr to Prince Muhammad A'ẓam Shāh*, f. 31.

[78] Brahman, *Chahār Chaman*, f. 26b.

[79] Bernier, pp. 154-161. The tutor was Mullā Jiwan.

enmity and suspicion. The Mughuls succeeded in raising the prestige of their dynasty to an extent that no one ever questioned their right to the throne, but they were not able to create a healthy tradition of smooth succession to the crown. The *shar'* does not recognize hereditary succession to monarchy and, therefore, does not provide for it; but then the Mughuls were the upholders of their right to rule the empire and had established widespread support for their right even in the religious circles.[80] If they could ignore the spirit of the Islamic law of succession by establishing a hereditary throne—and they were by no means the first to do this—they could as well have strengthened their House by going a little further and establishing a sounder tradition of succession. It may as well be mentioned here that the jurists also had failed to adhere to the main principle of election by not ruling out the succession of a son to the throne of his father; all that they had done was to lay down certain rules for election which were reduced to mere formalities. It is true that if the succession of a son had been legally barred, it would have taken away the right of a believer to rise to the privilege of becoming the ruler; but then by their refusal to face the realities and by sticking to the forms of law, they had mutilated the spirit of Islamic legal theory. The result, so far as the Mughul Empire was concerned, was to create a perennial source of conflict among the princes. In the beginning it brought the best men to the helm of affairs, but in the long run it frittered away the human resources of the dynasty and reduced its capacity to face difficulties and crises. 'Ālamgir I found himself so helpless that he could not even persuade his sons to agree to a division of his empire on his death to stop them from fighting after him; the emperor, a shrewd and experienced statesman that he was, must have realized that this also was a counsel of despair.[81] Bahādur Shāh was styled the heir apparent, but because of the relations between the brothers, 'Ālamgir I

80 Shaikh Ahmad of Sarhind, the Mujaddid-i-alf-i-thānī, tried to rejuvenate Islamic traditions of government, but nowhere does he question the hereditary nature of the monarchy; nor for that matter, does any other eminent theologian of the period. Perhaps they did not want to create more problems than they could manage.

81 Ashraf Khān, f. 7b.

was right in anticipating trouble after his death.[82] Akbar himself encouraged his grandson Khusraw to try to supersede his father, Salīm.

Some of the Rajput princes, because of their family relationship to the Mughuls, were treated as princes of royal blood and bore the title of *mirzā* or prince.[83] As they were not eligible for the throne being Hindus, they were safe from the risks of the life of a Mughul prince though not completely, because they also, owing to their relationship with the various contestants, were drawn into the conflict. Their stakes, however, were only slightly higher than those of other high officials.

The Mughuls have seldom been surpassed in the elegance and splendour of their court. They knew full well the psychological importance of maintaining the dignity of the monarchy, and they cultivated manners of speech and modes of behaviour which would not compromise it. Under the influence of their court came into existence a style of writing which could express the harshest sentiments in the politest language. The mellowness and elegance expressed in their architecture also pervaded their mode of living which had been cultivated almost into a fine art. All that was harsh and unpleasant was gradually eliminated, until at last the grit which makes soldiers and administrators ebbed out of the society which accepted their standards. The Mughul imperial family never lost its traditions of bravery, but little stamina was left in their followers and supporters.

The splendour of the Mughul court almost defies description. The marble halls of the fortress palaces of Agra, Dehlī and Lahore, overwhelming in beauty and dignity even today, are yet mere shells; when their builders held court in them, they were hung with the richest carpets and cloth mostly embroidered with gold; the canopies were made of rich materials supported by posts cased in gold or silver; the dresses of the officers were of silks interwoven with threads of precious metals or embroidered with

[82] Khawāfī Khān, ii, p. 444.

[83] *e.g.*, Mirzā Rājah Jai Singh, who was for some time incharge of 'Ālamgīr I's campaign against Shivājī.

gold; the qūrchīs and the mace bearers wore rich dresses and carried maces and staffs of their office encased in silver or gold.[84] The same splendour was maintained in royal processions and journeys.

The occasions when the populace could watch the spectacular processions or other functions were quite numerous. When in the capital or in a metropolitan city, the emperor rode out to the Jāmi' Masjid for his congregational Friday prayers; on the days of the two 'Ids he rode to the 'idgāh which was generally at some distance from the city.[85] The court travelled quite frequently, thus affording the countryside opportunities to see the processions formed in the journey. There were many occasions like the weddings of the princes when the metropolis was decorated; on several festivals fireworks and illuminations attracted the populace.[86]

The Mug͟huls enforced an exacting etiquette in their courts. During the long public audiences, the highest and the humblest were alike required to keep standing; only occasionally permission was granted to some princes to sit.[87] Persons admitted to private audiences prostrated themselves before the emperor, which degrading form of salutation was called a sajdah. Though the sajdah was prescribed only for the followers of the Dīn-i-Ilāhī in the first instance, the custom grew, until in Jahāngīr's reign, it had become quite common for persons admitted to a private audience to prostrate themselves before the monarch.[88] S͟hāh Jahān abolished the customs as being un-Islamic.[89] The curious fact is that he was advised not to do so. He compromised by prescribing the zamīnbūs, which differed only technically from the sajdah. In the latter the forehead touches the ground; in the Muslim belief it is reserved for God alone and offering it to any one else smacks of idolatry. The zamīnbūs was not invented by S͟hāh Jahān; it had existed in the days of the Abbasids. It consisted in placing the palms of

[84] Brahman, *Qawā'id-i-salṭanat-i-S͟hāh Jahān*, pp. 47, 48; 'Abd-u'l-Ḥamīd, i, p. 222.

[85] Kāẓim, p. 1098, the streets were decorated on the occasion of the Id, Brahman, *Qawā'id-i-salṭanat-i-S͟hāh Jahān*, p. 63.

[86] Kāẓim, p. 491.

[87] 'Abd-u'l-Hamīd, i, p. 146.

[88] Abū-'l-Fadl, *Ā'īn-i-Akbarī*, i, Ā'īn 74.

[89] 'Abd-u'l-Hamīd, i, p. 112.

the two hands on the ground and then kissing the backs of the two hands.[90] Humāyūn had instituted the taslim and the kornish; these continued to exist throughout the period. The former consisted in placing the back of the right hand on the ground and then raising it gently until the saluter stood erect when he put the palm of his hand upon the crown. The latter was simpler; the palm of the right hand was put upon the forehead and the head was bent downwards. The taslīm was the more common salutation offered to the monarch; on the occasions of presentation, or taking leave, or upon receiving a manṣab, a jāgīr, or a dress of honour, or an elephant or a horse, the rule was to make three taslīms; at other times only one was made.[91] When an imperial farmān was sent to a distant official, he came out to receive it and, on delivery, put it upon his head.

The Mughuls were extremely jealous in the matter of the respect which they thought was due to them, and severely reprimanded any failure on the part of a noble to show due humility or any assumption of prerogatives or customs by him which did not conform with the Mughul ideas of the limitations imposed by the protocol upon a subject.[92] Even powerful vassals like the rulers of the Deccan states were not spared.[93]

The Mughul patterns of polite behaviour came to be accepted all over the subcontinent and continued to influence notions regarding etiquette and good manners long after the empire ceased to exist.

The royal imperial household set the fashion for other dignitaries as well. The princely viceroys, the governors, the hereditary Hindu princes and other high officials maintained establishments which, within their capacity, were modelled upon the pattern of the imperial household. A visit to the Kachhwāha capital of Amber would show how closely some of the institutions mentioned here were imitated in the minor courts.

90 *Ibid.*

91 Abū-'l-Fadl, *Ā'īn-i-Akbarī*, i, Ā'īn 74.

92 Once a noble wore a dress so low that the skirts hid the feet. 'Ālamgīr I ordered that the skirts should be trimmed in the court, *Ruqqa'āt-i-'Ālamgīrī*, p. 46.

93 The Mughuls never addressed the rulers as sultans. They were often rebuked for exceeding the limits of tributaries.

CHAPTER IV

The Central Government

It has already been mentioned that the Mughul emperors were the pivots of their government; they kept almost all the threads of the administration in their own hands; yet it was impossible to rule such a vast empire single handed. Akbar prided himself unjustly upon being the author of most of his measures by saying that he was grateful to God that he had found no capable minister, otherwise people would have given the minister the credit for the emperor's measures. yet there is ample evidence to show that Akbar benefited greatly from the counsel of able administrators.[1] He conceded that a monarch should not himself undertake duties that may be performed by his subjects; he did not do this for reasons of administrative efficiency, but because "the errors of others it is his part to remedy, but his own lapses, who may correct?"[2] This is not in keeping with the Mughul methods of

[1] Abū-'l-Faḍl, *Ā'in-i-Akbari*, v, p 234.

[2] *Ibid.*, p. 243.

government, because they seldom delegated authority which they could keep in their own hands. Besides, they kept a careful watch upon the doings of their servants who were not independent in any sphere of their authority. The Mughuls did not possess any equivalent of a cabinet; the highest incumbents of office under them were heads of departments, rather than ministers. They were consulted severally as well as in undefined groups in matters for which they were responsible or even, if the monarch so desired, in matters of state generally on some occasions, but they had no right to tender advice, nor were there any institutions, the membership of which would entitle them to express views, whether accepted or not. Such of them could be sent for to tender advice as the emperor wanted to consult. It was, however, customary to consult some of them on important occasions; besides, in matters pertaining to their departments, they did express their views, and because they were experts, their opinions carried weight. It is not surprising, therefore, that the Mughuls designated only the higher officers of the department of Finance as ministers; the others were considered to be just high dignitaries and servants of the state.[3] The question of mutual consultation or of joint responsibility simply did not arise. Each one was responsible to the monarch.

Theoretically, at the head of the administration was the wakil, who was considered to be "the emperor's lieutenant in all matters connected with the realm and the Household." As such he was the emperor's chief adviser; he was also specially responsible for advising the emperor upon "appointments, dismissals, promotions and demotions. The financial offices were not under his immediate superintendence, yet he received the returns from the heads of all financial departments and kept abstracts of their returns."[4] In practice, however, such an office depends for its authority upon personal equation. These powers were exercised by Bairam Khān in the days of Akbar's tutelage; when the emperor

[3] The term wazir, meaning a minister, was used only for the diwāns, and, sometimes, for others holding high posts in the Revenue administration.

[4] Abū-'l-Fadl, *Ā'in-i-Akbarī*, i, p. 4.

grew up, he began to resent the wakīl's authority and brought about his downfall. No other wakīl was so powerful until the decay of the monarch's authority in the later days of the empire; mostly the office was ornamental; sometimes it was not even filled. Even when the wakīl did not have much power, he was influential as the highest official of the realm having access to the monarch and often his confidence. He could not exercise the final authority because of the monarch's interest in the details of administrative matters, but he was useful as a checking authority, because papers were submitted to him and he might be called upon to account for any irregularities or mistakes. The Mughuls were great believers in the policy of providing checks and balances in the exercise of authority by the officials; the wakīl, without having much authority himself, provided a supervisory agency at the top next only to the monarch.

The wazir, also called the dīwān-i-kul or dīwān-i-a'lā to distinguish him from the subordinate and provincial dīwāns, was the head of the fiscal administration of the empire. In theory he was subordinate to the wakīl; actually, however, he had independent authority.[5] Only when the monarch appointed an officer well versed in fiscal administration as the wakīl, could he exercise any supervisory authority over the dīwān. In exceptional instances the two offices were even combined; this, however, ran counter to the Mughul administrative theory.[6] The wazir's authority stemmed out of his expert knowledge. Monarchs were inclined to be more tolerant of the failings of experts than of others; financial experts were held in high esteem. The wazīr had to be strict with the highest officers in their financial dealings with the state and sometimes had to perform unpleasant duties by calling them to account. If the monarch desired orderly fiscal affairs, he had to give the wazīr support; the wazīr, on his part, had to be tactful and not too harsh in his dealings with the officials. This was even truer in the earlier period of the consolidation of the authority of the state. Khwājah Shāh Mansūr, whose execution was a miscarriage

[5] *Ibid.*

[6] *e.g.*, Sharīf Khān was given the two offices; Jahāngīr, p. 6.

of justice, had incurred the displeasure of the powerful officers because of his harshness. He was not removed until a trumped up charge of high treason, based upon forged evidence, brought about his execution. Even when Akbar believed in the truth of the evidence, he was sorry that he had to lose such a good officer.[7] He disliked Todar Mal's religious fanaticism; but the emperor did not permit his private feelings in the way of Todar Mal's promotion.[8] Once Dārā Shikūh violently rebuked the famous wazīr Sa'd-u'llah Khān for turning down his request for the grant of certain sums as irregular; when the matter was reported to Shāh Jahān by the appropriate authority, he censured the favourite prince and mollified the wazīr by expressing his appreciation and sending him valuable presents.[9] Sa'd-u'llah Khān and I'timād-u'd-dawlah were the greatest dīwāns in the history of the Mughul Empire and contributed considerably to its wealth and sound administration. In spite of Akbar's statement to the contrary, his dīwāns were responsible for many reforms in the administration and its procedures; these brought about efficiency in place of the chaos which had prevailed because of wars and disorders immediately preceding Akbar's reign.[10] When the emperor felt that a single person was not adequate for the responsibilities of this onerous office, another expert was associated with him; the second man occupied only a slightly subordinate position.[11] Sometimes the office was put into commission and two persons with equal authority were given charge of it.[12] Occasionally an officer was appointed who was higher than the dīwān, but who was not given the status of the wakīl or his authority; his supervisory powers were limited to fiscal matters. He was called ishrāf-i-dīwān or

[7] For the circumstances of Khwājah Shāh Manṣūr's execution vide Abū-'l Faḍl, *Akbarnāmah*, iii, p. 316.

[8] *Ibid.*, p. 158.

[9] Ashraf Khān, f. 31a.

[10] *e.g.*, Fath-u'llāh Shīrāzī's reforms in the 30th year and Todar Mal's rulings in the 27th year of Akbar's reign, Abū-'l-Faḍl, *Akbarnāmah*, iii, pp. 457-459, 381-383.

[11] *e.g.*, I'timād-u'd-dawlah's first appointment under Khān Beg; Mu'tamad Khān, p. 307.

[12] *e.g.*, Patr Dās and Shams-u'd-din; Muẓaffar Khān and Todar Mal; Abū-'l-Faḍl, *Akbarnāmah*, iii, p. 741.

mushrif-i-dīwān; Akbar once put Salīm in charge of supervisory duties of the fiscal administration and the dīwān was asked to consult him in all matters; this was done probably to acquaint the prince with the work.[13]

The wazīr had extensive powers. Though he was expected to send abstracts of financial statements to the wakīl, he was not his subordinate.[14] He did not have to seek his approval for his decisions from the wakīl. He took all cases for the emperor's orders directly to him. He was consulted by the monarch in almost all important matters, and, though his advice could be ignored, it must have carried weight.[15] Men like Sa'd-u'llah Khān and I'timād-u'd-dawlah were fully trusted by their royal masters. However great might have been the emperor's capacity for looking into details, many a matter must have been decided in accordance with the opinions of the wazīr. He was consulted in all important appointments; practically all fiscal posts were under his patronage. The appointment of the provincial governors and dīwāns was theoretically within his competence, though it is obvious that in such important appointments the wishes of the emperor must have played the decisive role. The officers of the smaller units like the sarkārs and the parganahs were also appointed by him in the first instance; they were formally installed with the emperor's approval, which the wazīr must have wisely sought before informing the incumbent or making the appointment public.[16] He kept a strict control over the provincial dīwāns and their offices and received for scrutiny detailed statements about the income and the expenditure continuously from the provinces.[17] The imperial treasuries also were under his control.[18] At the centre

[13] *e.g.*, Todar Mal in the 27th year of Akbar's reign, *Ibid.*, pp. 381; 158. For Salīm being entrusted with such duties, *Ibid.*, p. 839.

[14] Abū-'l-Faḍl, *Ā'īn-i-Akbarī*, i, p. 4.

[15] 'Abd-u'l-Ḥamīd, i, pp. 150, 151, 153; Ashraf Khān, f. 34 b; Kāẓim, pp. 1103, 1105 etc.

[16] Todar Mal's *Dastūr-u'l-'amal*, I.O.L.E, the 432, f. 29a; *Ḍawābiṭ-i-'Ālamgīrī* f. 31b.

[17] For details vide *ibid.*, ff. 31b-36b; also *Dastūr-u'l-'amal*, B.M. ms. or 2026, ff 18-20 a.

[18] Abū-'l-Faḍl, *Ā'īn-i-Akbarī*, i, p. 4.

the wazīr was assisted by three high officials; they had direct access to the monarch and were present in the dīwān-i-'ām as well as the dīwān-i-khās. They held almost independent charge of their departments and were directly responsible to the monarch. The wazīr had precedence over them and coordinated their work, but his control over them was not absolute. These officers were the dīwān-i-khāliṣāh, the dīwān-i-tan, also called ṣāhib-i-tawjīh, and the mustaufī.[19] To explain the functions of the dīwān-i-khāliṣah, it is necessary to say something about the khāliṣah lands. They have been erroneously called crownlands by many authors; in fact such land as was not given out in assignment at a particular time was called khāliṣah; there was no permanent demarcation; the same area could be khāliṣah at one time and jāgīr or assignment at another. The dīwān-i-khāliṣah, therefore, was in charge of all the revenues which the state received into its treasury and the sound administration of the sources of such revenue. The diwān-i-tan was responsible for the payment of salaries to the servants of the state whether in cash or in the form of assignments upon the revenues of certain areas called jāgīrs. The main function of the dīwān-i-tan was well defined by Shāh Jahān in his behest to Jaswant Khatrī, when the monarch said, "You should be a trusted judge between us and those who are being assigned jāgīrs."[20] It was his duty to prescribe an area which would yield the amount of the salary to the assignee so that neither he nor the state should be a loser. The mustaufī was the auditor general of the empire.

In another sphere, the mīr sāmān, also, was considered subordinate to the dīwān; but this was only a matter of precedence and formality. The mīr sāmān was dependent upon the wazīr in financial matters only; he took all matters up to the monarch directly.[21] His associate, the dīwān-i-buyūtāt, however, was really subordinate to the wazīr; he too had direct access to the monarch and, in all probability, represented the point of view of the dīwān's office of the financial aspects of the administration or expansion

19 *Ibid.*, 'Abd-u'l-Ḥamīd, i, p. 150.

20 Ashraf Khān, f. 51b.

21 Abū-'l-Faḍl, *Ā'īn-i-Akbarī*, i, p. 4; 'Abd-u'l-Ḥamīd, i, p. 146.

of the buyūtāt. He was also responsible for the proper administration of the internal finances of the buyūtāt. He drew the salaries of the staff from the treasury and disbursed them. He also made out the estimates of the expenditure twice a year and obtained the sanction from the wazīr and the monarch.[22]

The mīr sāmān was not only responsible for the efficient working of the buyūtāt but had other important duties as well. The menial staff of the palace and such household officers as were not on the state payroll received their monthly or annual salaries on his certification; he appointed the superintendents, accountants, cashiers of the various kārkhānahs and departments of the palace; he was responsible for seeing that the articles produced by the kārkhānahs were properly listed and stocked; the presents made to the emperor were registered by his department; the presents made by the emperor were provided by his office either from the stock of presents received previously or out of the produce of the kārkhānahs; he responded to the requests from the provinces for articles produced in the kārkhānahs and needed by the provincial authorities; he had lists of the precious articles in the treasuries; he drew up statements about the income from royal gardens, shops and houses; he was responsible for the realization of all dues from those who had leased such property; he fixed the daily rations of the various animals in the royal stables, menageries and aviaries; when the emperor ordered the award of a present, if it was not in cash, he certified its actual delivery; he was in charge of all celebrations of the weddings of the royal princes. When the property of an officer or dignitary was to be sequestered or taken into temporary custody, it was the duty of the mīr sāmān to do so. As many of these duties had their financial aspects, he had constant dealings with the dīwān and was, for this reason, theoretically his subordinate.[23]

More directly under the dīwān were the āwarjah nawīs and the mushrif of the treasury. The former kept the account of daily receipts and disbursements; the latter kept a record of the cash

[22] *Ibid.*, also Abū-'l-Faḍl, *Ā'īn-i-Akbarī*, ii, Ā'īn, 1; *Ḍawābiṭ-i-'Ālamgīrī*, ff. 22b, 23a.

[23] *Ibid.*, ff. 21-22a.

and other valuables in the imperial treasuries.[24] The wāqi'ah nawīs also was under the dīwān; his duties and functions will be described later. There was a dīwān for the ahadis as well to deal with their salaries.[25]

Of all the officers listed by Abū-'l-Faḍl as subordinate to the wakil, the mīr bakhshi is the most important. He was one of the most powerful officials of the state under the Mughuls; his subordination to the wakīl was only nominal. In importance he can be compared to the wazīr; he corresponded to the 'āriḍ-i-mumālik of the Sultans of Dehlī; the bakhshī was even more important because of the monolithic organization of the services in the mansabdārī system of the Mughuls. The word bakhshī probably comes from the Sanskrit word bhikshū, a word used for the Buddhist monks who had no worldly belongings and lived upon charity. Like the clergy of Medieval Europe, they were probably the only literates in an overwhelmingly illiterate population of Central Asia before its conversion to Islam; as such they were likely to be employed by monarchs and chieftains for keeping their records.[26] In the early organization of the Mongols, the main records would be about the number of the men and horses which a tribe or its chief was expected to bring to the muster when the monarch went out to fight. Essentially the duties of the bakhshī were of a similar nature; only with the change in circumstances with the organization of the manṣabdārī system, the record of the contingent expected from a manṣabdār had to be kept in a more elaborate form. Duties subsidiary to this main function also were added in course of time.

The mīr bakhshī was himself a highly placed manṣabdār and was responsible for the smooth working of the manṣabdārī system. It was his duty to see that able men were appointed as manṣabdārs. Though the appointments were made by the emperor, yet the candidates had to pass the bakhshī's scrutiny, because it was mostly he who presented candidates to the monarch. The candidates

[24] Abū-'l-Faḍl, *Ā'in-i-Akbari*, i, p. 4.

[25] *Ibid.*, ii, Ā'īn 4.

[26] Ibn Ḥasan, pp. 213-15.

were occasionally also sponsored by other manṣabdārs; the bakhshīs were, however, invariably asked to make a recommendation. Once a candidate was approved by the monarch, it was the duty of the bakhshīs to see that all the conditions of service were fulfilled. First of all a confirmation of the emperor's orders was obtained; then the necessary papers laying down in detail the rank and the salary of the candidate were prepared and handed over to the candidates, copies being also filed in the bakhshī's office. The appointee, then, had to produce the men, the horses, the beasts of burden and other accoutrement, which he was expected to maintain, for the bakhshī's inspection. If approved, the horses were branded, the men's descriptive rolls drawn up, and a certificate issued to the effect that the conditions laid down had been fulfilled; only then was the new manṣabdār entitled to draw his salary and allowances. The process of branding and the compilation of the descriptive rolls was technically called dāgh and taṣhīḥah; this was compulsory for the older manṣabdārs as well, who had to bring their contingents for periodical inspection. Any salaries paid without the certification that the contingent was in order were considered to be merely an advance payment subject to a final adjustment after the necessary inspection and certification.[27]

The mīr bakhshī was assisted by two other bakhshīs at the centre; he himself was also called the first bakhshī; his assistants were called the second and the third bakhshīs respectively. In the beginning one bakhshī was considered adequate to deal with the work, but in Shāh Jahān's reign the number was increased to three. Mostly all the three bakhshīs were in attendance in the various audiences of the monarch.[28] The work among them was divided in accordance with the ranks of the manṣabdārs.[29] The first bakhshī dealt with the royal princes and the highest manṣabdārs; the second bakhshī dealt with second grade manṣabdārs; the third with the lowest. There was a complex procedure for the

[27] Abū-'l-Faḍl, *Ā'in-i-Akbari*, ii, Ā'in. 11.

[28] 'Abd-u'l-Ḥamīd, i, pp. 146, 147, 153; *Dastūr-u'l-'amal-i-āgāhi*, f. 8a; Kāẓim, p. 1099.

[29] For details of the division of work, vide, *Ḍawābit-i-'Ālamgiri*, ff. 17-20.

division of the work regarding the preparation of the various papers and the maintenance of the records; the underlying principle seems to have been that there should be two authorities to check all the entries so that all mistakes should be eliminated. There were, however, some papers which were not considered important enough for this double check. A bakhshī was sometimes asked to accompany the army on an important campaign. The bakhshīs were also responsible for the recruitment and efficient maintenance of the directly recruited troops.[30] The bakhshīs have sometimes been described as paymasters general of the army; this is not correct, because the payment was made by the office of the dīwān-i-tan; only in exceptional circumstances, like a long campaign, did the bakhshī make payments mostly of ad hoc sums to the manṣabdārs. There is one instance on record when a bakhshī arrogated to himself the duties of the dīwān-i-tan and assigned jāgīrs, but this was considered to be irregular. The dīwān who permitted such a situation to develop was blamed for his inefficiency; the normal procedure was restored as soon as the facts came to light.[31]

The mīr bakhshī was kept informed of the main happenings in the provinces by the provincial bakhshīs; important items of the news received from them and the sawāniḥ nigārs were reported to the emperor.[32] The bakhshīs were responsible for assigning the duty of mounting guard on the palace to the different manṣabdārs.[33] In the evening when the emperor inspected the guards and the royal ensigns were brought out, the bakhshīs were in attendance.[34] There was a separate bakhshī for the aḥadīs.[35]

The department of religious affairs was under the ṣadr; his duties and functions will be discussed in a separate chapter. Normally he was also the qāḍī-u'l-quḍat, or the chief justice of the empire. One segment of the department of justice was under the

[30] Abū-'l-Faḍl, *Ā'īn-i-Akbarī*, ii, Ā'īn, 5.

[31] Shaikh Farīd Bukhārī was the offending bakhshī, for details vide Mu'tamad Khan, pp. 3,4.

[32] Ashraf Khan, f. 34b; 'Ali Muḥammad Khan, *Supplement*, p. 175.

[33] *Ḍawābiṭ-i-'Ālamgiri*, f. 18a.

[34] Kāẓim, p. 1105.

[35] Abū-'l-Faḍl, *Ā'īn-i-Akbarī*, ii, Ā'īn 11.

direct control of the emperor; this was the maẓālim, known as 'adālat under the Mughuls. The ṣadar was not subordinate either to the wakīl or the dīwān and held independent jurisdiction. The executive duties in connection with the dispensation of justice were under the mīr-i-'adl. In financial matters he was helped by the dīwān-i-sa'ādat.[36]

The procedure adopted for the transaction of business was lengthy and involved endless paper work and filing. This was true of the Mughul government at all levels; for this reason the Mughul government has been described by some modern historians as a government sustained by files. It is a pity that most of these files have perished for lack of preservation, disorders following the weakening of the central authority and a destructive climate. Our understanding of the working of the system would have been fuller if that material had endured.

Fourteen writers were employed by the court as wāqi'ah nawīses; there were also a few supernumeraries for emergent purposes. Two of them served every day; they were in continuous attendance and wrote down all that happened or was said. There was nothing too insignificant for them to record. As Abū-'l-Fadl states, "Their duty is to write down the orders and the doings of His Majesty." All that the monarch said, did or was reported to him was meticulously recorded; even the arrivals and departures of important officers and matters of every day routine were not omitted. Nothing that happened or was said was considered too trivial for the record. The next day the diary, after having been corrected by a senior official, was laid before the emperor and approved by him.[37]

This was the basic record; each item was then copied separately and given to those who were affected by the monarch's remarks or orders for their use; it was countersigned by the parwānchī, by the mīr 'arḍ, and by the person who had brought the matter up before the emperor. In this form the record was called a yāddāsht, a memorandum. It was then handed over to other copyists, who

[36] *Ibid.*, Ā'īn 10.
[37] *Ibid.*, Ā'īn 11.

kept the yāddāsht and made a proper abridgement of it; it was signed and sealed by the wāqi'ahnawīs, the risālahdār, the mīr 'arḍ and the dāroghah. This document was called a ta'līqah; the writer of it the ta'līqah nawīs. The ta'līqah was the basic certificate of appointment to all posts which required the royal approval.

The formal orders of the emperor were conveyed through farmāns. The orders of every high appointment were made out in the form of a farmān-i-thabtī; so were the grants of suyūrghāl. If the emperor ordered a cash payment, the farmān was called a barāt. The parwānchah was slightly different in form and was made out for the stipulation of the salaries of the royal consorts, female relations and the princes. The salaries of the aḥadīs and some officers of the Household also were fixed through parwānchahs. The general rule seems to have been that a salary which did not require a new sanad every year was fixed through a parwānchah. The farmān was quite an elaborate document. It bore the seals of several important officials, under whose jurisdiction the contents of the farmān or its drawing up might have fallen; the place of every seal was fixed in accordance with the status of the official; the monarch's name and seal appeared on the top.[38] The royal seal had the name of the reigning monarch in the centre; the names of his predecessors appeared in a circle around his own name. The lineal ancestors were mentioned up to Tīmūr. The seals of the ministers and other officials were affixed towards the end, generally on the reverse, the obverse being taken up by the text. The necessary endorsements appeared on the reverse as well. The usual procedure was dispensed with in drawing up a farmān-i-bayāḍī. The officers were not required to affix their seals; the royal seal was considered sufficient. This kind of farmān was used when its contents were secret and the monarch did not want to disclose them to all the officers who would have normally dealt with a farmān-i-thabtī.[39] Sometimes the emperor took the extra precaution of writing out the farmān himself.[40] The farmāns were

[38] *Ibid.*, Ā'īn 12; 'Abd-u'l-Ḥamīd, i, p. 148.

[39] Abū-'l-Faḍl, *Ā'īn-i-Akbarī*, ii, Ā'īn 13.

[40] 'Abd-u'l-Ḥamīd, i, p. 148.

always drawn up in beautiful calligraphy. The thabtī farmāns were of a routine nature; their language, form and style were stereotyped and their composition did not require much skill; hence they were drafted by subordinates and written by calligraphists. The formal correspondence with the heads of other states was always an essay in *belles lettres*. Sometimes the best writers were asked to draft them. Abū-'l-Faḍl has to his credit some of the letters he wrote on behalf of Akbar to 'Abd-u'llah Khān Uzbek, the ruler of Transoxiana. The Mughuls did not attach the same importance to a department of correspondence as the other Muslim dynasties had done before them; they did not have a dīwān-u'r-risālat of the Abbasids or a dīwān-i-inshā of the Sultans of Dehlī; but they had a munshī who was helped by a number of assistants.[41] Some important letters were drafted by the monarchs themselves; of these 'Ālamgīr I has left a collection of private and semi-official letters which show his mastery over Persian prose. Shah Jahān also wrote some letters himself. Sometimes the emperor added a few words to a farmān in his own handwriting to show his special favour.[42] The receipt of a farmān-i-bayāḍī was considered to be a mark of honour; the recipient came out some distance to receive it, put it on the crown of his head, prostrated himself, and rewarded the messenger according to the circumstances.[43]

Mention has been made of the risālahdār; this term does not refer to an office. Several officers were given the responsibility of certifying that the entries in the yāddāsht regarding the appointments of personnel under them or in certain capacities or regarding matters other than appointments were correct. Such persons had also to make an entry on the back of the farmān issued to formalise the order.[44] A farmān-i-thabtī was inoperative without such an entry and the certification of the dīwān.

The procedure adopted by the dīwān's office in making payments shows how many checks were provided against the possibility of

[41] *Ibid.*, Kāẓim, p. 1101.

[42] *Ibid.*, pp. 1101, 1102.

[43] Abū-'l-Faḍl, *Ā'īn-i-Akbarī*, ii, Ā'īn 13.

[44] Also called Ṣāḥib-i-risālah, *Ḍawābit-i-'Ālamgīrī*, f. 18a. Abū-'l-Faḍl, *Ā'īn-i-Akbarī*, ii, Ā'īn 10.

the defalcation of funds or wrong payments: it also demonstrates that in their anxiety to prevent fraud and mistakes, the Mughuls had made their system cumbersome. The traditions created by the Mughul bureaucracy have yet not been overcome in the subcontinent in spite of the need for greater dispatch in the modern conditions of society and the expanded requirements of government.

In the simple matter of the payment of salaries and allowances, after the ta'liqah had been made out, the money was paid by the officer in charge, or, in case the payment was to be in the shape of an assignment, the assignment order was made out by the dīwān-i-jāgīr in the form of a draft. This draft was approved and signed by the dīwān's accountant, the dīwān-i-tan, the mustaufī, the dīwān and the wakīl. In case it was an appointment to a manṣab and the conditions of the appointment required that the appointee should furnish a contingent and the animals for the carriage of the equipment, then the procedure was further complicated by the requirement of a previous inspection of the contingent and the beasts of burden by the bakhshī, the registration of the descriptive rolls of the soldiers and the branding of the horses. The bakhshī kept the ta'līqah and gave the candidate a sarkhaṭ, which was kept by the dīwān. In case a jāgīr was given in lieu of the salary—and this was done only when the emperor had given orders to that effect before—the dīwān passed orders that an appropriate assignment be made out. The determination of the salary was in itself a matter of calculation, because it was determined by the manṣabdār's personal rank, his sawār rank, the place of his posting and, on occasions of further payments, on the condition of his contingent at the time of the last inspection and even the date of the last inspection. The problem of matching an assignment with the determined salary in the area indicated posed another problem for the dīwān-i-tan. When he had found a satisfactory solution acceptable to the assignee and safeguarding the interests of the state, the necessary information was placed in the draft of the farmān. This draft needed the approval of the dīwān, the mustaufī the bakhshī and the wakil before receiving the royal approval. It had to be signed and endorsed by all the officials who had any jurisdiction in the matter. The barāts, being mostly made out for meeting the expenditure incurred in connection with the buyūtāt or other branches of the Household, were signed by the nāẓir, the dīwān-i-buyūtāt, the ba<u>khsh</u>ī, the dīwān and the mīr sāmān.[45].

The accounts of the empire were divided into three categories. The first, called abwāb-u'l-māl, dealt with all the income which accrued through the revenues or other sources. The record was not only kept up-to-date, but any departure from the normal, like an increase or a decrease, was explained, citing the causes. The second was called arbāb-u't-taḥwīl; this section dealt with the amounts spent in the Household; the name came from the fact that it dealt with the accounts of the people who had sums of money in their custody (taḥwīl) for meeting contingent expenditure, of which they had to render account. The third was called tawjīh; it dealt with the sums of money spent on salaries or the income of the assignments given in lieu thereof. The record was kept in the form of loose leaves in all these sections; this was technically called a daftar and was a collection of sanads, or vouchers showing payments. Thus a voucher could be taken out easily in case of doubt for inspection and examination.[46] Apart from the large number of statements, files, abstracts which continuously poured into the dīwān's office from the offices of the provincial dīwāns, there was a continuous flow of papers from the various departments at the centre. No money could by drawn from the treasury even by an officer authorized to keep imprest cash without a muqāsā, which was a certificate from the mustaufī that the sums of money previously advanced had been spent correctly.[47]

An essential part of the accounting system was the organization of the treasuries. There was a treasury at each parganah headquarters, at every provincial capital and several at the capital.

[45] *Ibid.*, ii, Ā'īn 11.

[46] *Ibid.*, Blochhmann thinks that Arbāb-u't-taḥwīl was in all likelihood Abwāb-u't-taḥwīl, (Eng. Tr, 1, p. 260, f.n. 2), but *Arbāb* seems to be correct, *Dastūr-u'l-'amal* or 2026 in giving the same sub-divisions has Arbāb-u'l-māl and Arbāb-u't-taḥwīl. Abwāb, plural of bāb, a door, a gate, metaphorically a channel, a source, a category; arbāb, plural of rabb, a sustainer, a keeper, a responsible authority.

[47] Abū-'l-Faḍl, *Ā'īn-i-Akbarī*, ii, Ā'īn 11.

All surplus of two hundred thousand dāms or more had to be submitted to the central treasury by the provincial treasurer. The central treasuries were in the charge of a treasurer general, who had a superintendent and a registrar working under him along with other staff. The central treasury was divided into twelve subdivisions, nine for different kinds of cash payments and three for precious stones, gold and inlaid jewellery. Each of the kārkhānahs had a separate treasury; this was done to facilitate the working of the buyūtāt and to relieve pressure from the main treasuries. The treasury for precious stones evaluated and classified the stones.[48]

The mints were well organized. The dāroghah, or the superintendent, was assisted by an expert staff. The ṣairafī, with a staff of ṣarrāfs, under him, determined the purity of the coins. This was important, because the Mughul coins represented the intrinsic value of the species in them. The Mughul coinage succeeded in achieving a very high standard of purity; the older Iranian standard of purity known as dah dahī, that is, ten out of ten, was changed by the Mughuls into twelve out of twelve; the methods of judging the purity of the species were improved; in addition to the ṣarrāfs, the mints employed banwārīs for testing the purity of gold. The amīn was the authority who decided the issue of purity if any difference of opinion arose among the other experts in the mint. There was a merchant to buy the needed bullion. Then there were the usual accountants and clerks; on the technical side there were workers in metals, assayers, die makers and others. By these methods, the Mughuls were able to achieve not only purity but also a high standard of beauty in their coins. Abū-'l-Faḍl mentions Mawlānā 'Alī Aḥmad of Dehlī as the master engraver of his days and says that he was unequalled in any country of the world; this judgement is justified by the aesthetic qualities of the Mughul coins. Abū-'l-Faḍl mentions twenty six gold coins, sixteen silver coins and four copper coins. Most of the gold coins were struck as novelties; for instance the sahansah weighing a little less than one hundred and two tolahs could serve little purpose as currency;

[48] *Ibid.*, i, Ā'īns 2 and 3.

indeed only three gold coins were in circulation and minted normally; these were the la'l-i-jalālah, its half and quarter. The la'l-i-jalāh was twenty two māshahs in weight. The silver coins were the rupee, weighing eleven māshahs and a half, and its half, quarter, fifth, eighth, tenth, sixteenth, and one twentieth. All these pieces were minted in round shapes as well as square. The square coin equivalent to a rupee was called a jalālah. The dām was the copper coin of the highest denomination; it weighed a little more than a tolah and eight māshahs; it had been known as a bahlūlī or a paisah; under the Mughuls there were forty to a rupee. Coins of the denomination of half a dām, a quarter and eighth were also minted. In case a coin had lost more than a small specified percentage of its weight, it was treated as bullion.[49] The main denominations continued under the greater Mughuls; Shah Jahān's reign saw even greater advance in the purity of the coinage and the coins retained their beauty.

The Mughuls were great builders; apart from the famous palaces, mausolea, mosques and gardens which they built, a large number of public buildings of a more modest nature were needed for the government and the convenience of the public. They built or repaired a number of forts and fortresses, bridges, roads, canals, inns and houses. The department of construction was under the general supervision of the mīr sāmān, because administratively it was one of the buyūtāt. However, sometimes a high official was asked to supervise the progress of some buildings. 'Ālamgīr I, when as a prince he was not posted away from the capital, was assigned this duty.[50] The emperors took a personal interest in the construction of the more important buildings; the architects showed their plans to the emperor who gave the final approval.[51] Most of the important buildings bear the unmistakable impress of the personality of the monarch under whom they were built. The works department maintained an army of architects, engineers, craftsmen, carpenters and workers in stone.[52]

49 *Ibid.*, Ā'īns 4-10.

50 *Dastūr-u'l-'amal-i-āgāhi*, ff. 33b, 34a.

51 'Abd-u'l-Ḥamīd, i, p. 149; Abū-'l-Faḍl, *Ā'īn-i-Akbarī*, i, Ā'īn 85.

52 *Ibid.*, i. Ā'īn 87.

The Mughuls did not have a seafaring navy worth the name; they never seem to have attached importance to the development of sea power, though they were seeing with their own eyes the consequences of neglecting it. However, this does not mean that they did not have a department. The head was called mīr-i-baḥr. He had the double duty of maintaining a fleet for fighting purposes and for policing the main inland waterways. The Mughuls had a few vessels which could have made voyages in the open sea, but they were generally used in the broader rivers or their estuaries; the smaller craft was used on the other rivers. The care and the regulation of the seaports as well as riverports was in mīr-i-baḥr's charge. The levy of tolls from the merchants using the rivers and the ports for the conveyance of their merchandise also came under his jurisdiction.[53]

[53] *Ibid.*, ii, Ā'īn 26; *Kaifiyat-i-ṣūbajāt-i-mumālik-i-maḥrūsah-i-Hindustān*, ff. 234-236.

CHAPTER V

The Manṣabdārī System

THE classical Muslim writers divided the servants of the state into three main categories: the fighters were aṣḥāb-u's-saif or the masters of the sword; the accountants, clerks and other workers in the offices were aṣḥāb-u'l-qalam or the masters of the pen; theologians and jurists were aṣhāb-u'l-'amāmah or men of the turban, this being an allusion to the dress which the doctors of religion wore. The last class was not exactly the servant of the state, though some of them served it in certain important capacities. The theory of their relationship with the state will be discussed later. The first two categories were in every sense members of the public services; they were organized by Akbar into a single service in which they had a defined place, a manṣab or a status. Literally the word mansab means a place or a position where something is fixed or placed and, therefore, in the technical context the word manṣab meant a station or a position in the system. Later the word also came to mean a function, a prerogative or even a duty, but all

tained only a contingent of twenty troopers. It is also significant that Badā'ūnī says that "every amīr should commence" with twenty troopers, meaning to say that a manṣabdār with the dhāt rank of five hundred could normally not hope to get a sawār rank of more than a hundred in the beginning.

There is another indication of a different nature. There is no record in the historical literature of the period of a measure to bring about a major change like the establishment of two different kinds of ranks in the manṣabdārī system. The passage in the *Pādshāhnāmah* does not imply a fundamental change like this; it only sets forth the alteration in the proportion between the contingents and the sawār ranks; it takes a difference between the number of the troops and the sawār rank for granted. If it were intended to reduce a hard reality to a symbol, the language would have been different. The discrepancy between the rank and the troops commanded has a long history so far as the Mughuls are concerned.

The Muslims very early adopted the system of organizing their armies on a decimal basis: the system adopted by the Mongols also was similar. Chingiz Khān is reported to have organized his troops into tens, hundreds and thousands. The larger units were combinations of thousands, a tūmān consisting of ten thousand. With the decline in the power of the Timurids, the familiar phenomenon of terms losing their original meaning and being used merely for prestige played its part in the military organization as well.[11] Under Bābur we read of tūmāns consisting of five hundred to a thousand persons.[12] This is a far cry from the original tūmān of ten thousand. It is a good instance of the difference between the nominal strength of a force and its actual numbers. The discrepancy continued at least in the earlier period of Akbar's reign. The number of troops which the officers must maintain was fixed for the first time in the eleventh year.[13] It is doubtful if this improved mattors until the manṣabdārs were asked to get their

[11] Viladimirtsov, pp. 58, 69.

[12] Bābur, pp. 170, 277.

[13] Abū-'l-Faḍl, *Akbarnāmah*, ii, p. 270.

horses branded and the description of their troops registered. Even then fraud could not be completely eliminated. The tradition of high sounding titles without concrete justification for it was deeply ingrained. Another manifestation of this tendency was the fact that when the empire was small under Akbar and the number of officers with high titles too many, assignments given to them in lieu of their salaries had to be inflated until they bore no relation to the reality.[14] This was corrected later, because it created administrative difficulties. There was, however, no need to cut down the high sounding titles to the actual size of the contingent.

Indeed there were advantages in not doing so. The intricacies of the organization were known only to a few; the population at large were impressed with the might of the empire and travellers carried tales of its grandeur. The propaganda value of exaggerated numbers seems to have been very much in the minds of the Mughuls; the salaries were shown not in rupees but in dāms, copper coins of which there were forty to a rupee. The same trend can be discovered in the method of the calculation of the salaries which find mention on a monthly basis, but which were drawn only by a few for the twelve months in a year. It seems, therefore, reasonable to think that Akbar could have found a propaganda value in making the sawār rank only a symbol standing for a multiple of the actual number of troops maintained by the officer. This trend is incontrovertibly present in the description of the dhāt ranks, because at no stage did they represent the number of troops actually commanded. Another authority, the *Ma'āthir-u'l-umarā* which has a parallel passage regarding Shāh Jahān's regulation also takes the dhāt and sawār ranks for granted and makes it clear that Shāh Jahān was responsible for the regulation regarding the proportions of a third, a fourth, and a fifth.[15] The English reports that Shāh Jahān started by lessening the "former livings" of the manṣabdārs of the previous reign and "impoverishing" his own manṣabdārs are in all probability partly based upon the results of his action in prescribing new proportions. This would confirm the

[14] Abū-'l-Faḍl, *Ā'īn-i-Akbarī*, iii, Ā'īn-i-dahsālah (Ā'īn 19).

[15] Ṣamṣām-u'd-dawlah Shāh Nawāz Khān, ii, p. 444.

dhāt sih hazār sawār (a commander of 3,000 personal rank; contingent 3,000) has to muster one-third (bring to the brand) (1000) cavalry. But if he holds an appointment in another ṣūbah, he has only to muster a fourth part. Accordingly, a chahār hazārī chahār hazār sawār (a commander of four thousand; contingent 4000) has only to muster 1000 cavalry.) At the time when the imperial army was ordered to take Balkh and Samarqand (1055 A.H.), His Majesty, on account of the distance of those countries, gave the order that as long as the expedition should last, each manṣabdār should only muster one-fifth."[7] This passage makes it clear that the term sawār in the context of an officer's title was a symbol which denoted a varying multiple of the actual number of horsemen commanded. The question arises if it was so in the reign of Akbar as an original feature of the system.

The writers on the manṣabdārī system have differed on this point. The majority have been misled by Blochmann's translation of the relevant portion of the *Ā'īn* and have uncritically accepted his version which has led them to erroneous conclusions. As the arguments of most of the writers are based upon this translation it is necessary to examine the text a little more closely. The *Ā'īn* by itself does not create any difficulty in believing that there could have been a sawār rank under Akbar denoting a multiple of the contingent commanded. In the revised version given above, the word sawār could very well stand for a sawâr rank rather than 'horsemen'. More information is, however, needed to justify fully such an interpretation of the text. Of the writers of that period, Badā'ūnī is of some help. He has a passage which says: "It was settled that every amīr should commence as a commander of twenty,.... and when, according to the rules, he had brought the horses of his twenty troopers to be branded, he was then to be made a commander of a hundred or more."[8] The question arises whether the proportion between twenty troopers and the command of a hundred horses has any constant significance and if this proportion

7 'Abd-u'l-Hamīd, ii, p. 506. The translation is Blochmann's, *Ā'in-i-Akbari*, Eng. tr., i, p. 244.

8 Badā'ūnī, ii, p. 190. Translation is from Blochmann, *Ā'in-i-Akbari*, *Eng. tr.*, i, pp. 242, 243.

persisted in the award of other commands as well. Another important question is whether Badā'ūnī uses the words amīr and commander of a hundred in any special sense. It is difficult to find a definite answer to the first question, excepting that it reminds one of the regulation mentioned in the *Pādshāhnāmah* regarding the minimum prescribed for the sawār rank. Badā'ūnī seems to imply that this proportion of twenty per cent was the maximum or at least the normal requirement, but there could be cases where a smaller proportion of troopers could earn a higher rank. Was the rank of a hundred the dhāt rank or a sawār rank? It is significant that Badā'ūnī does not use the word manṣabdār in this sentence; he uses the word amīr instead. Blochmann has independently reached the conclusion that the word amīr was not used for a commander of less than two hundred; this opinion is based upon the fact that Abū-'l-Faḍl does not list manṣabdārs who had a rank of less than two hundred.[9] There is, however, more definite evidence in Niẓām-u'd-dīn, who ought to know being the bakhshī. He adds a note to his list of manṣabdārs saying: "Let it be known that the title of amīr is given to all such as hold manṣabs from five-hundred upwards."[10] Badā'ūnī being a contemporary and having avowedly based his history upon Niẓām-ū'd-dīn's work could not have been unaware of this. It would, therefore, not be unjustified to think that Badā'ūnī uses the word amīr in its technical sense of a commander of at least five hundred. If that is so, the other rank of a hundred should be something different from the rank of five hundred. It seems, therefore, that the rank of five hundred is the dhāt or personal rank and that the other rank of a hundred is the sawār rank which. being based upon a contingent of twenty is a multiple of the contingent actually brought to the muster. If these conclusions are correct, the sawār rank as a symbol of the contingent maintained by the manṣabdār dates back to Akbar's reign, in fact to the very initiation of the system. The position of the amīr mentioned by Badā'ūnī would be described as a manṣabdār of the rank of five hundred dhāt and one hundred sawār though he main-

[9] *Ibid.*

[10] Niẓām-u'd-dīn, note added to the list of manṣabdārs.

and confers upon them high rank. Sometimes he increases the manṣab of a servant, but decreases his contingent. He also fixes the number of the beasts of burden. The monthly grants made to the manṣabdārs vary according to the condition of their contingents. An officer whose contingent comes up to his manṣab, is put into the first class of his rank; if his contingent is one-half and upwards of the fixed number, he is put into the second class; the third class contains those contingents which are still less..". This is a free paraphrase of the passage and embodies Blochmann's understanding of it rather than the real purport. A closer examination of the text reveals discrepancies in the translation and the full ambiguity of the text. It is necessary, therefore, to give a more literal translation to bring out the points at issue. It is unavoidable here to sacrifice idiom to get at the author's real meaning. Abū-'l-Faḍl says, "He recognizes (the merit of) some at first sight and confers at once a high rank. Sometimes he puts together a higher manṣab and less sawār. Through his knowledge of affairs he has prescribed the number of the beasts of burden. In accordance with sawār the monthly emoluments also became varied. Everyone whose sawār coincides with his manṣab is placed in the first class; whose (sawār) is half (of the manṣab) or over is in the second class· whose (sawār) is less (than a half) in the third class." Abū-'l-Faḍl is too brief in this passage, but then he takes the knowledge of the working of the system for granted. The following procedure seems to be implied. When a candidate was presented before the monarch for appointment to a manṣab, sometimes he thought that the candidate was good enough to be trusted with a command, and, therefore, was given a position of responsibility. In certain other instances he was given a higher rank than the number of horsemen which he was to command would justify. In accordance with the number of the horsemen in the contingent which the candidate was expected to maintain, he was placed within that rank and drew his salary.

The real significance of this passage does not lie entirely in the information which it contains regarding the subdivision of every rank into three classes; the most significant fact which emerges is that the manṣab did not convey the number of the troops commanded. If the manṣabdār was a panj hazārī, a commander of five thousand, according to this passage, he did not necessarily command a contingent of five thousand horsemen. If he was placed in the third class and even if sawār is translated as "horsemen", he obviously commanded less than two thousand five hundred. Thus, according to this passage, a commander of two thousand five hundred could conceivably command more troops than a commander of five thousand. It, therefore, follows that a manṣab signified a personal rank, not the number of troops commanded. To put it into the administrative jargon of the period, the manṣab denoted the dhāt rank of the officer. This is important because if any indication were to be given of the actual number of troops commanded by him, an additional nomenclature was necessary. This we find quite clearly in the titles of a later period, where they include both the dhāt or personal rank and a reference to the contingent commanded. An officer's name followed by a title like panj hazār dhāt chahār hazār sawār denoted his personal rank and had some reference to the contingent commanded by him. The reason why the word sawār has been left untranslated in the passage quoted from the *Ā'īn* above is that it does not necessarily mean troopers; it may mean a sawār rank. There is no doubt that a sawār rank did exist in Akbar's reign.[6] Several men have been mentioned both by Abū-'l-Faḍl and Niẓām-u'd-dīn with their dhāt and sawār ranks, and the words dhāt and sawār have been used in the context but it is still to be determined whether the word signifies troopers or has been used in a technical sense as a symbol, because when it is used under Shāh Jahān, it is only a symbol. Then the figure denotes a certain multiple of the actual troops commanded.

For understanding this feature fully, we have to turn to the *Pādshāhnāmah*, which says: "The following law was made during the present reign (Shāh Jahān). If a manṣabdār holds a jāgīr in the same ṣūbah, in which he holds his manṣab, he has to muster one-third of the force indicated by his rank. Accordingly a sih hazārī

[6] *e.g.*, Abū-'l-Faḍl, *Akbarnāmah*, iii, p. 739.

meanings grew out of the original idea of a station or rank within the organization. The explanation of the system would have been easy enough but for two complications. The first of these is that the word was not applied to any rank or station in the system, but only to the higher ones, or at least the lowest grades were not designated as manṣabs, though the principle underlying the system embraced the lowest servants as well. The second complication was introduced by the fact that the manṣab was defined in military terms, though the military definition was only a myth or at best a symbol. If an officer performed no military duties and the military obligations of the manṣabdārs did not apply to his case, the military definition of his grade was only a myth; if he was expected to fulfil the military requirements, the theoretical definition of his manṣab was only a symbol of his duties in this regard and of his actual contingent. As this confusion was further increased by subsidiary additions to the symbols, it is not surprising that the details of the system should have led to confusion as well as controversy.

The word manṣab in the technical sense of a rank had been used prior to Akbar's reign; it was in use in Central Asia; but it did not imply any elaborate organization like the manṣabdārī system.[1] The idea of paying some civilian officers by putting them on the military payroll was also not unknown, though there is no positive evidence that this was done uniformly in the Sultanate of Dehlī. Baranī does mention that the poets of 'Alā-u'd-dīn Khalji's court were paid by the dīwān-i-'arḍ, but this is the only evidence in favour of the maintenance of a common payroll for the civilians and the military personnel.[2] It might as well have been a special arrangement for some persons attached to the court in view of their having to travel with the sultan whenever he undertook a long journey. On the whole, it seems unlikely that the administration should have been complicated by putting all the civil officers on the military payroll and making the dīwān-i-'arḍ responsible for certifying that they had earned their salaries, when such a certificate from the immediate superior and the department con-

[1] Ḥaider Dughlat, p. 103.

[2] Baranī, p. 360.

cerned would be necessary anyhow. In any case the establishment of an organization wherein all superior officials should have their status defined in military terms was Akbar's own idea. He was perhaps inspired in the first instance by his father's division of all his servants into three categories of ahl-i-dawlat, or those who contributed to the might and strength of the state; ahl-i-sa'ādat, or those who served the state in the realm of religious and spiritual well being and ahl-i-murād or those who provided the monarch with cultural and literary diversions and were his companions for these purposes.[3] This would show that the civil and military servants of the state, apart from the religious and judicial officers, have been lumped together as ahl-i-dawlat.

The broad outlines of the system have been given by Abū-'l-Faḍl in the *Ā'īn*.[4] We are told that Akbar established sixty-six grades of manṣabdārs, ranging from the commanders of ten horsemen to those of ten thousand. The commands above five thousand were, however, limited in the first instance to the princes of royal blood. The fact that the grades worked out to be sixty-six gave the emperor great satisfaction, because this number represents the numerical value of the word Allah according to the well known method of *abjad* which assigns a numerical value to each letter of the alphabet. Originally designed for working out chronograms, it came to have a link with numerology in certain superstitious minds; as Akbar was fond of such pseudo sciences, he saw auspicious signs in this coincidence. An examination of the list of manṣabdārs given by Abū-'l-Faḍl reveals the existence of only thirty-three ranks in reality; the other thirty-three being only theoretical.[5] It seems probable that appointments were not made to all the theoretically possible ranks to simplify the working of the system.

Within each rank there were three subdivisions from the very beginning. The language of the *Ā'īn* is extremely ambiguous here. Blochmann translates the relevant sentences in the following manner: "His Majesty sees through some men at the first glance,

[3] Erskine, ii, p. 532.

[4] Abū-'l-Faḍl, *Ā'īn-i-Akbarī*, ii, Ā'īn 3.

[5] Vide *ibid.*, Eng. tr., Blochmann's note, vol. 1. p. 238.

title of mirzā or prince and he was not the only Rajput to do so The main point, however, is that commands higher than five thousand came to be conferred in Akbar's time upon others than the sons of the emperor. Under Shāh Jahān much higher commands came into existence. According to the *Pādshāhnāmah*, Shāh Jahān's four sons enjoyed commands respectively of twenty thousand, fifteen thousand, fifteen thousand, and twelve thousand; there were others among the higher officials who had commands of nine thousand, seven thousand and six thousand.[24] This seems to be true about the earlier period, because a later authority, the *Risālah-i-manāṣib* says that in the reign of Shāh Jahān "the manṣabs rose as high as the ranks of sixty thousand. Dārā Shikūh had (a manṣab of) sixty thousand (with a salary of) forty crore dāms; Shāh Shūja' and Awrangzib each had salaries of twenty four crore dāms; Murād Bakhsh had a salary of twelve crore dāms. It was also laid down in this reign that all the manṣabdārs having the ranks of sixty thousand down to six thousand shall be of the first class." There is a discrepancy between this statement and the table which follows wherein the salaries are given for the various ranks. The highest manṣab of sixty thousand has been shown to carry a salary of twelve crore dāms; whereas the salaries of all the princes are shown to be much higher. The salaries in the table find confirmation in other sources. It is difficult to explain or reconcile this data, but it seems certain that the princes enjoyed higher ranks and salaries than are shown in the *Pādshāhnāmah*.[25] Shāh Jahān himself had been given the rank of thirty thousand when he was a prince by his father.[26] According to Abū-'l-Faḍl's list in the *Ā'īn*, Akbar had one thousand and eight hundred manṣabdārs, of whom four hundred and twelve had commands of five thousand to two hundred and the rest of one hundred and fifty to ten.[27] The list is complete up to the time of writing only, because he himself lived to record in the *Akbar-*

24 'Abd-u'l-Ḥamīd, ii, p. 717.

25 Najaf 'Alī, ff. 11,12. *Kaifiyat-i-ṣūbajāt-i-mumālik-maḥrūsah-i-Hindustān* gives the same figures of salaries for the manṣabs as are common, f. 212.

26 Jahāngīr, p. 195. The rank was 30,000 dhāt 20,000 sawār.

27 Abū-'l-Faḍl, *Ā'īn-i-Akbarī*, i, Eng. tr. p. 239.

nāmah certain facts not mentioned in the *Ā'īn*. The *Pād*s*h*ā*hnāmah* says that Shāh Jahān's manṣabdārs numbered eight thousand; Khawāfī Khān gives some details regarding the time when Shāh Jahān fell ill and the war of succession broke out among his sons. At that time the empire had no one with the rank of seven thousand, there were six manṣabdārs with the rank of six thousand, fifteen with five thousand, fourteen with four thousand, one with three thousand and five hundred, forty seven with three thousand, twenty with fifteen hundred and fifty nine with one thousand.[28] It seems that the ranks above five thousand were bestowed only in exceptional circumstances, not more than four persons had ranks of seven thousand in the entire reign of Shāh Jahān.[29] Of course Khawāfī Khān does not include the princes. The number of manṣabdārs increased under 'Ālamgīr I, because he conferred a large number of manṣabs in the course of his war in the Deccan. The higher officers of the sultanates of Golconda and Bījāpūr were taken into imperial service after their absorption into the empire;[30] besides the emperor lured away many rebel chieftains into Mughul service by conferring manṣabs upon them. The increase in the manṣabdārs had an adverse effect upon 'Ālamgīr's administration, but under the circumstances it could hardly be avoided. The ranks under 'Ālamgīr I show a slight variation from Shāh Jahān's reign; manṣabs of twenty thousand, sixteen thousand, twelve thousand, ten thousand, nine thousand, eight thousand have been mentioned in addition to the usual seven thousand downwards.[31] The highest manṣabs were more a matter of the favour which the monarch wanted to show his sons. It is also mentioned that the manṣabs above five thousand were not divided into the three classes in accordance with the sawār ranks. The reason seems to be that there was no point in doing so, because there were so very few who enjoyed these manṣabs that complications of classification to determine precedence were deemed unnecessary.

28 'Abd-u'l-Ḥamīd, ii, p. 715; Khawāfī Khān, i, p. 759.

29 *Ibid.*, p. 758.

30 *Cambridge History of India*, iv, p. 286.

31 *Kaifiyat-i-ṣūbajāt-i-mumālik-i-maḥrūsah-i-Hindustān*, f. 212.

It was possible for a commander of five thousand to earn a salary which a commander of ten thousand would normally earn without crossing the line of seniority fixed by the dhāt rank. Within every dhāt rank there were three gradations, it is true, but in every gradation there was ample room for differences in pecuniary advantages. The emperor was the sole arbiter in giving promotions, but he had to keep in mind the feelings of his servants. The complexities of the system helped in keeping the older servants contented even if their value was not as great as their pretensions which had to be accepted when men willing to stake their future in supporting a struggling power were not too many.

In addition to the troopers mustered by the manṣabdārs, they had to maintain a certain number of beasts of burden.[22] These were elephants, camels and mules. Besides, they were also required to maintain carts for transport. The elephants were classified in accordance with their breeds and quality and a certain proportion was prescribed of each kind. Apart from the horses belonging to his troopers or provided for them the manṣabdār was expected to maintain in his own stables a number of horses whose numbers were prescribed, and which were classified in accordance with their breeds. The cost of maintaining these animals and the carts came out of the dhāt salary of the manṣabdār. The sawār rank made no difference to the number of animals which the manṣabdār had to maintain.

Not all the manṣabdārs were military officers. Those who held high civil posts were also manṣabdārs and were graded accordingly. Though the aḥadīs were not manṣabdārs; yet they were theoretically classified as soldiers and, like the manṣabdārs, drew their salaries from the common payroll for making disbursements to the military personnel. They also were employed as civil officers. If a post was considered high enough, a manṣabdār was appointed to it; if it was lower in status, an aḥadī was appointed; if it belonged to even a lower category, often a man of the status of a cavalryman or even an infantryman would be appointed. A manṣabdār serving in a civilian capacity generally had only

[22] *Ibid.*, ii, Ā'īn 3.

a dhāt rank, but this was not universal. As a mark of special favour, or for the purpose of promoting the officer within the same dhāt rank a sawār rank was also bestowed, thus making the system even more complex; because this rank could be purely fictitious in the sense that the incumbent did not command any soldiers, he only enjoyed the higher status and drew the higher salary. Sometimes, of course, a military officer was appointed to a civilian post for a short while and maintained his contingent.

The amalgamation of the civilian and military personnel into a single cadre has led some writers to believe that the Mughul government was a military government. Nothing could be farther from the truth, because there is no trace of military methods in the sphere of the civil administration. The functions of all civilian posts were well defined; nor were the rules and regulations under which the government functioned of a military nature. The Mughul government can be defined only as a bureaucracy. There are instances of some civilians trying their talent in military exploits sometimes with disastrous consequences and sometimes with conspicuous success, but the instances of warriors and generals succeeding as civilian bureaucrats are very few in Mughul annals. The Mughuls were wise in choosing their civilian officers so that their technical skills could be utilized to the greatest advantage.

It has been mentioned that Akbar established sixty six theoretical ranks ranging from commanders of ten to commanders of ten thousand and that he reserved commands of more than five thousand for the princes of blood. Akbar's three sons had commands from seven to ten thousand. In the fiftieth year of the reign Rājah Mān Singh was appointed to the rank of seven thousand dhāt and six thousand sawār, which is a clear indication that Akbar later did not restrict the commands higher than five thousand to his sons, as the *Ā'īn* says.[23] Rājah Mān Singh was related through marriage to the Mughul royal family, his paternal aunt being Akbar's wife. He may have been treated as a prince of royal blood. Later Rājah Jai Singh for the same reason bore the

[23] Abū-'l-Faḍl, *Akbarnāmah*, iii, p. 837; also Shāh Nawāz Khān, ii, p. 167.

first assumption is against the clear testimony of the *Pādshāh-nāmah* which mentions the difference between the dhāt rank and the troops commanded. It has even been suggested that the dhāt rank denoted the number of infantry commanded and the sawār rank referred to the number of horsemen under the command of the officer.[18] There is not a shred of evidence in support of that view; indeed all information points in a contrary direction.

It has been mentioned that the manṣab did not imply the assignment of an officer to any particular post; some posts, however, carried certain additional ranks with them. Such posts as well as ranks were called mashrūṭ or conditional; such a rank was taken away when the incumbent left the post. Those who were appointed to such posts were already the holders of a manṣab, which they held anyhow, ghair mashrūṭ or unconditionally; this latter was their permanent grade and did not depend upon their holding any office; when they were appointed to a post which had an additional manṣab attached to it, they held the additional mashrūṭ manṣab for that period. These posts were mostly governorships of provinces or the fawjdārīs of sarkārs.[19]

The question arises: why did the Mughuls adopt this complex system of grading their officers? Why did they not adopt a simpler method of uniform grading and imposing upon everyone the same requirements? Would it not have been much simpler if the dhāt and sawār ranks had coincided? Was it necessary to make the sawār rank as well merely a symbol of a much smaller reality? And, finally, what was the point in doubling an officer's contingent by the addition of another title rather than doubling his sawār rank? In particular the tamām dū aspah sih aspah rank went against the grain of Mughul methods of inflated figures for creating an impression.

There were historical reasons, as has been explained earlier, for the habit of hiding reality behind inflated figures. It was more honorific to call some one a commander of five thousand instead

[18] C. S. K. Rao Saheb, "A Note on the Mughul Military Terms" *Journal of Indian History*, August, 1935.

[19] *e.g.*, 'Ali Muḥammad Khān, *Supplement*, p. 169.

of a mere one thousand; the habit had grown up in the days of high pretensions and restricted means when the Timurids had lost power and the once great and mighty empire had fallen to pieces and its place had been taken by small kingdoms and states which found it impossible to maintain the old traditions. It was for this reason that the Mughul princes were styled sultans and men having twenty soldiers could be the commanders of five hundred. The manşab fixed the precedence of the officer. Irvine is right when he says that the object of the manşabdārī system "was to settle precedence and fix gradation of pay; it did not necessarily imply the exercise of any particular office, and meant nothing beyond the fact that the holder was in the employment of the state, and bound in return to yield certain services when called upon".[20] The custom of influential persons with troopers in their service or attached to them seeking employment at different courts had grown up earlier; a period of uncertainty on the fall of Tīmūr's empire made the troopers as well as their leaders anxious to find means of livelihood and avenues of adventure by joining any prince whose career promised them a future, or, at least, present security, however short lived. The Mughul Empire did not finally emerge from difficulties and restricted means until a few years after Akbar's accession. During all this time there were men who were too proud to accept humble appointments and yet whose pretensions were in accordance neither with their means nor with the financial resources of the state.[21] When the empire was able to bring some order into this chaotic position, the only method was to create a complex system, which would give the emperor a freer hand in rewarding talent without hurting the feelings of those who had come to enjoy prestige and seniority. The dhāt ranks were, therefore, meant to establish an order of precedence; within this framework, the more enterprising and the abler officers were able to do better, because there were so many different ways of determining their emoluments. Their salaries could range from five months in the year to twelve, and even these could be doubled.

20 Irvine, p. 4.

21 Abū-'l-Fadl, *Ā'īn-i-Akbarī*, iii, Ā'īn 19.

opinion that the previous proportion was lower.[16] In view of the proportion mentioned by Badā'ūnī in the passage which has been discussed above, the requirement of maintaining a third and a fourth of the number of the sawār rank would be a hardship, because the previous proportion demanded only a fifth in all circumstances. At least no other proportion can be established to have existed with the available evidence. It has already been mentioned that the existence of a hundred per cent proportion was highly improbable.

It is necessary to revert to the rest of the passage in the *Pādshāh-nāmah* a part of which has already been quoted. It proceeds to say that the actual contingent had a prescribed proportion of sih aspah, dū aspah and yak aspah soldiers depending upon the number of months for which the manṣabdār drew his salary in a year. The lowest was the manṣabdār within the same rank who drew his salary only for five months in the year. In a contingent of a thousand troopers, there were three hundred sīh aspah, six hundred dū aspah, one hundred yak aspah horsemen, if the manṣabdār drew his salary for twelve months; if he drew his salary only for five months in the year, all his troopers were yak aspah. These terms need a brief explanation. A sih aspah trooper had three horses; a dū aspah two horses; a yak aspah one horse. There were two thousand two hundred horses in the contingent of the manṣabdār who drew his salary for twelve months and one thousand horses in the contingent of the officer who drew his salary for only five months in the year, provided that his contingent numbered a thousand troopers. There were variations in the proportions of the sih aspah, dū aspah and yak aspah troopers in between.

There was a further complication. Some manṣabdārs were given an additional rank in which all their troops were dū aspah sih aspah. Normally a manṣabdār's rank was shown by giving his dhāt and sawār ranks after his name, for example, Ardshīr Khān, yak hazār dhāt shish ṣad sawār, meant that Ardshīr Khān was a

[16] W. H. Moreland, "Rank (Manṣab) in the Mogul State Service," *Journal of the Royal Asiatic Society*, Oct. 1936, p. 654.

manṣabdār with a personal rank of one thousand and a sawār rank of six hundred. If after the sawār rank the words dū aspah sih aspah or tamām dū aspah sih aspah were added, it meant that he mustered double the number of troops which he would have done without this additional rank in the proportion fixed for sih aspah dū aspah and yak aspah troopers in accordance with the number of months for which he drew his salary in the course of a year. The underlying principle would become clear by the following illustration. A manṣabdār with a sawār rank of five thousand would muster one thousand men of whom three hundred would be sih aspah, six hundred dū aspah and one hundred yak aspah; thus his contingent would have one thousand men with two thousand and two hundred horses, provided that he drew his salary for twelve months in the year. If the same person were given the additional dū aspah sih aspah rank, and he continued to draw his salary for twelve months in the year, he would muster six hundred sih aspah, twelve hundred dū aspah and two hundred yak aspah troopers, making a total of two thousand men with four thousand four hundred horses. He also drew twice the salary.

The dū aspah sih aspah rank could be conferred to cover the full sawār rank, in which it was generally preceded by the word hamah or tamām meaning 'all'; it could also apply only to a part of the contingent commanded, in which instance the number was mentioned. For example, in the illustration given above, if after the sawār rank chahār hazār dū aspah sih aspah is added, it would mean that the dū aspah sih aspah calculation is to apply only to four thousand of the sawār rank and not to the entire five thousand. It should also be mentioned that the dū aspah sih aspah rank never exceeded the sawār rank just as the latter never exceeded the dhāt rank.

Some of the conclusions arrived at in this discussion are against the opinions of certain writers. They have been misled in thinking that the dhāt rank must have denoted the number of the troops commanded; therefore they think that the sawār rank denoted an extra number of soldiers commanded.[17] The

[17] Irvine, p. 5.

The division of the manṣabdārs into ranks was not the only means of deciding precedence. Additional honours were conferred by the monarch. Of these certain titles were the best known to the general public. Almost invariably a manṣabdār was given an individual title upon a high ranking appointment. This was only a sign that the recipient had become an amīr, a man of distinction. Sometimes these titles were changed into more high sounding ones at the time of subsequent promotions. However, these titles were only an indication of the esteem in which the recipient was held by the monarch. According to Niẓām-u'd-dīn a manṣabdār was styled amīr on reaching the rank of five hundred; manṣabdārs reaching the rank of a thousand were considered to be sufficiently senior to be called umarā'-i-kibār, or great nobles. The title of amīr-u'l-umarā was held simultaneously by several manṣabdārs. The highest title seems to have been khān khānān which, normally was not held by more than one person at one time.[32] The Tuzuk, however, says that there was no title higher than that of the amīr-u'l-umarā for a servant of the crown.[33] This is, in all probability, true about the period after Akbar, because the *Pādshāhnāmah* uses it only for the senior most living officer. The same impression is conveyed by 'Ālamgīr I in one of his letters.[34] In addition to the titles, other distinctions were conferred in the form of permission to carry certain standards and display some insignia like beating kettle drums or playing the band in front of the manṣabdār's residence. A coveted honour was the māhī marātib, which consisted of two balls of steel called the kawkabah and a fish made of gold carried in front of the officer. When carried in royal processions, these standards were carried behind the monarch. Originally these symbols represented height and depth respectively and were meant to convey that the monarch had raised one of his humble servants to the heights of power and prestige.[35] Any one who presumed to display any

[32] Abū-'l-Faḍl, *Ā'īn-i-Akbarī*, Eng. tr., i, pp. 239, 240.
[33] Jahāngīr, p. 6.
[34] Ashraf Khān, f. 20b.
[35] Najaf 'Alī, f. 31a.

symbol of authority or dignity to which he was not entitled was sternly reprimanded and sometimes even publicly disgraced.[36] The protocol was strictly enforced by the Mughuls and, in course of time, when real power departed, the insignia and symbols of precedence became even more important in the eyes of those who were entitled to use them.

At the inferior level, yūzbāshīs or commanders of a hundred were divided into eleven classes depending upon their sawār rank; those whose sawār rank was equal to their dhāt rank were in the first class; every succeeding class denoted a decrease of ten in the sawār rank, until the eleventh had no sawār rank at all.[37]

The Mughul emperors were conscious of the worth of good officers and were extremely tolerant in dealing with them. Akbar did not like Todar Mal's religious bigotry, but he advanced him to the highest positions.[38] Shāhbāz Khān Kanbūh was too orthodox for Akbar's taste, but he also was not only tolerated but valued.[39] Ḥusain Khān Tukriyah showed extreme religious bias, but he was tolerated.[40] 'Ālamgīr I records that his father admonished Dārā Shikūh that he should treat the imperial nobles with consideration and should not be led away by the backbiting of selfish maligners.[41] 'Ālamgīr I recalls how Khān Jahān was opposed to him and how far he had gone in injuring the interests of the prince, but on his succession the monarch forgot Khān Jahān's opposition and treated him with consideration. "If an old servant is virtuous and sincere, he is like pure gold; but even if he has neither of these qualities, he should not be deprived of his livelihood," adds the emperor.[42]

The manṣabdārs were paid in two ways, naqdī or a cash salary, or in the form of an assignment of revenue corresponding to the

[36] 'Ālamgīr I once ordered that the robes worn by an officer should be shortened to a proper length; he had made the garment too long. *Ruqqa'āt-i-'Ālamgīrī*, p. 46.

[37] Abū-'l-Faḍl, *Ā'īn-i-Akbarī*, ii, Ā'īn 3.

[38] *Dastūr-u'l-'amal-i-āgāhī*, f. 8a.

[39] Abū-'l-Faḍl, *Ā'īn-i-Akbarī*, Eng. tr., i, pp. 401, 402.

[40] *Ibid.*, pp. 372, 373.

[41] Ashraf Khān, f. 45.

[42] *Dastūr-u'l-'amal-i-āgāhī* 'f. 11a, b.

salary, calculated in terms of money.[43] The assignment was called a jāgīr. No manṣab was hereditary, much less an office or a jāgīr. The monarch showed some consideration for the sons or heirs of a manṣabdār by granting him a suitable manṣab; but this was always in the lower rungs. If the young man had any worth, he could win his spurs and rise higher. There are not many instances of the sons of famous manṣabdārs rising very high. The sons could not demand any office or employment as a matter of right. A manṣab was at least for life; there were many promotions but few demotions and these also came in the wake of extreme inefficiency or an unexcusable lapse. "What I have planted with my own hands", Akbar is reported to have said, "I find it difficult to uproot."[44] Sometimes even rebellion and contumacy were forgiven, if the monarch was satisfied that the guilty man had sincerely repented. Of course treason was often punished with death.

The manṣabdār did not have a life interest in his jāgīr, It could be increased or decreased in accordance with his promotion or demotion, even in accordance with his ability to obtain the ba<u>khsh</u>ī's certificate that his contingent had been kept up in accordance with the conditions of service. Sometimes for reasons of his convenience or exigencies of administration, his jāgīr could be transferred from one area to another. The jāgīr was administered by the agents of the holder, the jāgīrdār. The office of the dīwān calculated the expenses of administering the jāgīr at ten per cent of the income.[45] The manṣabdārs who were paid through jāgīrs were given some concessions regarding the time which could be permitted to elapse between one muster and another, because it was realized that they did not have the same facilities regarding ready cash as those who received cash payments.[46] The jāgīrdārs were under the supervision of the central and provincial governments and were asked to carry out all the instructions issued from time to time. They had to bear even such responsibilities as the

[43] *Dastūr-u'l-'amal*, I.O.L. Ethe 432, f. 37b.

[44] *Dastūr-u'l-'amal-i-āgāhī*, f. 8a.

[45] Qābil <u>Kh</u>ān, f. 131b.

[46] *Dastūr-u'l-'amal*, I.O.L. Ethe 432, f. 37b.

construction of inns on the thoroughfares for travellers.[47] They were also held responsible for the development of the area; in one instance they were asked to build townships at strategic points and to plant colonies to stop highway robbery.[48] The government kept itself informed regarding the administration of the jāgīr through regular news writers and other spies.[49] There are instances of a jāgīr having been taken over because the government found that it was not being properly administered.[50] The government also took steps to ensure that its agrarian policies, specially its regulations regarding the methods of the assessment of the state demand on agricultural produce and its level, were enforced in the jāgīrs in the same manner as they were in the areas directly administered by the government.

This brings us to the question of the salaries of the manṣabdārs The *Ā'īn* has a table which gives the salaries of the manṣabdārs according to this table a manṣabdār of five thousand received a salary of thirty thousand rupees per month if he was in the first class; a first class manṣabdār of five hundred received two thousand five hundred rupees per month; a dah bāshī, or a commander of ten received a hundred rupees per month.[51] The *Pādshāhnāmah* gives the salary of a commander of seven thousand as two hundred and fifty thousand rupees per annum.[52] The figures given by some of the *dastur-u'l-'amals*, despite minor discrepancies, generally confirm the lower level of the *Pādshāhnāmah*[53] There is other evidence to corroborate the conclusion that salaries were reduced under Shāh Jahān. Taking into consideration the level of prices at that time these salaries sound fantastically high. In effect they were not as high as they look. First of all one should

[47] Jahāngīr, p. 3.

[48] *Ibid.*, p. 4.

[49] 'Alī Muḥammad Khān, *Supplement*, pp. 174, 175.

[50] *Ibid.*, p. 175.

[51] Abū'-l-Faḍl, '*Ā'īn-i-Akbarī*, ii, Ā'īn 3. The salaries are shown in rupees here, but officially they were calculated in dāms, *ibid.*, ii, Ā'īn 14.

[52] *Ibid.*, Eng. tr., i, p. 240.

[53] *Kaifiyat-i-ṣubajāt-i-mumālik-i-maḥrūsah-i-Hindustān* (f.n. 29) and Najaf 'Alī both give the salary of a manṣabdār of seven thousand as 14000000 dāms which is Rs. 350000 per annum. This is considerably higher than the figure of *Pādshāhnāmah*, but lower than the figures in the *Ā'īn*.

deduct the cost of the maintenance of the beasts of burden, carts, horses and other animals; then at least ten per cent of the gross income was taken up by the administration of the jāgīr, which increased if any special duty was imposed by the central government in connection with the administration. If there was a failure of the crops, the manṣabdār had to bear the loss. Then there were the complexities created by the sawār rank and within the sawār rank by the composition of the contingent. As has been mentioned earlier, only those whose contingent had the highest proportion of dū aspah and sih aspah soldiers drew their salaries for twelve months in the year; some went down as low as to qualify for only five months' salary in the year. For such persons the salaries shown in the tables have to be cut down to less than a half. Prince Awrangzīb complains in a letter to the wazīr Sa'd-u'llah Khān that if the portion of the salary which the manṣabdār received as his dhāt salary were further reduced, his capacity for recruiting more soldiers would be gravely affected.[54] In this letter he points out that formerly the manṣabdār was able to draw a fourth of his salary for his dhāt alone; under the new orders this proportion had been reduced to a twelfth or a sixth. The salaries, therefore, should not be taken at their face value, because if all the complex regulations are taken into view, they are found to be much smaller. It was for this reason that the manṣabdārs were often in debt to the state. When they found themselves in difficulties and were hampered in the discharge of their obligations, they could apply for a loan. If they returned it within a year, no charge was made; in the second year, the sum was increased by a sixteenth; in the third by one-eighth; in the fourth by one-fourth; from the fifth to the seventh by one-half; from the eighth to the tenth by three-fourths; after that the loan was doubled.[55]

The accounting system was complex; the manṣabdārs, apart from taking loans, drew money in advance for various government purposes; few died without falling into arrears or having to clear their account with the state. It was customary, therefore, for the

[54] Qābil Khān, f. 131b.
[55] Abū-'l-Faḍl, *Ā'īn-i-Akbarī*, ii, Ā'īn 15.

government to take into its custody all the belongings of the deceased manṣabdārs to recover its debts. After the accounts were cleared and the dues of the state recovered, the rest of the property was handed over to the heirs. This was a cumbersome and inconvenient method and must have resulted in hardship to the heirs and loss of money to the state. It has also given rise to the myth that the Mughul emperors claimed to be heirs to their servants and escheated their property. It was also believed by some Western writers that all land belonged to the crown. The question of the ownership of land will be discussed in another place; here it would be sufficient to say that this was an entirely wrong notion. The Mughuls did not claim the ownership of any land which did not belong to them for any special reason; the jāgirs were in an entirely different category. The manṣabdār had no rights in the land; he was assigned only the revenue accruing from that area in lieu of a salary in return for services rendered. As the posts were not hereditary, the jāgirs were taken away whenever the monarch thought it necessary and invariably at the death of the holder. The private property of the deceased was taken under custody pending an examination of the accounts and only that much was deducted as the manṣabdār owed to the state at his death.[56] In case he owed more than he left, his heirs were required to clear the debt; if they were not able to do so and were given manṣabs, they paid the state by instalments. Sometimes, they were permitted to keep the property left by the deceased and to pay his debts out of their own salaries by instalments. 'Ālamgir wrote off a large number of such debts when he found that the payment was causing hardship to some of the officers. Some of these debts had remained undischarged for more than two generations.[57] European travellers who came to the subcontinent with feudal notions of fiefs and hereditary rights in land misunderstood the working of the manṣabdāri system. Hence they put forward their theories regarding the monarch being the heir of his servants. Bernier used the manṣabdari system as a foil to dilate upon the virtues of the French

[56] 'Ali Muḥammad Khān, i, p. 268.

[57] Kāẓim, pp. 1082 - 1084.

hereditary nobility and, therefore, was too harsh in his criticism.[58]

The manṣabdārī system had many weaknesses, which contributed to the downfall of the Mughul Empire. It was inefficient as a military machine. The Mughuls depended upon the manṣabdārī system for the bulk of their armies; the inherent defects of a system which entrusted the supervision and the maintenance of the troops to such an extent to the officers could not have worked otherwise than weakening the army. The organization of all services into a single mammoth system could not contribute to efficiency, because the functions of a military machine are entirely different from the civil duties of other branches of administration. The inevitable result of the manṣabdārī system could have been either the militarization of the entire administration and the consequential abuses of a military rule or the surreptitious as well as ubiquitous inroads of the civilian red tape into the military services ruining its effectiveness and efficiency. The former contingency did not arise because of deep seated traditions of bureaucratic rule in the subcontinent and inherent in the Muslim methods of administration. The Mughul military machine, so efficient in the beginning, became more and more clumsy and useless as time went on. The manṣabdārs were quite often given civil responsibilities on one occasion and then transferred to military campaigns; so much so that gradually it came to a body of civilians trying to conduct military campaigns. Akbar not only amalgamated the services but he also seems to have thought that anybody could be a military commander. His friend Bīr Bar lost his life on the north-west frontier because he obstinately refused to heed the advice of men who understood military matters; men like Todar Mal and Abū-'l-Faḍl were asked to fight battles and lead military expeditions.[59] The Mughuls succeeded fairly well where they found that overwhelming numbers and resources could crush the enemy, but when they came across wily foes like the Marathas or guerrillas like the Pathan tribesmen, they found it difficult to deal with them. Then it was only the determination

[58] Bernier, *e.g.*, p. 230.

[59] For Bīr Bar's disaster Abū-'l-Faḍl, *Ā'in-i-Akbari*, Eng. tr. i. pp. 344, 345.

of an Akbar or an 'Ālamgīr I which could extract them out of difficulties.

The system had its strong points as well. The most important factor was that it was based upon a recognition of merit and encouraged ability. It has been mentioned that no office was hereditary; everyone had to begin at the lower rungs of the ladder and could rise to the highest if he possessed ability. The only exception was the appointment of the tributary chiefs like the Rajput princes. Even there talent and loyalty received adequate reward and mere chieftainship did not take the incumbent to the highest grades. The monarchs were fairly impartial in their encouragement of ability; they needed good servants and they encouraged them. The manṣabdārī system prevented the development of a feudal caste; however, it was not necessary to create this organization for this purpose. It weakened the tribal oligarchies which in the past had tended to grab power in times of stress though, as the emergence of the Saiyyids of Bārah shows, the Mughuls did not succeed in completely eliminating them. It put the Muslims, to some extent, at a disadvantage against hereditary rulers like the Rajputs in the continuity of traditions of power in the same families, but this need not have been a disadvantage, if the Muslim society had not displayed signs of decay. Its main advantage was that in spite of its weaknesses it strengthened the monarchy, because every manṣabdār could look only to the monarch for promotion and advancement. So long as the monarchs had the ability to utilize the leviathan created by them, they were supreme. The system was centered in the person of the monarch; when the monarchs found the sceptre too heavy for their inefficient hands, they could not wield such a large instrument. There are some who think that instead of a bureaucratic organization like the manṣabdārī system, a hereditary and feudal institution would have been better, because in course of time it would have snatched power from the crown and later passed it on to the people and established a democratic form of government; such thinking is grossly anachronistic and betrays ignorance of the trends of social development in the sub-continent at that time. Whatever its faults, the manaṣbdārī system did enable the Mug͟huls to give good government to the people.

In its basic conception the manṣabdārī system was a Turkish institution; it has affinities with similar institutions built up by the Mamelukes of Egypt and the Ottomans: it had little in common with European feudalism.

CHAPTER VI

The Armed Forces

THE Mughuls looked upon the cavalry as the main arm of their forces. In the beginning it was organized in a haphazard manner. Bābur and Humāyūn depended upon warrior leaders who had their own troops; every one of these leaders was paid in accordance with his importance, which was determined by the effectiveness of his contingent in war. During the first two reigns, the territories under the direct and effective control of the monarchs were not too far flung for the emperors to have reliable information regarding the condition of these contingents; in any case, almost continuous warfare provided an infallible test of their quality. These conditions began to change after the first few years of Akbar's reign, and some of the inherent defects of the system began to come to the surface. The officers failed to maintain the strength of their contingents; therefore, in the eleventh year of the reign all the officers were required to maintain the number of the troopers prescribed in each instance.[1] The salaries which were to

[1] Abū-'l-Faḍl, *Akbarnāmah*, ii. p. 270.

be paid to the troopers were also prescribed. These steps, however, proved ineffectual. The officers drew the salaries of the prescribed number of troopers without maintaining the full strength of their contingents. They would hire extra men at the time of the muster and dismiss them as soon as the inspection was over.

Akbar had been conscious of the existence of these malpractices for some time when he decided to impose further measures to eradicate the abuses in the nineteenth year of his reign.[2] The first of these was the establishment of the manṣabdārī system, which fixed the pattern for the higher officers. It gave them a well-defined rank and laid down well-understood obligations. Besides, Akbar ordered that the descriptive rolls of the troopers should be registered to prevent fraud; similarly the horses brought by the troopers should be branded to prevent their transfer to other troopers still awaiting registration. These measures were opposed by some of the officers, specially by Akbar's foster brother, Mirzā 'Aẓīz Kokah. Akbar punished the Mirzā by depriving him of his manṣab for sometime and putting him under house arrest. Other officials as well who had opposed the reform were left in no doubt of imperial displeasure; they were forbidden attendance at court for some time and were transferred to Bengal.[3] Thus by showing determination and strength, the emperor succeeded in enforcing these important measures. It is obvious that Akbar not only demonstrated in this way that he could not be thwarted in important matters, but also broke the power of the nobles by making them entirely dependent upon the throne. So long as the emperors were able to enforce these measures, the servants of the empire were not able to defy its mandates. This reform had also its counterpart in the field of revenue administration, because the system could not be expected to work satisfactorily unless the real income from the assignments given in lieu of cash payments for the salaries of the manṣabdārs and their soldiers was correctly defined. For this purpose, all assignments were temporarily taken over by the state and salaries were paid in cash.[4]

[2] *Ibid,* iii, pp. 116, 117.

[3] *Ibid,* pp. 147, 148.

[4] *Ibid,* p. 117.

Assignments were given again after a series of measures brought consistency and method in the calculation of the yield from every area. These reforms were of a basic nature and contributed in no small measure to the strength of the empire and the power of the monarch.

The *Ā'īn* has an important passage regarding the different categories of officers and soldiers, a proper understanding of which depends upon a correct interpretation of the text; hence it is necessary to insert a faithful translation here:

"As this group was large in numbers, (the emperor) divided it into several categories . . .

"The branding of horses was prescribed for some, and the recognition of status and the registration of descriptive rolls came into great vogue;

"Some were assigned to (a commander) to obey him and to accompany him;

"Those who were capable of (serving) individually were trusted (to do so) and were called aḥadīs;

"Some were considered to deserve leadership and were appointed as leaders;

"And many worthy persons in want of resources were granted the wherewithal for mounts, and such were given the assignments without the horses receiving the brand;

"The Tūrānīs and the Irānīs are given twenty-five rupees and Indians get twenty rupees, and those who are employed as workers of the khāliṣah fifteen rupees;

"And these are called barāwardīs;

"And some who find it difficult to find men are given under them those who have already submitted (their horses) to branding, this category is known as dākhilīs;

"In the contingents of dah hazārīs are included up to hazārīs, of haft hazārīs up to haft ṣadīs, of panj hazārīs up to panj ṣadīs, of panj ṣadīs up to ṣadīs; a manṣabdār of less than this rank is not included in the contingent of a higher rank;

"And some are given as auxiliaries, and they are known as kumakīs;

"Today all emphasis is upon branding, and such soldiers are superior."[5]

The first division according to this passage is the basic one between the officers and the troopers. Those who were considered capable of holding a command were expected to bring their contingents for approval. Those who were approved had their descriptive rolls registered and their horses branded. This was intended to be the regular procedure. Special circumstances, however, found recognition in other methods of recruitment. A number of men were considered to be too good to be employed merely as soldiers, and therefore were given a higher rank, though not of an officer. They were called aḥadīs. The manṣabdārs who brought their men to the muster and fulfilled all conditions or approved applicants for manṣabs who were in a position to fulfil the requirements received their assignments and drew full salaries in accordance with the rules. There were, however, men considered fit for commands but lacking the resources for raising a contingent. If they had men who, given good horses, would have been good cavalrymen, they were provided with the means for purchasing horses. These men were paid only the basic salary for horsemen and were not given the higher salaries which were drawn by men bringing their own horses. These soldiers were called barāwardīs; some of them were attached to manṣabdārs; others were employed by the state in essentially non-military duties. The *Ā'īn* gives the salaries of those who had to perform military duties under the manṣabdārs and also of those who rendered service "on the k͟hāliṣah lands." It should be remembered that the principle of giving a rank to civilians was not limited to the manṣabdārī system; there were many civilians in subordinate positions who had military ranks. Some were classified as aḥadīs; others as ordinary troopers, and yet others as infantrymen; though none of these were expected to fight as a part of their normal duties. At the lower levels, however, it was rare for a man to be transferred from civil to military duties.

There were candidates for manṣabs who were not in a position

[5] Abū-'l-Faḍl, *Ā'īn-i-Akbarī*, ii, Ā'īn 1.

to furnish any men. Similarly there must have been a class of troopers who have not been mentioned directly by Abū-'l-Faḍl; many deserving men must have come with horses who were not sponsored by any manṣabdār. These men, if found deserving, were recruited and then assigned to those manṣabdārs who had not furnished their own contingent. The lower manṣabdārs who were given such troops served as part of the contingent of higher manṣabdārs. The commander of a thousand could serve in the contingent of a manṣabdār of ten thousand, a commander of seven hundred under a commander of seven thousand, a commander of five hundred under a commander of five thousand, and a commander of a hundred under a commander of five hundred. This would show that in case of commanders of dākhilī troops, a kind of a graduated command could, at least theoretically, be built up; though it seems unlikely that commanders of more than a thousand had contingents of dākhilī troops alone without any tābīnān or barāwardīs.

Some manṣabdārs were assigned duties which required a larger number of troops than the size of their contingents; in such instances they were given assistance in the form of an additional number of directly recruited troops which did not form part of their permanent contingents. Such troops were called kumakīs, or auxiliaries. They differed from the dākhilīs only in not being permanently attached to that manṣabdār. Thus the main divisions of the cavalry were the manṣabdārs, the aḥadīs, the troopers recruited and maintained by the manṣabdārs known as tābīnān, the barāwardīs, the dākhilīs and the kumakīs. The main features of the manṣabdārī system have been discussed in the previous chapter; here it would suffice to discuss the other categories of the cavalrymen.

The aḥadīs were so called because they were employed individually and did not form part of any manṣabdār's contingent. They were, in the words of the *Ā'īn*, "among the immediate servants of the emperor". These were men who were not given manṣabs, but who were considered too good to be employed as ordinary troopers. In the beginning some aḥadīs maintained as many as eight horses, but later the maximum was fixed at five horses. They had a separate bakhshī and a separate dīwān; besides a manṣabdār with a high rank was entrusted with their general supervision. They did form an elite corps, because they were paid higher salaries than ordinary soldiers; but they were employed mostly singly and quite often on non-military errands.[6] Many civilians had the ranks of aḥadīs, being employed in administrative and clerical capacities. In fact though they were sometimes good soldiers, they were not organized as a fighting force and were employed mostly for household duties. Towards the end with the decay of the emperor's authority, the aḥadīs had so little to do, that their name became a byword for laziness and passed into the language for an extremely lazy person. During the period of vigorous administration, however, they had plenty of work. Indeed Abū-'l-Faḍl tells us that an officer was assigned the duty of bringing a few good candidates every day for appointment as aḥadīs. As late as Bahādur Shāh I's reign, it was found necessary to recruit four thousand and seven hundred extra aḥadīs.[7] The reasons are obvious; they were needed to fill many of the intermediate posts in the administration and to do a large number of Household duties.

The most important class of troopers were the tābīnān, or the soldiers who were furnished by the manṣabdārs and formed their contingents. They were the bulk of the Mughul cavalry and indeed the most important part of the fighting machine. In the first instance they were recruited by the manṣabdār; then they were mustered for inspection by the bakhshī and sometimes even by the emperor. The horses were examined by an expert and their quality was determined. The trooper's salary was fixed in accordance with the number and the quality of his mounts. Ten troopers were placed under the command of a dahbāshī, a commander of ten. A contingent of ten cavalrymen was so composed that the number of horses exceeded the number of men. This was achieved by classifying troopers as yak aspah, or having a single horse, dū

[6] *Ibid*, ii, Ā'īn 4.

[7] Irvine, p. 44.

aspah, or having two horses, and sih aspah, or one having three horses. In the beginning there were chahār aspah soldiers as well who mustered as many as four horses each, but this category was discontinued later. The proportions varied at different times. In the beginning of Akbar's reign the mark was to have two chahār aspahs, three sih aspahs, three dū aspahs and two yak aspahs, thus having a total of twenty five horses for ten soldiers. This seems to have been abandoned as being unrealistic, and the proportion of three sih aspahs, four dū aspahs, and three yak aspahs was prescribed, which brought the number of horses down to twenty for every ten troopers.[8] This was further changed in course of time; for under Shāh Jahān we find that the highest proportion was three sih aspahs, six dū aspahs and one yak aspah making a total of twenty two horses for ten troopers. This ratio was maintained by a small number of manṣabdārs in their contingents. The ratio varied in accordance with the number of months in the year for which the manṣabdār was entitled to draw his salary. The ratio mentioned above of twenty-two horses for ten men was maintained by those who drew their salaries for twelve months in the year; those who drew their salaries only for eleven months maintained twenty horses for every ten men. Those who were entitled to a salary for ten months or less had no sih aspah soldiers in their contingents; the ratio worked out at eighteen, sixteen, fourteen and a half, twelve and a half, and eleven horses per ten men in the contingents of those who received salaries for ten, nine, eight, seven and six months respectively each year. Those who received salaries for only five months every year maintained only yak aspah troopers, and, therefore, they had ten horses for every ten men.[9] This is obviously a more complicated system than the one mentioned in the *Ā'īn* when every contingent of ten soldiers had twenty horses.

The question arises here whether the basic difference between the original system and the one we find under Shāh Jahān of the proportion of horses varying from contingent to contingent in

[8] Abū-'l-Faḍl, *Ā'īn-i-Akbarī*, ii, Ā'īn 5.

[9] 'Abd-u'l-Ḥamīd, ii, p. 507.

accordance with the number of months for which the salary was drawn by the manṣabdār originated in some form under Akbar. The system of not paying the full twelve months' salary in the year did exist in Akbar's reign. The *Ā'īn* mentions that the aḥadīs did not draw their salaries for twelve months; it is not unlikely that the practice extended to the manṣabdārs as well; but we have no positive record of the fact.[10] It is a little doubtful that such a complexity as the payment of salaries for some months in the year and varying the number of months in accordance with the proportion of horses to men should have been introduced all at once. We have seen that the original ratio of twenty-five horses for every ten soldiers was altered under Akbar for being unrealistic; as the details of the system were still in an experimental stage, it is not outside the realm of probability that the idea of having a uniform proportion of twenty horses for every ten men also should have been abandoned fairly early as being impractical, because to find thirty per cent men among the troopers who would bring to the muster three horses each and another forty per cent who would bring two horses each, specially when they had to purchase the horses themselves, could not have been easy at any time. Akbar himself permitted the recruitment of barāwardī troopers, who knew horsemanship but could not afford to purchase horses. This is an indication that the state did not have too large a supply of applicants for appointment as troopers who had their own horses; among such as did have their own horses, it would be difficult to find such a high proportion of men with more than one horse. The shortage could not have been felt quite in the beginning, when the recruitment started, because those who had already been employed would seek confirmation under the new regulations, but when it came to men hitherto unemployed seeking employment, the situation must have altered and gradually it must have been found essential to change the original regulation. As the system of recruiting barāwardī troopers existed throughout the period, at no time could the supply of men bringing their own horses have been too

[10] Abū-'l-Faḍl, *Ā'īn-i-Akbarī*, ii, Ā'īn 4.

great.[11]

These considerations lead one to believe that the system originated under Akbar. There is no positive record of a change in that reign because the main writings on which we depend for information had been completed before the change, which must have evolved over some years. It is not possible at any stage to find out exactly the proportion of horses to men in an overall estimate of the cavalry, because we have little evidence. We know the names and ranks of manṣabdārs for certain periods, but we do not know for how many months each of them drew his salary; nor do we have a record of the number of horses.

There has been some unnecessary controversy regarding the responsibility for paying the tābīnān. Some of the earlier Western writers believed that the manṣabdār paid the tābīnān out of his personal salary. With the present clarity of the position regarding the sawār rank, it is obvious that the dhāt salary could not have included the salary of the tābīnān. The evidence contained in various *dastūr-u'l-'amals* which give details of the payments made to the manṣabdārs for the tābīnān should have set the controversy at rest; actually the *Ā'īn* itself makes it clear when, in connection with the regulations regarding the renewal of the brand, it lays down that a manṣabdār promoted to a higher rank received an immediate increase in his dhāt salary, but the payments on the basis of his increased contingent were made to him only after the first muster.[12] Three farmāns existing in Jaipur archives make it amply clear that the manṣabdār received extra sums of money or assignment for paying the tābīnān. He was responsible for the disbursement alone.[13]

The next important class of the troopers were the barāwardīs. When they were attached to a manṣabdār, he was responsible for disbursing their salaries, but he was reimbursed for the amount

[11] It existed under Shāh Jahān, vide Moreland, "Rank (Manṣab) in the Mogul Sta e Service". *Journal of the Royal Asiatic Society*, 1936, p. 662; they are also mentioned in *Dastūr-u'l-amal-i-nawīsindagī*, f. 144 b. quoted by Irvine p. 10; baradari is obviously an error for *barāwardī*.

[12] Abū-'l-Faḍl, *Ā'īn-i-Akbarī*. ii, Ā'īn 8.

[13] W.H. Moreland, "Rank (Manṣab) in the Mogul State Service" *Journal of the Royal Asiatic Society*, October 1936, pp. 645-466.

so spent. The proportion of three sih aspahs, four dū aspahs and three yak aspahs mentioned by the *Ā'īn* seems to have been imposed upon the barāwardī contingents in accordance with evidence contained in some dastūr-u'l-'amals.[14] This seems to be probable in view of the reasons given in a previous paragraph regarding the difficulties involved in maintaining this proportion in the contingents of tābīnān. Moreland's assumption that the barāwardīs were all yak aspah, therefore, does not seem to be justified.[15] The dastūr-u'l-'amals sometimes use the phrase tābīnān-i-barāwardi for barāwardī troops placed under a manṣabdār; it was obviously coined to distinguish this class on the one hand from the tābīnān who brought and maintained their own horses and those barāwardīs who were not attached to manṣabdārs. The number of barāwardī troops increased after Akbar and formed part of the contingents of a growing number of manṣabdārs.

In the beginning the tābīnān, which literally means 'followers', were generally men who had been attached to him for some time; sometimes they were bound to him by tribal ties or they came from a common homeland. A manṣabdār sponsored them when he sought service; they were known to him and he could rely upon their loyalty and support. This was truer in the beginning when the Mughul nobility had not had sufficient time for assimilation with those who had lived longer in the area; but the tradition continued; either the manṣabdārs who settled down built up new ties or the local elements seeking service like the Rajputs or the Saiyids of Bārah had their own tribes and clans and preferred men who thus had close ties with them. In spite of these factors the number of troopers who failed to find manṣabdārs who would be willing to have them as their tābīnān continuously decreased and towards the end seems to have almost disappeared. In the beginning the odd troopers who had their horses were recruited as dākhilī troops and were placed under the command of mansabdārs who could not bring their own tābīnān. Towards the end of the

[14] e.g. *Dastūr-u'l-'amal-i-nawisindagī*, f. 144 b quoted by Irvine, p. 10.

[15] W.H. Moreland "Rank (Manṣab) in the Mogul State Service", *Journal of the Royal Asiatic Society*, October 1936, p. 662.

period the dākhilīs find little mention. This is true of kumakīs as well.

The *Ā'īn* mentions the salaries of troopers. Those who came from Central Asia or from Iran received a higher salary, in all probability to make it attractive for these foreigners to migrate to the subcontinent. The Muslim empires of this region always encouraged migration from Muslim lands to strengthen themselves. The foreigners were paid twenty-five rupees every month; the Indians were given twenty rupees if employed in a military capacity. These salaries were subject to a deduction of five per cent, which the manṣabdārs were entitled to charge as administrative commission for overhead charges. There was a further deduction of a month's salary every year for paying the cost of the horse and other equipment given by the state until the debt was discharged. The state charged a profit of fifty per cent upon the price of the horse, but because the government purchased horses at advantageous prices, the trooper was said to have paid a fair price. The tābīnān who brought their own horses were paid, in addition to their salary, allowances compensating them for their horses and their maintenance in accordance with the quality of their mount. Those who mustered more than one horse were asked to maintain a beast of burden as well which was assigned to them, for which they received a further allowance.[16] The salaries seem to have been reduced during later reigns. The tables in some *dastūr-u'l-'amals* give the figure of two hundred rupees per annum for each trooper.[17] After making allowances for several deductions which were made in the salaries on various accounts, this sum works out to be only a little less than twenty rupees per month. It is not unlikely that minor deductions other than those mentioned earlier in this chapter were also imposed. Awrangzīb mentions the salaries as twenty rupees, seventeen and a half rupees and fifteen rupees in the Deccan during his viceroyalty.[18] The round figure of two hundred rupees per annum for a soldier in all probability

[16] Abū-'l-Faḍl, *Ā'īn-i-Akbarī*, ii, Ā'īn 5.

[17] *Ḍawābiṭ-i-'Ālamgīrī*, f. 46 b, *Dastūr-u'l-'amal-i-nawisindagī*, ff. 144b, 148b, quoted by Irvine p. 10.

[18] Qābil Khān and Muḥammad Ṣādiq, f. 131b.

represents the average of the various scales of the salaries.

The Mughuls relied upon the systems of maintaining descriptive rolls of the soldiers and branding the horses.[19] The first was a most effective method because the officers were experts in describing the general appearance as well as the distinguishing marks of individuals; verification of troops through this process was called taṣḥīḥah. The tradition of registering descriptive rolls for certain police purposes has endured in the subcontinent and proves fairly effective even now, when, because of finger prints, the utility of the method has been diminishing for some time. The horses were branded every time they were mustered for formal inspection by the bakhshī; this was called dāgh. The normal regulation was that the manṣabdār should bring his troops every year for inspection and the repetition of the brand. Fines were imposed for delays in bringing horses to the muster. If a manṣabdār made a delay, he would lose ten per cent of his salary for the period of the delay. It is, however, certain that there were exceptions to this rule. The manṣabdārs posted in difficult areas could not possibly comply with these regulations; sometimes it was impolitic to require a manṣabdār to leave his duties and to arrange for a muster.[20] Awrangzib, as the viceroy of the Deccan, mentions in a letter to the wazīr Sa'd-u'llah Khān that it was he who introduced the system of dāgh and taṣḥīḥah in the provinces of the south and that before that these regulations had not been enforced in the area. The reasons are obvious; the area was still in the process of being conquered and the manṣabdārs were not in a position to submit to the regulations of descriptive rolls and branding.[21] In the beginning various marks were tried for branding the horses; ultimately, however, it was decided to have separate numerals for the various categories of personnel concerned: the princes, the manṣabdārs and the troopers of various kinds. On every subsequent occasion, the brand was simply repeated.[22] The system

[19] A description roll was called either ḥuliyah or chehrah, both meaning physiognomy or countenance. Branding was called dāgh.

[20] Abū-'l-Faḍl, *Ā'īn-i-Akbarī*, ii, Ā'īns 7 & 8.

[21] Qābil Khān and Muḥammad Ṣādiq, f. 131b.

[22] Abū-'l-Faḍl, *Ā'īn-i-Akbarī*. ii, Ā'īn 7.

of branding was introduced in the subcontinent by Sultan 'Alā-u'd-dīn Khaljī. Subsequently, with the weakening of the central authority it fell into disuse and was later revived by Sher Shāh.[23] Akbar saw the advantages of the system and adopted it. It remained in force until the crumbling of the imperial authority. There were, as has been pointed out, certain exceptions. Some of the servants attached to the court were required to bring their horses every eighteen months; those mansabdārs whose jāgīrs were very remote were required to muster their horses once in twelve years; however their salary was reduced by a tenth after the sixth year. If a manṣabdār was promoted to a higher rank and three years had elapsed since the last muster, he received an increase only for his dhāt salary. Other allowances were increased only after the first muster.[24]

The cavalry was the most effective arm of the Mughul armies. Bābur's victories against Ibrāhīm Lodī and Rānā Sāngā owed much to his superb use of the tulughmah manoeuvre with his swift cavalry which wheeled round the Indian armies and took them in the rear.[25] The cavalry continued to play an important role in all Mughul victories, but towards the end, it deteriorated in keeping with the general trends of decay. When the Mughul cavalry came into conflict with European armies, its real weaknesses were revealed. Apart from corruption and internal jealousies which became such a feature of the later days of the Mughul Empire, there were two factors which would have put the Mughuls at a disadvantage at any time. The first was a lack of cohesion. The troopers were personally brave, and indeed even up to the very end of the empire they did not lose this quality, but they knew only to fight in a big mass or as individuals. The impact of ten thousand troopers riding en masse was not only a formidable sight to behold, but its impact upon the foe was very great; but if, by some device, this mass could be broken into fragments, it became helpless. They did not know how to form their ranks

[23] Irvine, p. 46.

[24] Abū-'l-Faḍl, *Ā'īn-i-Akbarī*, ii, Ā'īn 8.

[25] Bābur, pp. 473, 569. Tulughmah=flanking movement.

again after a dispersal or to muster to the support of a small group which might have been isolated and put in danger of being overwhelmed. European observers were also struck in the later days by the fact that the troopers were unwilling to place themselves in danger in spite of their bravery; this they rightly attributed to the anxiety of the soldier for his mount. If he were to lose his horse, he would lose more than just an expensive mount; he would lose the chances of further employment at a reasonable salary.[26] This factor came into operation when the employers were reluctant to replace the horses of their troopers even though they might have been lost in battle, often because of restricted resources. In that period one reads of rebellious troopers whose salaries had been long in arrears, partly because of empty treasuries, partly because it was considered politic to keep back the salary so that the trooper should not transfer his loyalty to another employer. Even in the heyday of the Mughul rule, the trooper could not be entirely indifferent to the fate of his horse and the fact that it represented a good portion of his assets must have exercised a restraining influence over his qualities as a soldier. Awrangzib describes the difficulties of the tābinān posted in the Deccan during his viceroyalty in which he pointedly draws attention to the scarcity of horses and their high prices in that area and the hardship to which a trooper was put to be able to furnish a good horse.[27]

The trooper was required to take a certificate, called a saqṭ-nāmah, when his horse died, so that he might receive the full allowance up to the time of the loss of the animal. In case the trooper failed to produce such a certificate, the deduction was made from the date of the last muster. To prevent fraud, the hide of the animal had to be produced before the officer issuing the certificate; he put down a full description of the dead animal in the certificate. In many cases the portion of the skin bearing the marks of the brand was forwarded with a report to the headquarters. A slightly different procedure was adopted when a horse

[26] Irvine, pp. 233, 234, who quotes various western observers.

[27] Qābil Khān and Muḥammad Ṣādiq, f. 131.b.

was discarded because of some injury or of old age; but the report, called a barṭarfī in this instance, had to be sent to the headquarters for record.[28]

The Mug͟huls maintained extensive stables. A manṣabdār of high rank was given the post of atbegī, also called āk͟htahbegī; he was responsible for seeing that the Imperial Household and the government never remained short of suitable horses.[29] A comparatively small number of chosen horses was kept for the emperor's own use and that of the princes. These were called k͟hāṣah horses. Each stable of these was called a chihlaspī and contained forty horses. Six such stables were maintained. There were separate stables of horses for the use of the princes, of Turkic courier horses and of those bred in the imperial studs. The other horses were kept in stables classified in accordance with the prices of the animals.[30] The atbegī's post was held by no less a person than K͟hān K͟hānān Mirzā 'Abd-u'r-Raḥīm under Akbar. Each stable had a superintendent or a dārog͟hah; the incumbents of these posts varied in their ranks in accordance with the importance of the stables; they could be manṣabdārs of the rank of five thousand to aḥadīs. Each stable had its accountant and registrar, the mus͟hrif, who kept the accounts and also acted as the registrar of the rolls of the horses and other documents. Then there was the usual technical staff for keeping the horses and the saddleries in proper trim.[31] There were separate stables for horses lent to persons for definite errands. These men were called bārgīr; they knew how to ride, but were not required to keep horses and were supplied with horses only for specific purposes.[32] The total number of foreign bred horses in the imperial stables in the reign of Akbar was twelve thousand.[33] As large number of horses were being given away as presents and sold to troopers, the supply was kept up by importing horses on an extensive scale from various countries

[28] Irvine, p. 24; Abū-'l Faḍl, *Ā in-i-Akbari*, ii, Ā'īn 4.
[29] *Ibid.*, i, Ā'īn 53.
[30] *Ibid.*, Ā'īn 50.
[31] *Ibid.*, Ā'īn 53.
[32] *Ibid.*, Ā'īn 54.
[33] *Ibid.*, Ā'īn 49.

which were famous for their horses, specially 'Irāq and Turkestan. The Sultans of Dehlī had established excellent traditions of horse breeding in the subcontinent and fine horses were bred in Kachh, Panjab, Rajputana and Bihar. The Mug͟huls maintained a well organized department for the purchase of horses which encouraged both the importers and the native breeders.[34]

The other arm to which the Mug͟huls came to attach increasing importance was the artillery. Some writers have attached exaggerated importance to the role of the artillery in the conquests of Bābur, who did not have many pieces and the few he had were not too effective. Humāyūn had twenty-one pieces in the Battle of Qanauj; by now S͟her S͟hāh had the superiority in artillery.[35] The Deccan had made greater advances in artillery than the North, because of the contacts with the Turks and the Persians. The best artillerymen were recognized to be the Europeans who had by now settlements on the Western coast. Abū-'l-Faḍl recognizes the importance of artillery. The guns were "carefully distributed over the entire empire, each province being supplied with the suitable variety of pieces". Artillery was considered necessary for "the seige of fortresses and naval actions."[36] The artillery was under the mīr ātis͟h, who was an officer of high rank. Jahāngīr mentions that he appointed Patr Dās as his mīr ātis͟h and ordered that three thousand pieces of cannon and five thousand artillerymen should remain with the monarch at the headquarters.[37] In addition to the mīr ātis͟h there were several other officers attached to the artillery. There was a dārog͟hah and a mus͟hrif; the former assisted the mīr ātis͟h in his executive duties and the latter was an accountant and record keeper; the dārog͟hah was a manṣabdār.[38] 'Ālamgīr I appointed a manṣabdār as dārog͟hah and promoted him to the rank of eight hundred d͟hāt and four hundred

[34] *Ibid.*, Ā'īn 49.

[35] Ḥaider Dug͟hlat, p. 474.

[36] Abū-'l-Faḍl, *Ā'īn-i-Akbarī*, i, Ā'īn 36.

[37] Jahāngīr, p. 10.

[38] *Ḍawābiṭ-i-'Ālamgīrī*, f. 26 b.

sawār.[39] Patr Dās was a high official under Akbar, who had bestowed the title of Rāi Rāyān upon him; when Jahāngīr appointed him as his mīr ātish, he gave him the title of Rājah Bikramājit. Awrangzīb was ordered by Shāh Jahān to recruit for him some artillerymen in the Deccan and then to send them to the capital.[40] The sultanates of Bījāpūr and Golconda were known for the excellence of their artillery.[41]

Abū-'l-Faḍl speaks highly of Akbar's artillery; he says that, with the exception of Turkey, there was no country which was so well equipped with artillery as the Mughul Empire.[42] This statement is, however, not borne out by other evidence. Abu-'l-Faḍl is too vague. He mentions that some of the guns were very large and required several elephants and a thousand cattle to transport one of them. Such unwieldy pieces could not be of much use in a battle. The largest piece of that period which still exists is the mulk maidān at Bījāpūr; this gun was made by the government of the sultanate. It and its twin played some part in the Battle of Tālikota; their main contribution must have been to frighten the animals as well as the men in the ranks of the foe with their noise; the long intervals at which they could be fired and the small area of destruction wrought by their solid balls were serious handicaps. The Mughul artillery improved as the result of the contacts with the Deccan as well as with the Europeans. Irvine seems to be correct in his opinion that 'Ālamgīr I had a better artillery than his predecessors.[43] He showed an understanding of its working and personally supervised its location and working in the sieges of the strongholds of the Deccan.[44] The Mughuls, however, were never able to catch up with the West. In the anarchy after the reign of 'Ālamgīr I, the contending powers in the subcontinent used artillery increasingly; even where they adopted Western methods, they did so with less efficiency than the Europ-

39 Qābil Khān and Muḥammad Ṣādiq, f. 40 a.
40 *Ibid*, f. 35a.
41 *Ibid*, f. 35b.
42 Abū-'l-Faḍl, *Ā'in-i-Akbari*, i, Ā'īn-36.
43 Irvine, p. 116.
44 Ashraf Khān, f. 19a.

eans. The local artillery was clumsy and some times too heavy for man euvring and could not be fired often enough. The pieces were mounted clumsily and the heavier pieces were so heavy that they could not be moved in the rainy season at all and even in the dry weather their progress was so slow that they were useless in an emergency. This explains why the European artillery, being mobile and manageable and capable of being fired more often, struck such terror in the native ranks. The native powers had almost a superstitious faith in their own pieces and an unholy terror for the artillery of the foe and did not contest a battle with a clear knowledge of the limitations of artillery.[45] It must be added that the morale had deteriorated in the days of the anarchy. The weakness of the artillery as an arm was, however, not a new factor. The Mughul artillery was never a match for the artillery of the Turks and later for that of the European countries.

The infantry like the cavalry had many men who were not soldiers. They performed various duties. Some of them were porters; as they were armed, they can be considered to be soldiers; they did not take part in battles. There were the kahārs, who carried the various means of conveyance like the pālkis, takht-i-rawāns, dolis, etc., upon their shoulders. The khidmatiyahs guarded the environs of the palace and ran small errands. They belonged to a Hindu caste; the word khidmatiyah means a servant. Their chief was given the title of Khidmat Rā'i. These men also were not proper soldiers. Similarly the mewrahs who were runners were used to carry messages. As they were also used for military purposes, they could be called soldiers, though they were hardly combatants. They were also employed as spies. Wrestlers and athletes who performed for royal amusement are also classified by Abū-'l-Faḍl as infantrymen; they were not soldiers at all. There were several kinds of gladiators who used their traditional weapons with great skill. Some of them used cudgels Even today in many a town the processions in connection with Muḥarram, the anniversary of the martyrdom of the Prophet's grandson Ḥusain at Karbalā, contain parties of gladiators who give

[45] Irvine, p. 116 et seq.

exhibitions of sword dances and combats with cudgels. It is doubtful if their utility in battles could ever have justified their inclusion in armies. As a form of sport, these skills were entertaining and useful. Even today some of these skills are learnt not only for sport but also for personal defence like jujitsu, specially by the people in the countryside where firearms are not easily available to the populace. The slaves belonging to the emperor also have been classified as infantrymen; though only a few of them could have been used for military purposes.

The real infantry consisted of matchlockmen and the archers. Akbar maintained at the court a body of twelve thousand matchlockmen Their administration was organized into a department with a registrar, a treasurer and a superintendent. There were four grades of minor officers who were paid salaries varying from two hundred and sixty dāms to three hundred dāms. The soldiers were divided into fifteen grades, three grades being classified as a class. Their salaries varied from one hundred and ten dāms to two hundred and fifty dāms. This provided ample room for promotion. The archers were some times more effective in the battle than the matchlockmen, because the matchlocks were still not very efficient. They became heated after being fired and had to be left to cool before they could be loaded again. Some infantry was also given to the manṣabdārs as dāk͟hilī troops. A fourth of such contingents consisted of matchlockmen, the rest were archers. Ten archers were under a mīrdahah who received a salary ranging from one hundred and twenty dāms to one hundred and eighty; the common archer's salary was from a hundred dāms to one hundred and twenty dāms. Some of the infantrymen were classified as nīmah sawārān or half troopers. These were mostly the infantry used as dāk͟hilī troops. Pioneers, carpenters, ironsmiths and other workers were also treated as infantry; those who had military duties to perform were not the only ones to be thus treated. The infantry was the weakest arm of the Mug͟hul fighting machine. Infantrymen were not properly trained, had little sense of discipline and gave way at the first contact with the enemy's cavalry. The impression created by the early European observers is that the Mughuls placed little reliance upon their infantry. The piyādahs, as the foot soldiers were called, were used mainly for civilian purposes. They came from the lowest ranks of society. The better class of infantryman was called a nīmah sawār, so that he might be saved from the indignity of being considered a mere infantryman.[46]

Abū-'l-Faḍl mentions yet another class of troops. He says,"With some the emperor is content if they submit; he does not exact much service from them; in this manner many a wild dweller in the country-side were led into good fortune; and the zamīndār troops are more than four million and four hundred thousand men. . .". A great deal of speculation has resulted from this passage among scholars, specially because Abū-'l-Faḍl is so specific not only about the total number, but he also gives numbers for every administrative area when he describes it. If these had been well organized troops, Abū'-l-Faḍl would have given a more detailed description of their functions and salaries. Actually, the brief sentence contains the essential information; to disentangle its meaning, it is necessary to give a short historical background.[47]

It was a well understood old tradition in the subcontinent that villages were held responsible for the maintenance of peace in their neighbourhood. If a highway robbery or murder took place in the vicinity, the local population was called upon to find the culprits and to recover the looted property. If they failed in doing so, they were asked to compensate the victim. This obligation was based upon the theory that in a sparsely populated countryside, a crime like that could not be perpetrated without information leaking to the inhabitants. The village notables were paid a commission on the revenue as their perquisities for these duties.[48] As a part of these duties, the village headmen were also expected to cooperate with the government in the general maintenance of peace. If there was a nest of robbers to be destroyed, the headmen

[46] Abū-'l-Faḍl, *Ā'in-i-Akbarī*, ii, Ā'īn 6; *ibid*, i, Ā'īn 40.

[47] *Ibid*, ii, Ā'īn 1.

[48] 'Ali Muḥammad Khān, *Supplement*, pp. 228, 229.

furnished armed men to cooperate with the government troops. If any village turned refractory or created mischief, the headmen of the neighbouring villages were required to cooperate with the authorities. The government had a record of the number of men who could be expected from an area; this was based on the number of dwellings in that locality. It is this potential manpower, only a portion of which was expected to come to the help of the authorities in case of a local emergency which is called the zamindār army by Abū-'l-Faḍl. This is the reason why this category of troops finds little mention elsewhere. In later days some of the native chiefs brought this rabble to increase the bulk of their troops against other chiefs; against Europeans they proved of a negative value, because they were the first to disperse and run away and thus created panic among other troops. Such a rabble did not have even standard arms, and the curious medley of weapons which they bore were of poor quality. However, the Mughuls do not seem to have used such troops for fighting against properly equipped forces. They were employed for police purposes alone. The existence of such troops on paper was utilized by Akbar's court jurists as a justification for the abolition of the jiziyah, because such dhimmīs as choose to fight for the Muslim state are not required to pay that tax.

In the beginning the Mughuls placed some reliance upon elephants in their battles. The elephants were clad in armour to protect them from the enemy's missiles; gradually the elephant was used to carry light guns so that a better aim could be taken from the height which the animal afforded.[49] Elephants were also used by the generals in battles so that they might tower above others and direct the progress of the combat more effectively. The troops could see them and this inspired confidence; because many a battle was fought for a person rather than a cause. If the monarch or prince were killed, the troops saw no reason to endanger themselves any further. His presence on the elephant inspired them to greater effort. The advantages of the general being clearly visible

[49] *Ibid*, i, Ā'īn 41; *ibid*, Ā'īn, 36. A gun carried on an elephant was called gajnāl.

to his own troops were more than nullified by the dangers to which he exposed himself. From the beginning he was the main target for the archers and the musketeers of the other side and all attempts were made by the enemy to destroy him. If he were hit or found it advisable to get down from the elephant, his troops gave way and fled. Dārā Shikūh was not the only general to suffer from such a contingency. Nādir Shāh was amazed that the Mughul generals should take such risks. Elephants continued to be used as beasts of burden throughout the period; they were particularly useful in moving some of the heavy pieces of artillery of which the Mughuls were so fond.

The other animals used for military purposes were camels, mules and oxen. Specially trained dromedaries were the swiftest means of transport for generals if they wanted to reach some place quickly. Akbar surprised both his friends and foes by covering the distance between Agra and Gujrat in record time riding a dromedary.[50] Camels were also used for carrying small pieces of artillery.[51] Oxen were used to draw guns and other wagons. They were also used as pack animals. The mule has always been known for its strength and capacity to carry large loads over long distances. The art of breeding these animals was well known and widely practised; this was all the more necessary because the mule does not reproduce itself and every animal is the result of cross breeding. Mules were used for transport as late as the Second World War. The Mughuls maintained well organized stables for all these animals. Their diet was carefully regulated; veterinarians were easily available; the monarchs took personal interest in their stables of various animals, in particular horses and elephants.[52]

The commissariat was not organized officially, except for the household and the immediate followers of the general, there was no central kitchen. The army, even when it was moving, had a bazar, where cooked and uncooked food was available to any

[50] Smith, pp. 117, 118. From Delhi to Ahmedabad he took nine or eleven days.

[51] Guns carried on camels were called *shutarnāls* or *zambureks*, Irvine pp. 135, 136.

[52] Abū-'l-Faḍl, *Ā'īn-i-Akbarī*, i, has details about the stables of these animals, Ā'īns 61-71.

purchaser. The soldiers bought from the shops all that they needed. The bazar was kept supplied with stocks of food by the banjārahs, a community of traders who specialized in this kind of trade. The state kept some control over prices; the war against the Marathas harassed the Mughuls so much because the Marathas were effective in cutting out supplies from the Mughul camp.

The Mughul armies moved slowly; sometimes, when they were obliged to make forced marches, they moved a little more quickly. Akbar once covered four hundred and fifty miles at the head of three thousand horsemen in eleven days and, at the end of the journey, fought two decisive battles in one day. This was exceptional. In later days military movements were generally slow. The reason was that a Mughul army seldom moved as a purely combatant force. The bazar was essential for the army if it was to subsist. Very often the general's family and household moved with him. The Mughul armies were not troops on the maroh but cities of canvas on the move, which made quick movement difficult. The camp was a vast concourse of tents; every soldier had his own tent, small in dimensions, yet part of the equipment to be moved and fixed. The nobles had elaborate collections of tents; if the monarch himself happened to be moving with the army, he had a miniature replica of the essential sections of the imperial residence moving with him. The movement was orderly and well organized, yet it was too cumbersome for military purposes.[53]

The Mughul armies were drawn up in a conventional order for battles. The ingenuity shown in the earlier days by the Mughul conquerors like Bābur had gradually given place to stereotyped strategy. In the front were the qarāwal or skirmishers; at their back was the harāwal or the vanguard. It was also called muqaddamat-u'l-jaish. To its right and left, jutting out well forward were two small wings placed in such a way that they might give support to the qarāwal in case of need or act as a protection for the left and right wings of the harāwal, the bulk of which was stationed

53 *Ibid*, Bernier, pp. 358 et seq. gives a good description.

in the centre. Behind the harāwal was the qalb, or the centre of the main force. To the right and left of the qalb were the maimanah and the maisarah, or the right and the left wings, also called rāst and chap. The qalb, the maimanah and the maisarah were sometimes called the ghol, because this was considered to be the main section of the battle array. The general almost invariably took his position in the qalb. Behind the qalb was the rear guard, which also had the duty of guarding the camp.[54] The ranks were kept in order by a small group of officers who carried the instructions of the general to other officers and kept an eye on the ranks so that they did not create confusion by acting in an undisciplined manner. In later days they came to be called nasaqchīs, or the maintainers of order.

The Mughuls constructed forts at strategic places; the principles of military architecture were well understood. Advantage was invariably taken of a helpful natural feature; where, as in the plains of Northern provinces, such features were not common, they were sometimes created artificially. Fortresses were generally placed near sources of water supply, a curve in a river was an asset. The fort was put upon an eminence, and if one did not happen to be in the vicinity, an artificial mound was created by piling up earth; the area from which it was excavated created another feature, that of a marsh or a lake, which was useful in defending the fort. Forts were generally surrounded with moats; outside the moats, sometimes a thick jungle of bamboo or some thorny bushes or trees was planted to delay the approach of a hostile force. If the climate was not favourable for this purpose, a veritable forest of stone blocks was planted to obstruct the cavalry. The gates were stout and barred with beams of wood or even of iron; there were sometimes several concentric walls; in any case the approach to the citadel was tortuous and long. The walls were machicolated and mounted with parapets. The forts were strong and capable of standing long sieges. Many

[54] *Dastūr-u'l-'amal-i-nawisindagi*, f. 164 a. The small body interposed between the right wings of the harāwal and ghol seems to be a mistake in view of the Mughul insistence upon symmetry.

towns had protective walls around them. The forts were more often starved out than taken by assault because of their intrinsic strength and also stout defence. If the walls were breached or the walls scaled the defenders did not give up the fight and often succeeded in repulsing the attack. The arts of laying a siege and standing it were well understood. Sandbags were used to find a passage through a moat; covered paths, called sabāṭs, were built to enable the attackers to give battle to the defenders at closer quarters. Scaling ladders, mining and cannonading were used. The besieged sometimes sallied out to fight the besiegers. The sieges were, however, long drawn affairs in most cases; the methods of cutting water supplies and starving out the besieged were considered more effective, because they were less expensive in human losses.[55] Sometimes bribery and corruption proved to be effective methods of attack as well as defence. Towards the end this was so common that it undermined the integrity of the Mughul officers themselves and the monarchs, specially 'Ālamgīr I, had to be extremely vigilant.

The total strength of the Mughul army under Shāh Jahān has been mentioned as two hundred thousand mounted soldiers and forty thousand foot soldiers.[56] This number excludes the non-military personnel of grades lower than that of a manṣabdār. The figure for mounted soldiers includes eight thousand manṣabdārs, seven thousand aḥadīs and mounted musketeers and one hundred eighty five thousand tābīnān of the princes and the manṣabdārs. The foot soldiers were artillerymen, musketeers, grenadiers and archers. The number of cavalrymen has been calculated in accordance with the regulation of the proportion of the tābīnān to the sawār rank prescribed by the monarch.

Mention has been made of the mīr-i-baḥr and his duties. The Mughuls did maintain a few seaworthy boats but they seldom ventured out into the open sea. They were manned by sailors whose experience was generally limited to large rivers. On the

[55] Irvine, pp. 260 et seq, 270 et seq.

[56] 'Abd-u'l-Ḥamīd, ii, p. 715; Najaf 'Alī, f. 28b.

rivers, both in fighting and in maintaining supply lines they rendered good service. The fleet was called nawwārah. It was the duty of the mīr-i-baḥr's department to build bridges of boats when such bridges were either needed by the army or for the maintenance of normal communications. The Mughuls employed a number of half caste Portuguese in their nawwārahs to deal with the pirates on the coast of Bengal and relied upon the Abyssinian rulers of Janjira on the West coast.

The Mughul military machine was not efficient. They succeeded in building up the empire because they were pitted against foes who were even weaker and who could not match their resources to those of the Mughuls. The repeated failure of the Mughuls to hold Qandahār against the Persians was a sad commentary upon their military efficiency. They were equally unsuccessful against the Uzbeks. They changed too slowly; their methods had become inelastic. Even when faced with foes like the tribesmen in the north-west frontier or the Marathas, the Mughuls failed to adapt their methods to the new situations; it took all the energy of a man of an iron will and unparalleled determination like 'Ālamgīr I to reduce the tribesmen and bring the Marathas to bay.

CHAPTER VII

Finance

THE Mughuls developed sound traditions of financial administration. Their sources of income were well defined and so were the channels of expenditure. The system was built up by able administrators, some, but not all, of whom were of foreign origin. They had inherited well tried traditions and principles which were based upon Islamic legal theory worked out in conjunction with local ideas and customs. Sher Shāh had revived some institutions and reformed others and had left an efficient financial administration. The anarchy following the collapse of the Sūr dynasty had not completely wiped off these traditions, yet there had grown up abuses which Akbar undertook to remove with vigour. He also improved upon the previous institutions and developed them to a higher level of efficiency. Essentially the system was the same as had been built up by the Sultans and corresponded to the classical Muslim pattern.

The jurists of Islam have divided the legal sources of the income of the state into two broad categories. The first of these consists of those dues which a Muslim pays as his religious obligation and which the state collects to expend in an organised and orderly manner; the second category includes the legitimate taxes which the state is entitled to collect for administrating the affairs of the inhabitants of the area under its control. The former classification applies to 'ushr and zakāt; the latter includes jiziyah, kharāj and such other taxes as the state can legitimately raise. Of these 'ushr and kharāj will be discussed in a subsequent chapter.

The zakāt is prescribed by the Qur'ān upon all Muslims who have a modest minimum of wealth which is technically called the niṣāb. This was calculated as 1350 English grains of gold or 9450 English grains of silver or any other form of wealth of an equivalent value which the owner had in his possession for an entire year. The believer is required to pay a fortieth portion of it for charitable purposes. As the poor and needy among the kith and kin of the person required to pay are considered more deserving than strangers and because it is a virtue to make such grants secretly, the state often has not insisted upon the collection of this levy and has left it to the conscience of the believer to discharge his responsibilities in this regard. The response has been exceptionally good among the Muslims of the subcontinent throughout history. The Muslim jurists have worked out elaborate tables regarding the niṣāb as well as the amount of the zakāt due upon it for various forms of wealth; the underlying principle of paying a fortieth of such wealth as has been in the possession of a believer for at least a complete year has been maintained. As the Mughuls did not collect this kind of zakāt, it is not necessary to discuss this topic any further.[1]

The jiziyah has been mentioned in the Qur'ān in the general sense of a tax; the word has an ancient origin in the Aramaic form of gezit. It came to be used early in the history of Islam in the sense of a poll tax levied upon the non-Muslim residents of a Muslim state. The Muslims probably adopted it from the areas which they conquered, because poll tax had existed in both the

[1] For a fuller discussion vide Aghnides, Chapter II.

Eastern Roman Empire and the Sassanid Empire. The Muslims imitated the Roman practice of exempting Roman citizens from the payment of the poll tax; they had nothing corresponding to the Roman citizenship, hence they substituted Islam for it. Its main purpose in the beginning was to meet the expenditure of administering the conquered territories where the non-Muslims were dominant in numbers. The earlier Umaiyids, for instance, levied it from such Muslims as well who belonged to the conquered peoples. They resisted the pressure of those who considered this act un-Islamic and wanted all Muslims to be exempted. The Umaiyid reluctance was based upon financial grounds. At last orthodoxy won and the Umaiyids had to limit the levy of the jiziyah to non-Muslims. This act was more in accord with the doctrines of the days of the Republic when the brotherhood of the Muslims was a cardinal principle. The payment of jiziyah was looked upon as a symbol of submission to the political power of Islam; as indeed the payment of taxes is always the recognition of the authority of the state. It was from the basic concept of submission to the political jurisdiction of Islam that some extremists among the jurists drew their exaggerated notions regarding jiziyah being an instrument of humiliation for the dhimmīs.[2] It is also wrong to argue that jiziyah was the price which every non-Muslim was required to pay for being permitted to live in a Muslim state; this was neither the theory nor the fact.

The way the jurists worked out the principles is capable of only one interpretation: that it was a tax paid in lieu of the discharge of the responsibility of defending the state in which the dhimmī lived against external foes and internal disturbers of peace, because to fight such foes was the religious duty of Muslims which could not be imposed upon non-Muslims. It has been a cardinal principle of Islamic law that any religious obligation of the Muslims could not be imposed upon non-Muslims. This seems to be the only explanation for the fact that the jiziyah was imposed only upon those who were capable of bearing arms for the state and who did not actively serve it in any capacity. All women, minors, slaves,

[2] Baranī's views in *Tārīkh-i-Fīrūzshāhī* (p. 290) quoted so often illustrate the point.

religious hermits and priests were exempt; so were the blind, those incapable of work, the insane and the incapacitated. If a person had been ill for half a lunar year or more, he was not required to pay. Those who served the state either in a military or a civil capacity were also exempt.[3] The view, therefore, that the jiziyah was a tax paid in lieu of service to the state which the assessee would have been called upon to defend if he were a Muslim is correct. The monarch could call upon any able bodied Muslim to fight for the state and it would be his religious and legal duty to do so; after accepting the jiziyah from the dhimmī, the monarch could not ask him to render any service; if the dhimmī, of his own accord, decided to serve the state, the monarch, after accepting the offer of service could not demand the jiziyah from him.[4]

The jiziyah had a chequered history under the Mughuls. Akbar abolished it. The argument seems to have been that all the citizens of the Empire, irrespective of their faith, were liable to serve it, hence it would be unjust to levy jiziyah. Mention has been made of a record of persons liable to be called up in connection with the zamīndār troops. Akbar's advisers could argue with justification that if able bodied persons could be called upon to serve in a military capacity, they could not be required to pay jiziyah.[5] The abolition continued to remain effective during the next two reigns. Shaikh Aḥmad of Sarhind, the Mujaddid-i-alf-i-thānī, however, was not of this view. He looked upon jiziyah as an institution of Islam and agitated for its reimposition. This was a part of his general campaign to fight laxity and heterodoxy at all levels, because he was perturbed at the loss of political power incurred by orthodoxy in the Empire. Along with his other endeavours, his efforts in connection with jiziyah also succeeded in convincing a large number of politically important persons and groups that the abolition had been un-Islamic; the reimposition, however, did not come until the reign of 'Ālamgīr I. As he himself was so

[3] 'Alī Muḥammad Khān i, p. 296.

[4] This is why 'Ālamgīr exempted servants of the state, *ibid.*

[5] Akbar's abolition, Abū-'l-Faḍl, *Ā'īn-i-Akbarī*, ii, Ā'īn 11. Zamīndār troops have been discussed in Chapter VI.

strongly orthodox, he reimposed the tax.[6] He had considerable difficulty in making the measure effective. All taxes, whatever their justification, tend to be unpopular if they are revived; jiziyah seemed to have no justification in the eyes of the Hindus. It galled because it was discriminatory. If the tax had never been abolished, the Hindus would not have felt it so much because it had become a part of the pattern of life; but its abolition proved that it need not have been so. 'Ālamgīr I, however, made it a matter of principle, because in his mind the question was tied up with the bigger problem of restoring the political power of Islam and the maintenance of its institutions. Shāh Jahān was also orthodox, but he had seen fit not to reimpose jiziyah; it is conceivable that he did not consider it legally necessary and was conscious of the political difficulties involved. As has been pointed out, it was possible to find a legal justification for not imposing the jiziyah and looking upon the collective responsibilities borne by the populace as their contribution to the defence of the realm.

The doctors of the orthodox school and with them 'Ālamgīr I seemed to think that the willingness to serve the state or even actual service exempted individuals and not the entire community.

The exemptions laid down by the jurists and mentioned earlier in this chapter were respected by 'Ālamgīr I. The amount of the tax levied as well as the basis of assessment was in accordance with the rulings of earlier jurists. The assessees were divided into three categories in accordance with their wealth. Those in possession of ten thousand dirhems or more were considered to be wealthy; those who had less than ten thousand but more than two hundred dirhems were classified as belonging to the middle class; those who had less than two hundred dirhems but enough, in addition to the cost of maintaining themselves and their dependents, to pay the tax were considered to be poor. The first category was required to pay forty-eight dirhems per annum; the second twenty-four; and the third twelve.[7] These seem to have been the rates for the urban areas; in the countryside the government

6 'Alī Muḥammad Khān, i, p. 296.

7 *Ibid.*, also, *Dastūr-u'l-'amal*, B.M. or 2026, ff. 53 b, 54 a.

levied a flat charge of four percent of the state demand upon agricultural produce.[8] If the agents of the government failed to collect the jiziyah from any one for an entire year, he could not be charged the sum later.[9] A dirhem was roughly 550 English grains of silver. The amounts collected were never too large; for instance the province of Gujrat which had large non-Muslim commercial communities raised only five hundred thousand rupees in jiziyah.[10] 'Ālamgīr's feelings in the matter of jiziyah can be gauged from the fact that one of his officers remitted large quantities of revenue from agricultural produce; but because this was done to help the peasants in times of difficulty, the monarch approved of the action. He, however, censured Amānat K͟hān for remitting the jiziyah; for, argued the monarch, he had faced many difficulties in the reimposition of the jiziyah and he did not like to see his endeavours nullified in that regard.[11] The Emperor had been frustrated in his attempts because of the non-cooperation of the many Hindu officials who were in charge of collecting the revenue in many parts of the Empire.

The jiziyah was again abolished by Bahādur S͟hāh I. Thus the tax was levied only for a part of the time during which the dynasty was strong. 'Ālamgīr did not look upon it as a source of income, because as such it was insignificant. To him its imposition was a political measure, a matter of principle, the symbol of the prevalence of the law of Islam in his domains. Today the Muslim society does not think that jiziyah as understood in the Middle Ages is an essential part of the polity of Islam, but this was not so in the days of 'Ālamgīr; with him it was a matter of conscience; hence he made it an integral part of his policy.

It has been mentioned that the Mug͟huls did not levy zakāt on property and left it to the conscience of the individual to use the sum due from him in the furtherance of the benevolent and charitable purposes for which it was intended. Generally, taxes left to

[8] 'Alī Muḥammad K͟hān, i, p. 298.

[9] *Ibid.*, p. 304.

[10] *Ibid.*, p. 297.

[11] K͟hawāfī K͟hān, II, p. 378.

the discretion of the individual tend to be forgotten, but such has been the hold of religion upon the Muslims of the subcontinent that the vast majority of those liable to pay do so even today and the zakāt has lived all this time as an institution. It does not, as it did not in the days of the Mughuls, bring any money to the public exchequer, but it does help the state insofar as it shares with it the burden of relieving distress. One form of zakāt, however, was imposed, though only occasionally. This was a tax on the import and export of commodities. Muslim traders paid two and and a half per cent on the value of the commodity imported; Christians and Jews paid three and a half per cent; Hindus were required to pay five per cent; if Christians and Jews belonged to non-Muslim countries and thus did not possess the status of dhimmīs, they were charged four per cent.[12] In the seventh year of his reign, Akbar abolished this duty on a number of articles which were of daily use: these included foodstuffs; medicines; perfumes; textiles made of linen, cotton and wool; accessories made of leather; utensils made of wood and copper; canes and bamboos and anything else which was judged to be an article of necessity for the people. Animals and arms were excluded from the exemption.[13] The farmān embodying these orders lays great emphasis upon the importance of trade and commerce and the need for their protection by rulers. The exemption was later extended to cattle.[14]

Jahāngīr continued the policy and did not levy zakāt. He mentions that the tax was abolished in all his dominions, even in the border provinces of Qandahār and Kābul, though the zakāt on the imports and exports was the main source of revenue in these areas.[15] Jahāngīr casually mentions that the income from zakāt exceeded "tens of millions"; the figure seems to refer to dāms and not rupees in view of the figures mentioned under 'Ālamgīr I. In this emperor's reign we find that

12 'Alī Muḥammad Khān, *Supplement*, p. 183.

13 Farmān quoted in *Oriental Miscellany*, 1798, p. 26.

14 Abū-'l-Faḍl, *Ā'īn-i-Akbarī*, iii, Ā'īn 11.

15 Jahāngīr, pp. 4,22

the zakāt was levied upon all merchandise of a value higher than the legal niṣāb of fifty two rupees and a half representing the value of 9450 English grains of silver. This minimum must have been exempt all the time.[16] In the eighth year of his reign the Emperor abolished the zakāt so far as Muslims were concerned, but the non-Muslims continued to pay the tax at the higher rates levied from them.[17] The zakāt was, however, reimposed upon Muslims as well in the twenty-fifth year of the reign.[18] Orders were issued to assess the tax at the time of the sale of the merchandise; later these orders were rescinded and the older method of making the assessment at the time of the original purchase was revived.[19] Under 'Ālamgīr I, the term zakāt was given up so far as it concerned the non-Muslims, because it was felt that zakāt could not be levied from them as it was purely a Muslim tax and had religious significance. It is often mentioned by the rate of the tax, chihl dū, or two in forty, which being five per cent of the value of the commodity was the rate.[20] When mentioning the higher rates for the non-Muslims, the *Mir'at-i-Aḥmadi* calls the tax kharāj which confirms the views expressed here regarding the reasons for the discontinuation of the use of the term zakāt when the tax was levied from non-Muslims.[21] The sultans of Dehlī had levied a similar tax and had called it zakāt for Muslims as well as non-Muslims; they had discriminated against non-Muslims by charging the higher rates prescribed by the jurists for them.[22]

The Mughuls seem to have levied the legal tax of a fifth upon minerals and certain categories of treasure trove. All unstamped bullion or coins, bearing the imprint of monarchs who ruled before the Muslim conquest buried in the earth and discovered now, had to pay twenty per cent share to the state; the rest belonged to the owner of the land, irrespective of his being a Muslim or a

16 'Alī Muḥammad Khān, i, pp. 258, 259.

17 *Ibid.*, pp. 266, 267. Also *Dastūr-u'l-'amal*, B.M. or 2026, f. 57a.

18 'Alī Muḥammad Khān, i, p. 298.

19 *Ibid.*, p. 340.

20 *e.g.*, *ibid.*, pp. 258, 259.

21 *Ibid.*, *Supplement*, p. 183.

22 I. H. Qureshi, *The Administration of the Sultanate of Dehli*, p. 98.

dhimmī. The finder, if he was not the owner of the land, had no share. There was no tax on a treasure trove bearing the imprint of a reign subsequent to the Muslim conquest. The theory was that if the treasure had not been hidden at the time of the conquest, it would have fallen into the hands of the Muslim army and the state would have collected a fifth of it as its share.[23]

The Mughuls do not seem to have enforced the Islamic tradition of sharing the war booty with the soldiers. The jurists prescribe a fifth of the booty as the share of the state and the rest goes to the soldiers. This was based on precedents when the soldiers were unpaid volunteers and did not receive regular salaries from the exchequer. As the soldiers in the Mughul armies were full time paid servants of the state and were not unpaid volunteers, they were not given any share in the booty, except perhaps that to which they surreptitiously helped themselves without being detected.

The property of persons dying heirless and intestate was taken over by the state and earmarked for charitable and benevolent purposes.[24]

These, in addition to kharāj and 'ushr, which will be discussed in the next chapter and which were the mainstay of the financial resources of the Mughul Empire, were the taxes recognized by the shar' and were based upon precedent. It would appear from this discussion that the Mughul emperors did not violate the rulings of the jurists regarding the structure of taxation in any flagrant manner. The two instances were the abolition of jiziyah and the denial of their share of the war booty to the soldiers. Both of these measures had some legal justification, however controversial. The jurists are divided upon the question whether the state can raise taxes which are not mentioned in the shar'. There are some who think that the only legitimate sources of income for the state are the taxes which are based upon the precedents set up by the pious caliphs on their understanding of the Qur'ān and the sunnah. These precedents have been worked out, interpreted, enlarged and explained by the jurists and form part of the Islamic Law. This was the view adopted by Fīrūz

23 *Ibid.*

24 Jahāngir, p. 4; 'Alī Muhammad Khān, i, p. 268.

Shāh who limited himself to "only those taxes which are mentioned in the shar' and which find mention in religious books." These he describes as the kharāj, the 'ushr, zakāt, jiziyah, heirless property, and a fifth of minerals and war booty.[25] This view has often prevailed, but there have been authoritative opinions holding that the state has the right to raise additional taxes if it finds that it needs a larger income to meet its obligations.[26] As Muslim states have often resorted to additional taxation, the writers on Muslim administration have classified the extra imposts on the following basis.

The legitimate revenue derived from the recognized demand of the state on agricultural produce was called māl; anything demanded from the cultivator is wujūhāt, if it comes to the state treasury; if the additional impost is of the nature of perquisites of officers, it is furū'āt; this last category, if demanded against the orders of the state, was illegal. The taxes raised from manufactures and merchandise apart from the zakāt were jihāt if they were of financial importance; minor imposts raised by the central government and all imposts raised by the local authority were called sā'ir jihāt.[27] The distinction between the jihāt and the sā'ir jihāt was never clear. They also used the term abwāb for all additional burdens upon the people. The abwāb also came to be divided into two broad categories: those which were permitted and those which were prohibited. It would, therefore, be easier if the cesses are discussed as a whole. The only exception is the tax which was levied upon the non-Muslims in lieu of the zakāt upon merchandise. It was called chihl dū, as has been mentioned earlier. Under 'Ālamgīr I, it was classified as sā'ir jihāt.[28]

The method for the assessment of the zakāt on merchandise and the chihl dū, was as follows. All sales were required to be made in prescribed markets. The sultans had called these places sarā'i 'adl; the Mughuls called them by the Hindi name of kathehrahs, which literally means palisades. It seems that the area was enclosed

[25] *Futūḥāt-i-Fīrūzshāhī*, B.M. or 2039, f. 300 b.

[26] I.H. Qureshi, *The Administration of the Sultanate of Dehli*, p. 130.

[27] Abū-'l-Faḍl, *Ā'in-i-Akbarī*, iii, Ā'īn 7.

[28] 'Alī Muḥammad Khān, *Supplement* p. 183.

in a palisade. There were separate kathehrahs for different commodities. Each kathehrah had an amīn, a mushrif and a taḥwīldār. The amīn arbitrated in cases of dispute regarding the assessment, the mushrif was the accountant and the taḥwīldār was the treasurer. Later a dāroghah was added who was the superintendent and head of the organization. Towards the end of the reign of 'Ālamgīr I a karorah was put in charge of the administration of the kathehrah and the dāroghah was made subordinate to him, which shows that the volume of business had grown. An expert in the trade, called muqīm, assessed the prices of the commodities; he received a commission of 3/4 per cent. There was a qānūngū in every kathehrah, who kept a record of the trends in the price of the commodity concerned. A waqā'i'nigā rrecorded all the news including the prevailing prices and sent this information independently to the court.[29] The interests of the traders were watched by an officially approved headman or choudharī, who was enjoined "to keep the traders happy with his considerate behavior and conduct."[30] Because of the difference in the rates levied, some Muslims passed off the merchandise belonging to non-Muslims as their goods. Officers were specially warned to prevent such malpractices.[31] The places where grains and foodstuffs were sold were called mandwīs. As taxes were imposed or remitted, a kathehrah or a mandwī was controlled or decontrolled but it seems to have continued to exist as a place of trade and business. The government made frequent remissions in cases of necessary commodities if a rise in their price caused hardship to the people.[32]

We read again and again about the abolition of various cesses. The significant fact is that these lists of the prohibited cesses overlap to a remarkable extent. Fīrūz Shāh gives a long list of the imposts which he abolished; some of them can be traced back to the days of Kautilliya; many of them are also found in the lists of the cesses prohibited or remitted by the Mughul

29 *Ibid., Kaifiyat-i-ṣūbajāt-i-mumālik-i-maḥrūsah-i-Hindustān*, f. 233 b.

30 *Ibid.*, f. 223 b.

31 *e.g., ibid.*, f. 233 b.

32 *e.g.*, Kāẓim, p. 1082.

emperors.[33] This shows that they had become so ingrained in the tradition of the land that irrespective of the policy of the emperor, the people went on paying them to their immediate officers. The abolition of such cesses became extremely difficult, because if the money did not go into the imperial treasury, it tended to find its way into the pockets of the minor officials. Most of the imposts, however, seldom found their way into the imperial treasury; they were in the nature of perquisites charged by local officials. The cesses, therefore, may be divided into two broad categories: those which at any particular time happened to be recognised as a legitimate source of revenue and, therefore, were collected by the treasury and taken into account as a source of income; and those which were raised for their own benefit by the local officials as their fees with the cognizance of the state or illegally against the orders of higher authorities When we read of the abolition of cesses by emperors, we find that the imperial farmans do not always make the position clear. When a tax like the jiziyah was abolished, there was no doubt about its real abolition: similarly when the state abolished a duty or cess which came to its treasury and the assignees of certain areas had no interest in it, the chances were that the order was effective. The difficulty arose not so much in areas which were directly administered by the state, but in areas under the control of the assignees. The existence of the news writers posted at various places did act as a deterrent, because we read of officials censured for even minor lapses. 'Ālamgīr I went to the extent of appointing special officers to see that the forbidden cesses were not collected.[34]

In spite of these precautions, there were instances of such cesses being not only levied by the assignees but also being shown in the documents of assignments issued to them as a part of the revenue

[33] For lists of taxes abolished by Fīrūz Shāh and of those mentioned by Kautilliya, vide I. H. Qureshi, *The Administration of the Sultanate of Dehlī*. Appendix H.

The list of taxes abolished by Akbar appears in Abū-'l-Faḍl, *Ā'īn-i-Akbarī*, iii, Ā'īn 11. For those abolished by Jahāngīr, Jahāngīr, pp. 3,4,22. For those abolished by 'Ālamgīr I, 'Ālamgīr I's farmān dated 22 Jamādi I, 1075 A.H. quoted in *Oriental Miscellany*, 1798, pp. 30-32; *Ḍawābiṭ-i-'Ālamgīrī ff.* 136-138; 'Alī Muḥammad Khān, i, pp. 259-264, 288; Khawāfī Khān, ii, p. 88; Kāẓim, p. 1082.

[34] *Kaifiyat-i-ṣūbajāt-i-mumālik-i-maḥrūsah-i-Hindustān*, f. 230b.

assigned.[35] This must have happened because of misunderstandings regarding imperial orders and sometimes because of the central ministry's anxiety to keep a proper balance between the expected income and expenditure; such disregard for the imperial orders brought no return to the officers concerned. The task of matching an assignment to the salary was complicated in any case and it is likely that officials instead of making a new calculation of valuation without the cesses sometimes adopted the short cut of including the cesses. Another reason might have been the fact that 'Ālamgīr I had created so many new manṣabdārs for political reasons, specially to entice Maratha chieftains into imperial service that the dīwān-i-tan was hard put to it to give assignments to all the new appointees.[36] Another reason why 'Ālamgīr I was not fully successful in suppressing the cesses was that he was exceedingly lenient and did not take extreme measures against the defaulting officers.[37]

The most burdensome of these cesses was the rāhdārī, a toll levied upon the transport of goods from one place to another. The assignee or the chief through whose jurisdiction the merchandise passed supplied an escort to defend the merchant from highwaymen and charged a fee for the escort. The fee charged by an individual assignee or chief does not seem to have been high, but the cumulative effect upon the cost of commodities which had to travel long distances was oppressive; in extreme cases where the merchandise had to be transported very far, the expenses incurred would exceed the original price of the goods.[38] Another tax was the fee charged when stolen property was restored by the authorities to the rightful owners having been recovered from the thieves. If the property could not be recovered the owner had to be compensated by those in whose jurisdiction the theft or the robbery had taken place. A fee as high as a quarter of the debt was charged from those who were helped in recovering debts. The other imposts were not high. They were of the nature of

[35] Khawāfī Khān, ii, p. 89.

[36] *Ibid.*, p. 36.

[37] *Ibid.*, p. 88.

[38] *Ibid.* p. 89. The picture painted here refers to the conditions created by Maratha anarchy.

octroi on sales of various commodities or a small rent charged for government land on which petty pedlars arranged their stalls. 'Ālamgīr I also abolished the tax on Hindu pilgrims who went to bathe in their sacred rivers like the Ganges and the Jumna.[39] The orders regarding the abolition of special perquisites to officials on various occasions could be set at nought by corrupt officers in distant areas in the same way as it was done by their successors under the British when the communications had improved so well. The central government exercised vigilance and punished guilty officers, though it did not succeed in eliminating such practices. A small perquisite went so far in expediting business that it was impossible to root out the evil. These unlawful perquisites had such hoary traditions that they were deeply ingrained in the habits of the people. Such perquisites as were recognised by the state were an indirect source of income to the government, because they saved so much money in salaries. The most important of these were the commissions charged by the computers of prices in the various kathehrahs and mandwīs and remuneration to certain officials maintained by the villages for keeping their records.

It was customary for a new appointee to one of the hereditary offices to pay a small amount of money at the time of his appointment. Hereditary chiefs of small principalities and officers attached to the villages and the different kathehrahs and mandwīs who succeeded to offices of profit which brought them commissions and lawful perquisites made such offerings called pes͟hkas͟h.[40] In case of rulers of large territories like the sultanates of Golconda and Bijāpūr the pes͟hkas͟h was large, but then the imperial presents on such occasions were also considerable. Tributary rulers and chiefs paid regular sums to the agents of the emperor as tribute. These sums were the result of agreements concluded at the time of recognition and sometimes subsequent succession to the office.

A considerable source of income was through the presents which were made to the emperor on various occasions. Sometimes these presents were very rich; but every one who had audience of

[39] *Ibid.*, p. 88.

[40] *Kaifiyat-i-ṣūbajāt-i-mumālik-i-maḥrūsah-i-Hindustān*, ff. 220a, 223b.

the emperor for the first time or after a long leave of absence made some present to the monarch. Sometimes it was as low as a single gold coin. This brought large sums of money and valuable commodities to the imperial treasuries, but there was little net gain if any at all, because it was customary for the monarch to bestow even more valuable presents upon the donors. Several times a year the emperor gave away robes of honour which were invariably accompanied with some jewellery, occasionally of very high value. The monarch also made presents of elephants and of valuable horses. The manṣabdārs and others who made presents were generally the gainers in these exchanges of presents.

The Mughul equivalent of a budget was a complicated system of separate treasuries for various heads of revenue, which were earmarked for different heads of expenditure, estimation of expected income under various heads and consequent expenditure. The main divisions of the treasury under 'Ālamgīr I were khazānah-i-'āmirah, khazānah-i-baqāyā, khazānah-i-ṣadaqāt and khazānah-i-jiziyah. To these may be added the special treasury where the property of those dying heirless and intestate was deposited. The khazanah-i-'āmirah was also called bait-u'l-kharāj. This was the general treasury and received the revenue from various sources. The khazānah-i-baqāyā was earmarked for the deposit of the sums recovered from those who had taken loans or who had not been able to clear their accounts with the government. This treasury also dealt with the taqāwī loans advanced to cultivators in times of difficulty to enable them to cultivate their lands. The khazānah-i-ṣadaqāt kept the zakāt received from the Muslims levied upon their merchandise. The khazānah-i-jiziyah was, as its name implies, the repository of the sums realised as jiziyah. These two sources, as well as the property of those dying heirless and intestate, went to finance charitable and benevolent expenditure. The expenses of the government were met from the khazānah-i-'āmirah. The khazānah-i-baqāyā was used for advancing loans.[41]

The estimation of likely income from the various sources was an integral part of the financial administration of the empire.

41 'Alī Muḥammad Khān, *Supplement*, pp. 178, 179.

The likely income from the various cesses was also estimated and formed part of the valuation of assignments. There were figures of the yield of revenue from all sources and any serious lag in the actual income was a cause of inquiry. The entire system of assignments could be worked only with the help of proper valuations. As the valuation depended so much upon the methods of agrarian administration, it will be discussed in some detail along with that topic; here it would suffice to say that every geographical unit of administration had its valuation which recorded the expected income for a year. It took into consideration all the factors which were likely to affect the yield as well as the sources of income. The Mughul valuation was built upon the schedules of average yield per unit area of cultivation calculated upon figures of decennial averages based upon the returns regarding actual yields for that period. This was a progressive procedure bringing the figure up-to-date. The estimates of non-agricultural income also were based upon the record of the previous income from the same sources for a number of years. The system of valuation was particularly useful in giving assignments in lieu of salary.

The total revenue of the empire was estimated to be 5,131,353,000 dāms under Akbar; 8,800,000,000 dāms under Shāh Jahān; and 13,599,963,822 dāms under 'Ālamgīr I. There were 40 dāms to a rupee.[42]

The Mughuls adopted various methods of payment. A fair number of disbursements were made in cash. A proper pay order was made out and the treasurer concerned made the payment on obtaining a receipt. The other method was of paying salaries through assignment of the revenue of a particular area. The categories of revenue were specifically mentioned in the order giving the assignment. Generally all the sources of revenue of an area were assigned, making it easier for the assignee to administer the area assigned to him and to prevent the difficulties which arise in cases of divided authority. Sometimes, however, certain sources were reserved; such sources were called pā'ibāqī.[43] If for some reason

[42] Najaf 'Alī, ff. 21-25.

[43] Ashraf Khān, f. 46 b.

an area given as an assignment to a jāgīrdār had to be temporarily reduced, the area so taken out of the jāgīrdār's jurisdiction was called pā'ibāqi as well.[44] There seems to have existed some division in the records of the ministry of finance between the areas which were intended to be kept khāliṣah, producing the cash income for meeting such expenditure as was not designed to be met through assignments, and the areas which were earmarked for being given out as assignments. There was some convenience in adopting this method, because the range of salaries was fairly well defined except in the case of a few exceptionally favoured individuals and the ministry had carefully tailored assignments to such needs. If a part of the area so demarcated was left unassigned for some reason, it also was included in pā'ibāqī. Such a division had another advantage; it saved the ministry the unnecessary task of transferring a host of officials on the occasion of making new assignments. The pā'ibāqi areas were administered like khāliṣah areas by karorīs and amīns.[45] Normally if the assignment was not for the entire revenue, only the state demand upon agricultural produce was assigned; the collection of the other dues was left to the jāgīrdār, but he had to keep an account and paid all the sums to the amīn of the pā'ibāqī.[46]

Those who received their salaries in cash were better off because they were saved all the bother of administering an area, which was not a part of their normal duties. It was like a civil or military officer of the government simultaneously trying to discharge his duties and being bothered with the administration of a large personal estate for maintaining himself. A man may mismanage his personal property with only financial loss to himself, but a jāgīrdār had to be vigilant over his agents, because any abuse of authority by them would be reported and he would be held responsible for their shortcomings. Besides it was financially a poor bargain, because the administration cost roughly a tenth of the income which came out of the assignment, though the assignment was only for the amount of the salary.

44 *Kaifiyat-i-ṣūbajāt-i-mumālik-i-maḥrūsah-i-Hindustān*, f. 229a.

45 *Ibid.*

46 Ashraf Khān, f. 46 b.

Besides, the assignment was made out on jins-i-kāmil, or the total expected yield, and did not take into consideration the losses from natural calamities and other causes of poor crops or total failures; though the jāgīrdār was prevented from realising revenue irrespective of the actual produce, because, though under the ḍabṭi system the produce was estimated upon the basis of decennial averages, in case of total failure the peasant paid nothing, and when the loss was only partial, he was guaranteed his expected share as the minimum. The jāgīrdār, therefore, suffered heavily in case of decline in production. It is not surprising that the manṣabdārs were generally in debt to the state.

The Mughuls also made grants for benevolent purposes to the learned and the pious. Such grants will be discussed fully at the appropriate place; it would suffice here to mention that the grants were made either in cash or in the forms of assignments. These assignments were different in nature, because whereas such assignments were not made in perpetuity and sometimes they were taken away, yet they were more lasting than the jāgīrs. For one thing, the assignees were not transferred from one place to another and, therefore, there was no need to shift the assignments; besides, if the traditions of scholarship and piety continued in the family, the heirs of the deceased scholar were left in possession of his assignment. These assignments were given in the form of revenue free land. Part of the land granted was always uncultivated and it was the grantee's duty as well as in his interest to get it cultivated. The land was granted out of a pool of land in every area which was earmarked for this purpose and was defined as īmah land. The pool was enlarged by giving hitherto uncultivated area as a part of every grant. In īmah land, the assignee had the rights of the cultivator and did not have to pay any dues to the state; thus he had an interest in it unlike that of the jāgīrdār in his assignment. The īmah lands were excluded from the jāgīrdār's assignment as they yielded no income to him. The assignment was known as suyūrghāl or madad-i-ma'āsh. The cash allowances given for similar purposes were called rūzīnah or waẓīfah, respectively depending whether they were calculated on a daily basis or were awarded for longer periods.[47]

A few assignments were given in perpetuity by Jahāngīr to some officers. These were called al-tamghā assignments. This was a freak revival of an old Timurid tradition. These grants were so called because they were made out under the al-tamghā seal. The extent of such grants is not known; they could not have been extensive and must have been granted as a mark of special favour; they were the exception and not the rule.[48] Al-tamghā assignments were also made for pious purposes; their extent also was not great.[49] On the whole the Mughuls, during the days of the vigour of their empire, were averse to creating hereditary interests.

Another method of payment which the Mughuls adopted from the traditions of the land was to pay commissions on revenue for certain duties performed. This was true of the assessors of the value of the goods sold in kathehrahs and mandwīs.[50] Of the same nature were the perquisites paid to the village headmen for assisting in the collection of the revenue and for helping in the maintenance of peace. Many officials at the local level were engaged not upon a fixed salary, but upon a proportionate commission upon the collected revenue. This was wise because it made the officers interested in the collection of the revenue; abuse was prevented by limiting taxation to the demands and prescribing their rates by the state. Any infraction by the jāgīrdār or the officials could be easily detected by examining the records of payment kept by the patwārī, the village registrar and accountant. This petty official maintained, apart from other papers, an account of payments made by every peasant in the village. On receipt of any complaint, the officer concerned was removed, and a barāmadnawīs was appointed to

47 Chhatar Mal, f. 42 b. The proportion was as high as 75% uncultivated; 25% cultivated. Originally 50% land was uncultivated under Akbar, Abū-'l-Faḍl, *Ā'īn-i-Akbarī*, ii, Ā'in 19. *Also, Kaifiyat-i-ṣūbajāt-i-mumālik-i-maḥrūsah-i-Hindustān*. ff. 229. 230.

48 Jahāngīr, p. 10. Al-tamghā originally was stamped in vermilion, hence the name, because Al in Turki is red. Jahāngīr kept the name but changed the colour into gold. Later the distinction of colour was dropped.

49 Khwājah Yāsīn, f. 49 a.

50 'Alī Muḥammad Khān, *Supplement*, pp. 183, 228; *Dastūr-u'l-'amal*, B.M. or 2026, f 45 b. *Kaifiyat-i-ṣūbajāt-i-mumālik-i-maḥrūsah-i-Hindustān*, f. 219b. etc.

check the papers of the patwārī and compare them with the record maintained by the officers realizing the revenue. This invariably revealed any infringement of the rules, and the culpable officer was punished. On the retirement of an officer, a barāmadnawīs was appointed as a matter of course.[51]

The Mughuls built up large reserves. Their expenditure, except in times of stress, was always kept lower than their income. The great wealth that fell into the hands of Nādir Shāh after all the deterioration in the standards of administration and the power of the central authority which followed 'Ālamgīr I's reign shows how large the Mughul reserves originally must have been. The large sums of money which changed hands among the contestants for supremacy in the subcontinent after the decline of the Mughul empire is another index. There is no record of a campaign or a project having been thwarted for lack of resources in an emergency. This shows that the Mughuls built up large reserves and husbanded their resources with prudence. The Mughul system of financial administration was complicated, but it served its purpose of the prevention of the defalcation of public funds. The principles of accounting and auditing were well understood. There was little attempt at streamlining the accounting methods, but perhaps distances and slow communications of the period stood in the way.

The resources of the empire were at the service of the emperor in theory. It would be uncritical to think from this that the expenditure incurred upon the person and the household of the emperor was undefined or ill organized. The ladies and the princes of the imperial family had their fixed salaries; beyond that they could not draw any money without imperial sanction, which was not always forthcoming even in the case of favourites.[52] The emperor himself had definite sums appropriated for his needs and seldom exceeded such appropriations. That he could, if he so desired, exceed the original appropriations, was in itself a psychological reason for not doing so too often or beyond certain limits; his first concern even from the strictly selfish and personal point of view was to keep himself

[51] *Ibid.*, f. 221a.

[52] *e.g.*, Dārā Shikūh's demand was refused by Sa'd-u'llah Khān, who was supported by Shāh Jahān, Ashraf Khān, ff. 30b, 31a.

on the throne and this could not be achieved by squandering his resources. The stronger Mughul emperors were men who fully understood the principles of sound administration and knew how to control expenditure both at the government level and in the personal sphere. The allocations for personal expenditure sometimes took the form of the assignment of the revenue of some area for some particular purpose; for instance one reads of the assignment of a certain sum of money out of the pā'ibāqī revenue of a parganah for the imperial wardrobe in the reign of 'Ālamgīr I.[53] This must have been only one of several assignments for this purpose.

When the monarch is absolute in his authority, the question of the existence of a privy purse is merely a matter of accounting or financial administration and does not have a constitutional importance. The main factor in such instances is whether the monarch spent money upon himself to the detriment of the efficiency of the administration. The Mughuls did not, so long as power was in their hands, indulge in such personal excesses; but they did maintain standards of splendour which have few parallels in history. Today the upkeep of such magnificence by a monarch would be criticized as wasteful, but this was not so in those days in the subcontinent. The splendour which surrounded the monarch in that period was an institution of great importance because of its public appeal and its psychological impact. Apart from other factors, the magnificence of the Mughul court created the halo around the monarch which made the dynasty stable and raised its prestige so high that it became a legend with the people in spite of its inherent military weakness. The Mughul monarchy was an expensive institution but it justified the expenditure by giving peace and good government to a subcontinent which had been a prey to anarchy before the Mughuls and which relapsed into anarchy as soon as their authority weakened.

[53] *Kaifiyat-i-ṣūbajāt-i-mumālik-i-maḥrūsah-i-Hindustān*, f. 231a.

CHAPTER VIII

Agrarian Administration

THE best organized branch of the Mughul government was its agrarian administration. The Mughuls devoted so much attention to agrarian matters because the state demand on agricultural produce was the mainstay of Mughul finance, which was natural in a land where the economy was mainly agricultural. Agrarian administration has received the closest attention of various governments established in the subcontinent throughout history; only when anarchy or disorders made efficient government impossible, did agrarian administration receive a setback. Sher Shāh devoted considerable attention to it after the breakdown following the anarchy preceding his reign; therefore Akbar did not have to search very far for previous traditions. He, however, increased its efficiency and introduced some far reaching reforms.

The basis of the Mughul agrarian system was the recognition of the fact that the prosperity of the empire depended upon the well-being of the peasant. Throughout the historical literature of the period, this sentiment is ubiquitous. He was to be protected, encouraged and helped. The level of agricultural production was to be not only maintained but also continuously increased.

It was taken for granted that the state was a sharer in the produce; its right to demand a portion of the yield was universally accepted. This tradition precedes the dawn of history in the subcontinent. The recent discovery at Moenjodaro of a large building for storage has led archaeologists to believe that there was a large pool of grain which could not but be common property, perhaps of the government, because the remains suggest organization and rigidity of a nature which would be impossible without a well obeyed government. It does not seem beyond the pale of probability that this was the share of the government in agricultural produce. The *jātakas* which certainly embody a good deal of ancient traditional folk lore take such a demand for granted. The earliest literature, whether in the form of the *nītishāshtras* or records of a secular nature, also does so. When the Muslims entered the subcontinent, they found the tradition well established. As the concept was embedded in their own tradition as well as legal system, they did not question it.

The Hindus had developed in the course of time several methods of assessing the share of the state. The simplest of these was to divide the produce between the state and the peasant. When the crops were reaped, they were stacked and then the share of the state was taken out. This could be done before or after thrashing; Abū-'l-Faḍl calls the former batā'ī or bhāolī, and the latter lāng batā'ī. If the crops were divided while still standing by dividing the area of the field, it was called khet batā'ī.[2] It is obvious that these are the simplest methods of sharing. The difficulty in this process is that it is lengthy and cumbersome. More convenient methods were, therefore found for assessing the share of the state and the first of these was appraisement of the yield to determine the share of the state. This was less cumbersome; it extended the

[1] *e.g.*, 'Ālamgīr I's farmān to Muḥammad Hāshim, *Oriental Miscellany*, 1798, pp. 51, 52.

[2] Abū-'l-Fadl, *Āīn-i-Akbarī*, iii, Ā'īn 5.

time available for assessment. With experience the appraisers would be able to determine the likely yield fairly accurately. In any case, the peasant could always ask for actual division of the crops if he was dissatisfied. In course of time the appraisers as well as the peasants came to know how much of a commodity a unit area produced in a locality; they had only to measure the area cult vated to determine the yield. This method was called measurement. It had the advantage that the assessment could be made any time between the sowing and the harvesting of the crops. The peasant was left free to deal with his crops as he liked, and he did not have to await the convenience of the officials who would be too busy at the time of the harvest. Thus there were three basic concepts: of sharing in various ways, of appraisement, and of measurement. These methods were developed in remote antiquity and find mention in the *jātakas*.

When the Muslims entered the subcontinent, they did not find any of these methods antagonistic to their own ideas. The Muslim jurists were not unaware of the main idea of sharing, because it corresponded to the Muslim kharāj-i-muqāsimah, which had been in vogue for some time in the lands of Islam. The methods of determining the share of the state which they found in vogue in India were logical and reasonable and similar to their own methods. The stage was, therefore, set for the fusion of some of the basic factors in the Hindu and Muslim traditions of agrarian administration.[3]

The Muslim jurists divided agricultural land into three categories. The first of these was 'ushrī. These were lands belonging to the Muslims from the earliest times and those which were permitted by the state to become 'ushrī later; generally these were waste lands which had been brought under cultivation with the permission of the state by Muslims. There were various restrictions upon even a waste land becoming 'ushrī. No kharājī land could become 'ushrī, even if it was purchased by a Muslim or its owner turned a Muslim. There were some 'ushrī lands within the Mughul Empire, but their extent was not large. They were

[3] For Hindu parallels and the developments under the sultans, a more detailed discussion will be found in I.H. Qureshi, *The Administration of the Sultanate of Dehli*, Chapter VI.

mostly lands in the hands of religious men or Muslim scholars; very few of these paid ʻushr to the state, because they were generally given free of the liability to pay revenue; but some did. Their extent was not large enough to affect the system to any degree. The second category was of the kharājī lands. All land cultivated by the non-Muslim subjects of the empire was kharājī: besides, all land cultivated by the Muslims, which was not ʻushrī—and very little was ʻushrī—was kharājī. A third category was that of ṣulḥī lands. As these lay outside the subcontinent, there is no need to discuss their nature. Later some Muslim states developed a category called arḍ-i-mumlikat, of which the ownership vested in the state. There is no mention of this category in the historical literature of the Muslim period in the subcontinent. This category, also, may, therefore, be dismissed. The only two categories found during the Muslim rule in the subcontinent are the ʻushrī and kharājī lands.[4]

The ʻushrī lands paid either a tenth of the gross produce or a twentieth, depending upon the methods of irrigation available. As their extent was limited the rest of the discussion will be devoted to kharājī lands. The kharāj was of several kinds. During our period, the most prevalent category was the kharāj-i-muqāsimah, or a defined proportion of the gross yield. In point of time, perhaps the first category to come into existence was the kharāj-i-waẓīfah, or a fixed demand, irrespective of the actual yield, either in kind or in cash or in both. The caliph ʻUmar had levied from the area of Sawād a kharāj partly in cash and partly in kind. A third category of kharāj is mentioned, the kharāj-i-muqāṭiʻah. This was also levied in the form of a fixed demand, but it differed from the kharāj-i-waẓīfah in one important respect. The kharāj-i-muqāṭiʻah under ʻĀlamgīr I was a device to persuade a cultivator to bring more land under cultivation; whereas the kharāj-i-waẓīfah was the full demand, arrived at between the peasant and the state and applied to lands which had been under cultivation for some time, the kharāj-i-muqāṭiʻah was fixed very low for a prescribed period to encourage the cultivator to work upon hitherto unculti-

[4] *Ibid.*, also Abū-'l-Faḍl, *Ā'īn-i-Akbarī*, iii, Ā'īn 7.

vated land. All these forms of kharāj were subject to the law that the cultivator could not be asked to pay more than a half of the gross produce to the state. 'Ālamgīr I interpreted this in connection with the kharāj-i-waẓīfah as an injunction to guarantee to the cultivator a full half of the expected normal average yield, so that, at times of a calamity or failure of crops, whatever might have been the fixed demand, only that much of it could be realized as left with the peasant a half of the average yield. The state was entitled to its demand if a person who had undertaken to pay kharāj-i-waẓīfah did not cultivate his field without adequate reason. In case the cultivator, for reasons beyond his control, had failed to cultivate his land, or, after cultivation, to save his crops from destruction or damage, he was not obligated to pay the kharāj, even though the kharāj-i-waẓīfah was normally independent of the act of cultivation. The nature of the kharāj could not be changed without the consent of the cultivator.[5]

It will be noticed that the kharāj-i-muqāsimah was not different in its basic concept from the Hindu methods of sharing. There are reasons to believe that the principle of a fixed demand also was not unknown under the Hindus; it was natural for a method of a fixed demand to grow up as the result of long experience regarding the productivity of an area; it would be particularly convenient in case of commodities of a perishable nature. As a result of these similarities in the two systems, they were integrated. The Muslim Empire adopted the native system and assimilated it into its legal theory; the Hindu cultivator did not bother about the legal theory so long as he did not find the system strange or oppressive. In the history of the Muslim Empire, there is no record of even a theoretical conflict between the two systems, so great was their assimilation. The Mughuls had found the main features of the agrarian administration well established. The systems of sharing, appraisement and measurement were taken up by them. In certain fields the method of a fixed demand, which may be called contract, was also in vogue. Hence there is a continuity of tradition in the history of agrarian administration during the

[5] Muḥammad Hāshim Farmān, op. cit., pp. 50-60.

Muslim period. There were changes, but not of a fundamental nature.

Akbar devoted considerable attention to agrarian administration. He was forced to do this because the conditions threatened to become chaotic unless reforms were introduced. This was not the result of any inherent basic shortcomings of the system. Akbar inherited a number of officers who had grandiose titles and pretensions which were out of all proportion to the financial resources of the empire. They claimed large salaries and were not willing to compromise with their dignity by accepting smaller but more realistic emoluments. The prevalent method of payment was by assignment. The only way in which the ministry of finance could meet this situation was to inflate the valuation of the assignments. If this were done in a uniform manner, the difficulties could not have multiplied, but because individual valuations were arbitrarily increased to meet every situation as it arose at the time of giving an assignment to a particular officer, the ministry soon lost track of reality. Even if this had not been done, there was the problem of possessing reliable figures after a breakdown in the administration which followed the violent change of the ruling dynasty. The Mughuls also seem to have insisted upon the prices of various commodities being approved by the ministry of finance before the local authorities could accept the cash equivalent of the demand from the peasant. This naturally resulted in hardship and dissatisfaction. Besides, the valuation of every assignment was in terms of money and it was necessary to keep track of prices for reaching a correct figure of the income expected from an area, which was its valuation. Another factor in the valuation was the determination of the average yield per unit area of cultivation and a record of the area which was brought under cultivation. The method of measurement needed schedules of average produce to make it effective; the Mughuls had adopted the schedules in use under Sher Shāh, but they needed revision for various reasons. Akbar's empire was expanding and new areas were coming under the control of the Mughuls. These new territories were to be assessed for their likely income; even in the older areas productivity did not remain constant for long periods of time. The element of delay had to be eliminated, which could be best done by finding out a method of further expanding the time during which the likely yield from an area as well as from every field could be determined with fairness and accuracy. The answer to these problems was found in a comprehensive reform, which took these matters into consideration.

The first of these was further to standardise the units of measurement. A yard, called a gaz, was adopted consisting of forty-one digits. An area of such sixty yards square was called a bīgah. The reform did not lie in adopting a new scale, but in standardising the existing ones. To bring greater uniformity the old practice of measuring lengths with a rope was given up, because it shrank when exposed to contact with moisture; instead bamboo rods joined together with iron rings were used which were less affected by moisture.[6] Then the land was classified according to the length of its cultivation. If it had been continuously under cultivation, it was called polaj. If it was left uncultivated only for a short time to recover its strength, it was called parauti. Chāchar was land left uncultivated for three or four years. Any land which was not cultivated for a period longer than that was called banjar.[7] The purpose of this classification was to encourage the cultivation of abandoned and fallow land.[8] Polaj paid the full dues; parauti was treated as polaj when it was cultivated. When banjar land was brought under cultivation, only a nominal demand was laid upon it in the shape of a ser or two of the yield per bīgah. In the second year this demand was raised five sers per bīgah. In the third year it paid a half of the normal demand; this was gradually raised until it paid the full demand in the fifth year. This principle was maintained throughout the period.[9] The chāchar was treated on the same basis; when it was cultivated it was treated as banjar land would have been treated when it was just as far from becom-

[6] Abū-'l-Faḍl, *Ā'īn-i-Akbarī*, iii, Ā'īns 7-10.

[7] *Ibid.*, Ā'īns 11-13.

[8] *Ibid.*, Ā'īns 12, 13; Abū-'l-Faḍl, *Akbarnāmah*, iii, pp. 381, 382.

[9] Kewal Rām, f. 164b; *Ka fiyat-i-Ṣūbajāt-i-mumālik-i-maḥrūsah-i-Hindustān*, f. 239a Muḥammad Hashim Farmān, op. cit., pp. 55, 56.

ing polaj. For instance if a field had been lying fallow for three years, it was two years from becoming polaj after it had been cultivated for the first time again; it, therefore, paid what the banjar land would pay after having been in cultivation for three years.[10]

The cultivated areas had also to be grouped in accordance with the similarity in climate and other natural factors which would make them fairly homogeneous from the point of view of productivity. Each area had a common dastūr, a schedule of average produce. Apart from this there was no other division or classification on the basis of productivity, nor, indeed, was any necessary. The opinion that all land was further classified into three categories based upon productivity relies upon a wrong reading of the text of the Ā'īn. In every area where a single schedule applied, sample cuttings were made of the best, the middling and the poor crops, the figures were added and a third of the total was considered to be the *medium* produce, called ḥāṣil or maḥṣūl. This should not be confused with the *average* produce which was determined in a different manner.[11]

This brings us to the major reform which is embodied in the Ā'īn-i-dahsālah. This was the most basic and far reaching reform undertaken during the Mughul regime. In the beginning figures for the fifteenth to the nineteenth years of the reign were collected from the local records; the ministry of finance which seems to have possessed accurate data for the period following supplied the figures for the twentieth to the twenty-fourth years. The data collected consisted of the medium yield for each area, the prices at which the peasants had commuted the demand in kind into cash, the area cultivated and the crops grown. The first two are mention-

10 Abū-'l-Faḍl, *Akbarnāmah*, iii, p. 382.

11 The difficulty has arisen because a stop was inserted in Blochmann's text of Abū-'l-Faḍl, *Ā'īn-i-Akbarī*. iii, Ā'īn 11, after the word زبون in the following sentence:

در دوے نخستین گزیده و میانه و زبون هر جنس را فراهم آورند و سوم بخش آن محصول پندارند

For a fuller discussion vide I.H. Qureshi, *The Administration of the Sultanate of Dehlī*, Appendix C. For the method adopted in choosing areas for sample cuttings vide Abū-'l-Faḍl, *Akbarnāmah*, iii, p. 382; also Kewal Rām, f. 165a.

ed explicitly, the last two are implied as the logical sequence of the process involved. It should be remembered that the objective was to find a satisfactory basis for formulating the state demand, to find its equivalent in cash and to draw up a more satisfactory valuation so that the state should know how much income it could expect normally and have a more accurate basis for making out the assignments. All the confusion had arisen in the beginning of the reign because of the falsification of the data; the collection of all the figures involved was essential for putting the financial administration of the empire on a sound basis. The first step was to create fresh schedules by taking the medium produce for ten years, adding up the figures, dividing the total by ten and thus calculating the average annual yield of a homogeneous area. This was a progressive method, because every year the figure of the medium produce for the first year was taken out and the figure of the medium produce of the new year was added, and thus the figure of the average yield for the next year was calculated. This process made it more convenient to assess the state demand because the time for calculating it was considerably lengthened and the state and the peasant could calculate it simply on the basis of the area cultivated and the crops grown. The cash equivalent of the demand was also probably calculated on the basis of the decennial average of the prevailing prices. These calculations produced what was technically called the jins-i-kāmil, or the expected full yield. The realization was much less, because remissions were made for total and partial failures of crops every year. The valuations were based upon the jins-i-kāmil. In case the failure happened to be serious, commissioners known as amīns were sent by the government to assess the extent of the damage and to recommend the amount of remission.[12]

The method of assessment in the preceding paragraph was called the ḍabṭī system and was encouraged by the government; it, however, did not completely replace the older methods of sharing; appraisement also came in whenever the extent of damages

[12] For a fuller discussion of controversial problems in this connection vide Appendix A.

to the crops by natural or other calamities had to be assessed. Indeed, if for any reason, an area had ceased to produce the normal yields either for a year or for longer periods continuously, the assessment had to be based either upon sharing or appraisement and the ḍabṭī system had to be suspended. Sharing was called by the Mughuls, ghallah bakhshī.[13] In the course of time another method grew up. When a holding had paid state demand over a number of years, in ten or twelve years, it became quite apparent what the average payment had been, and the state and the cultivator came to an agreement whereby a fixed sum was paid and the area cultivated and the crops grown were not taken into consideration; this was contract and was known as nasaq.[14] The nasaq was not group assessment, because it was arrived at between the state and the peasant.[15] The Mughul Empire did not permit group assessment or tax farming when it had the vigour to enforce its orders upon its officers and local authorities. The chieftains who continued to function as zamīndārs fall into a different category altogether.

This brings us to the question of the level of the state demand. Akbar fixed a third of the gross produce as the state demand; but from the beginning the level was not uniform in all the parts of the empire. The rate of a third applied to the major part of the area under control when this level was fixed. In actual fact the level varied between an eighth and a half.[16] Apart from certain 'ushrī areas, whose extent was not large and which paid a twentieth or a tenth, the prevailing level in the Ajmer area was a seventh, whereas in Gujrat it was a half. 'Ālamgīr I explains in a farmān that the peasant was to be guaranteed a half of his average produce, so that in cases of calamities and shortages,

[13] *e.g.*, Abū-'l-Faḍl, *Akbarnāmah*, iii, p. 459; *Dastūr-u'l-'amal*, B.M. or 2026, f. 22b.

[14] For a fuller discussion vide *Indian Culture*, Calcutta, January 1937, pp. 543-45.

[15] Abū-'l-Faḍl, *Ā'in-i-Akbarī*, iii, Ā'īn 5 prohibits group assessment. It was rare even in the days of the anarchy following the decline of central authority.

[16] Abū-'l-Faḍl, *Ā'in-i-Akbarī*, iii, Ā'īn 11, the Province of Ajmer paid from one eighth to one seventh, *ibid.*, description of ṣūbah of Ajmer; Gujrat paid one-half.

the state could only realize what was left after leaving the minimum of a half of the average produce to the cultivator.[17] This view was based upon the ruling of the jurists that the state could not take more than a half of the yield in kharāj. It is not clear if this was the practice before this monarch as well, or if it was introduced for the first time by him. There is no record of such a ruling in the earlier literature; but because it is grounded in the shar', its existence in the previous reigns is not impossible.

Fruit gardens were treated in a special manner. A flat rate of Rupees 2-3/4 per bighah was charged, even if the trees did not bear fruit. Exception was made if the orchard was planted with grapes and almonds, in which case the demand was realized only when the plants bore fruit.[18] Sometimes, if it were found that the orchard was not sufficiently productive, a fifth or a sixth of the net produce was claimed. If the maintenance of the orchard cost more than the value of the yield, no charge was made.[19]

The ḍabṭi and nasaq systems envisaged payment in cash. Even in ghallah bakhshī, the share of the state could be commuted in cash. The state demanded cash and its success can be determined from the fact that one does not read of large state granaries dotted over the countryside as was the case earlier. Indeed Akbar had to levy part of the demand in kind, only ten sers from each bighah of cultivated land, to build up reserves of grain for emergencies like famines and also for the use of the government, like the movement of personnel.[20] In certain places the text of the Ā'īn mentions the system of naqdī in antithesis to ḍabṭī; this seems to have been used as a variant of nasaqī because it was a lump sum payment and was not based upon detailed assessment.[21] If a cultivator did not cultivate his land and used it for pasturage, he

[17] Muḥammad Hāshim Farmān, op. cit., p. 60.

[18] *Ibid.*, p. 66.

[19] *Oriental Miscellany*, 'Ālamgīr I's farmān, p. 48.

[20] Abū-'l-Faḍl, *Ā'īn-i-Akbarī*, ii, Ā'īn 21.

[21] Moreland, (*Agrarian System of Moslem India*, Appendix D) is of the opinion that nasaq was group assessment. This is not correct. Moreland depends on evidence that contradicts him. If Akbar prohibited group assessment, how could it become a recogized method? Nasaq *with headman* (italics are mine) should not be confused with nasaq in general.

was asked to pay a small tax on every head of cattle.[22]

The difference between the khāliṣah lands, the jāgīrs and the pa'ibāqi has already been explained. The jāgīrdār was only the representative of the government; he was not a middleman. He realized only the prescribed state demand. Certain areas were called ghair 'amalī, or unadministered.[23] These were the territories of the tributary chiefs, called zamīndārs, who administered their territories themselves and whose agrarian administration was not under the supervision of the central government. The Mughuls tended gradually to encroach upon the autonomy of such rulers; a well known method was to enroll them as manṣabdārs and to give them their hereditary territories as jāgīrs. However, not all autonomous territories were brought under control in this manner. In cases where the state succeeded in treating the tributaries as manṣabdārs the mere weight of traditional relationship between them and the cultivators must have militated against the effectiveness of the control of the central government. The minor zamīndārs were under more strict control and some of them had been reduced to little better than mere recipients of a small commission upon the revenue. Where the control was effective, the state insisted upon the enforcement of its measures. Then if the zamīndār demanded more from the peasants than the legitimate demand, or oppressed the peasants otherwise, the state interfered. As new zamīndārs, on succession to their position, obtained the consent of the central government, and also because of their weak position *vis-a-vis* the empire, the state was able to increase its authority continuously.[24] The kind of zamīndāri system introduced by the British was unknown.

The state tried to protect the peasant from the exactions of its officers as well as from the local authorities. Every peasant entered into an agreement with the state. The agreement was embodied in two documents: the pattah was drawn up by the officers re-

[22] Abū-'l-Faḍl, *Ā'īn-i-Akbarī*, iii, Ā'īn 5. The tax was 6 dāms for buffaloes and 3 dāms for cows per annum. Cattle which had not calved were exempt.

[23] Lachhmī Narāyan Shafiq, ff. 14b-16.

[24] *Kaifiyat-i-ṣūbajāt-i-mumālik-i-maḥrūsah-i-Hindustān*, f. 221; Qābil Khān and Muḥammad Ṣādiq, f. 42a.

presenting the state or the manṣabdār, it mentioned the area under cultivation, the crops and the amount of the demand; the qubūliyat literally, acceptance, was drawn up by the peasant, repeating the details of the pattah and denoting the peasant's acceptance of the assessment. The former was retained by the peasant and the latter was deposited in the local revenue office.[25] This procedure ensured that the peasant knew how much was expected from him and he could not be imposed upon by any dishonest officer. In case it was discovered that any sums had been recovered from the cultivator which he was not legitimately expected to pay, a barāmadnawīs was dispatched from the provincial headquarters or the capital to make inquiries and to examine the accounts.[26] Detection was easy, because all the payments by the cultivators were meticulously recorded by the village accountant.[27] In case the officer was found guilty he was punished and was made to pay the sum exacted from the peasant back to him. The state could not have succeeded completely in its efforts to prevent corrupt practices, but its vigilance did exert a healthy influence upon the agrarian administration.

The general attitude of the state towards the peasant was one of benevolence; it was realized that the prosperity of the empire depended upon his welfare and prosperity. The army had strict orders to avoid any damage to the crops; when some damage was unavoidable, commissioners were appointed to assess its extent and compensation was paid to those affected. In case of difficulties or calamities the peasant was advanced loans, called taqāwī, to enable him to cultivate his holding.[28] This was repaid in convenient instalments. Remissions of revenue were quite common; whenever it was felt that the cultivator was adversely affected by circumstances, steps were taken to afford him relief. It was not only the loss of crops which was taken into consideration;

[25] Forms of these documents are available in *Dastūr-u'l-'amal*, B.M. or 2026, ff. 23, 24.

[26] *Ibid.*, ff. 33, 34; *Kaifiyat-i-ṣubajāt-i-mumālik-i-maḥrūsah-i-Hindustān*, f. 221a.

[27] Abū-'l-Faḍl. *Ā'īn-i-Akbari*, iii, Ā'īn 5.

[28] Kewal Rām, f. 164 b, *Kaifiyat-i-ṣubajāt-i-mumālik-i-maḥrūsah-i-Hindustān*, f. 219 b, etc.

when, for instance, the court moved from Lahore in the forty-third regnal year, it was felt that the higher level of prices would no longer prevail, hence Akbar reduced the rate of the demand.[29] This seems to indicate that the commutation of the state demand into cash was done on the decennial average of prices, because if the current prices had been the basis, no reduction would have been necessary. Remissions because of natural calamities were too frequent to be mentioned.[30]

The Mughuls were extremely anxious to expand agriculture and special concessions in the demand were made if a cultivator brought new land under cultivation.[31] Officers were instructed to encourage the cultivators to expand their holdings. To ensure such efforts by the officers, newly cultivated areas were shown separately in the statements submitted to the higher authorities.[32] The policy of the government was that no cultivated land should be permitted to become barren and uncultivated.[33] The state also tried to improve the quality of the crops.[34] The Mughuls continued the policy of the sultans to introduce new crops into the subcontinent. Jahāngir introduced the cultivation of pineapples and several new varieties of grapes.[35] Potatoes had been introduced in the previous reign and soon gained popularity. Guavas and custard apples which grow so profusely today in certain parts of the subcontinent were introduced by the Portuguese and their cultivation was encouraged by the Mughuls. Tobacco also was introduced by the Portuguese and spread rapidly. The honeydew variety of the melon, a native of the colder regions, was successfully cultivated in the plains of North India. Muḥammad Riḍā of Khurāsān who raised the first crop was rewarded and honoured by Shāh Jahān.[36]

[29] Abū-'l-Faḍl, *Akbarnāmah*, iii, p. 747.

[30] *e.g.*, *ibid.*, p. 534.

[31] Vide supra under banjar and chāchar lands.

[32] Areas newly brought under cultivation were called *iḍāfah*, those already under cultivation were called *dakhl*. *Dastūr-u'l-'amal*, B.M. or 2026, f. 29a.

[33] Muḥammad Hāshim Farmān, opp. cit., pp. 54 et seq; also Abū-'l-Faḍl, *Ā'in-i-Akbari*, iii, Ā'in 5.

[34] *Ibid.*

[35] Jahāngir, pp. 5-7.

[36] Khawāfī Khān, i, p. 757.

The Mughuls were obliged to keep up the agricultural produce of their empire for economic reasons. The Mughul Empire was an exporter of foodgrains, specially rice and wheat; its trade in manufactured goods was also extensive. It was necessary to maintain the level of agricultural production for feeding the population at home, to export the agricultural products and to supply the raw material for the extensive industry. At that time the subcontinent had a thriving industry in textiles; it clothed the entire population of the littoral of the Indian Ocean extending from the Indonesian archipelago to Africa; it also exported cloth to Europe and even to distant America. It also had the monopoly of the shipbuilding trade so far as the lands washed by the Indian Ocean were concerned; Indian built ships reached the ports of Europe. In addition, the Mughul Empire exported leather goods, sugar and candied fruit. All this industry engaged a large proportion of the population because those were not the days of elaborate machines and all work had to be done by human hands. It is estimated that the subcontinent did not have a population of more than a hundred million at that time. The number of people who cultivated the soil was not too large proportionately. Hence there was the ever present danger of agricultural production falling below the needed quantities and thus affecting both industry and the food situation. The Mughuls, therefore, insisted that the fields should be cultivated and if a peasant was not able to cultivate his land, the state made arrangements to get it cultivated for him and deducted the cost of cultivation as well as the state demand from the yield of the holding.[37] For the same reason the state undertook the construction of irrigation canals and reservoirs. Irrigation works were put in charge of local officers called dāroghahs of canals who were entrusted to keep them in good repairs.[38] The state does not seem to have demanded any extra amount as water rate, because no such demand finds mention in contemporary records; the government was content with sharing the increas-

[37] Abū-'l-Faḍl, *Ā'īn-i-Akbarī*, ii, Ā'īn 5; Muḥammad Hāshim Farmān, op. cit., pp. 54 et seq.

[38] *Kaifiyat-i-ṣūbajat-i-mumālik-i-maḥrūsah-i-Hindustān*, f. 225a.

ed yield with the cultivator, who, however, was expected to help the state with his work in the maintenance of the canals. With the same end in view if a jāgīr was not managed properly so that the yield went down, it was resumed for better administration.[39]

The peasant was the owner of his holding. The theory that the state was the owner of all land grew up during the period of anarchy and was not only too readily accepted by the British but was almost sponsored by them. In the eighteenth century considerable research was made by native jurists as well as administrators under the patronage of the British on agrarian matters; parts of the results of this research are still available in the archives of Europe and the subcontinent. It seems that the views of those who held that the peasant was the owner of the land did not find favour with the new rulers who had their own policies to justify and perpetuate. This alone can explain some of the far fetched arguments found in some writings. During Muslim rule in the subcontinent the legal position that the peasant was the owner of his holding was never questioned. All contemporary literature bears this out; the *Ā'īn*, the law books and the dastūr-u'l-'amals are all unanimous on the point[40] This does not mean that there was no landless labour; such labour was employed by the peasant during harvest time when extra hands were needed; it was also employed upon lands held as suyūrghāls by scholars and divines who themselves could not work upon their holdings. The availability of such labour was a determining factor in the size of the holding even when more land was available for cultivation. If some of these were settled permanently as tenants, called mazāri', they became hereditary, and were entitled to sell or transfer their rights. The ordinary peasants had all the rights which are associated with ownership.

The peasant in the subcontinent had certain advantages over his compeer in Europe and many other parts of the world. Serfdom in any form was unknown; the peasant as well as the landless labourer was free to go anywhere he liked. Indeed the availability

[39] e. g. Qābil Khān and Muhammad Ṣādiq, f. 53a.

[40] For a more detailed discussion vide Appendix B.

of cultivable land and the freedom of movement guaranteed reasonably good behaviour on the part of the local authority even in times of anarchy. The migration of peasants was not unknown in cases of the breakdown of law and order in any area on the approach of an invader or local tyranny.[41] The peasant was not too docile; it took a century of anarchy and large scale robbery and plunder to break his spirit; later landlordism imposed by an efficient government, in course of time, made him submissive and reconciled to petty persecution on the part of landlords and others. Peasants were not averse from taking up arms if they felt that they were being unjustly treated.[42] They could resort to such resistance because the difference between an army and an armed rabble was proverbially too small, specially when the peasant bore arms almost as a part of his dress. The presence of tropical forests in the neighbourhood of the villages further helped them if they took up arms; bamboo clumps and thorny cacti tended to make impenetrable walls in conjunction with acacia and other thorny bushes.

The peasant, during the days of the Mughul Empire, was independent and even pugnacious and had to be treated with respect and consideration. The government relied so much upon his cooperation that it could not be otherwise. Not only was he the main source of income; the local administration was based upon his cooperation. The traditions of self-governing village communities date back to prehistoric times; the Mughuls, like their Muslim predecessors, respected them and made them a part of their administrative system. It was with the cooperation of these communities that the agrarian administration could function; without the village accountant and qānūngū, the machinery could not work. Similarly the government depended upon the peasant communities for the maintenance of law and order in the countryside. Any contumacy on the part of a community was dealt with by the local officials in which they were helped by the neighbouring villages.[43] Such cooperation could not be forth-

[41] Bābur, pp. 487, 488. Also *ibid.*, f.n. 2 on p. 487.

[42] Kewal Rām, f. 165.

[43] Vide Chapter XI.

coming if the peasants had not felt that the government was in the right. The cooperation between the government and the cultivators could, in the ultimate analysis, be based only upon ties of common interest. The Mughuls understood this, hence they devoted so much attention to agrarian administration.

The peasant was left with sufficient margin after he had paid the state demand upon his produce to enable him to live in modest comfort. In the greater part of the subcontinent the weather does not make too great a demand upon the resources of the villager. For the major part of the year he does not need too much clothing; a good deal of the time can be spent outdoors, and, therefore, a tradition grew up of simple homesteads and meagre furniture. This simplicity had constituted the pattern of life for centuries and had become deeply ingrained in the habits of the people. It led several European travellers who visited the Mughul Empire into thinking that the lack of elaborate furniture and spacious houses was an index of the poverty of the people, though they themselves record similar facts about the lives of people who were apparently in affluent circumstances.[44] The wellbeing of the peasant in the subcontinent at that time expressed itself in good food, and feasting on the occasion of the numerous Hindu festivals and ceremonies like weddings, births and even deaths. The investment of the extra wealth often took the form of jewellery for the women and hoarding. The grinding poverty which is now associated with the peasantry is the legacy of the anarchy followed by the exploitation by uncontrolled landlordism which remained dominant for more than two centuries and the general impoverishment of the economy under the East India Company.[45] The situation was further aggravated by the continuation of habits which had been cultivated in the days of plenty and the perpetuation of social behaviour which were the creation of prosperity into days when that prosperity had disappeared. The extravagance of the

[44] *e.g.*, the facts that rich Hindu merchants were usually scantily dressed; even Hindu rulers traditionally wore few clothes before coming under the influence of the Muslims.

[45] Maratha armies and Pindārī freebooters mercilessly plundered the villages.

Indian peasant on such occasions has added to the great load of indebtedness that he has carried for so long after his impoverishment.

In the days of the Mughul Empire he was helped by several factors. His holding was of a reasonable size because there was not so much pressure upon the land. The total population was not more than a hundred million in the entire subcontinent; out of this a fair number was engaged in industry and trade. Government service absorbed some; others were teachers, religious men and scholars, artists and labourers. The peasant's own family found employment in spinning and other handicrafts when there was no work in the fields. The cattle, which were a source of additional income, were easier to maintain because there was no dearth of pasture land. The forests were of great economic benefit to the peasant. He had a perennial source of fuel, timber, certain flowers and herbs of commercial value, honey and even some fruit. All that was needed to put up a homestead was available in the forest and could be secured for the labour of collecting it and transporting it where it was needed. The prosperity of the Mughul Empire finds an index in the plentiful supply of commodities and the prevalence of low prices. The brilliance and the opulence of the Mughul Empire which so struck the Western travellers was based upon the wellbeing and prosperity of the peasant. The agrarian administration of the Mughul empire played no mean a part in keeping the peasant contented and happy.

CHAPTER IX

Justice, Hisbah and Police

The basic purpose of the organization of the community of Islam has always been the facilitation of the pursuit of virtue. The determination of the rights of individuals and groups is a necessary corollary of such a purpose, because virtue implies fulfilment of social and civil obligations. Therefore, from the day that a few disciples gathered around the Prophet and sought his guidance in matters spiritual and mundane the foundation was laid of an embryonic government including an organ for the dispensation of justice. From these meagre beginnings there grew up a tradition and a pattern of the administration of justice in the Muslim world which produced one of the greatest systems of law in history.

The function of the institutions for the dispensation of justice in any society is the determination of the rights of individuals and groups to resolve the disputes that may arise between them. The criminal jurisdiction of such institutions is but a corollary of this function, because every criminal infringes the rights of others and the society needs protection against anti-social activities. Conversely, it has to be determined if the accused is really guilty, and, if he is found guilty, the nature and seriousness of his crime have to be determined and proper punishment has to be prescribed. So far as these aspects of justice were concerned, they were called qaḍāyā and formed part of the jurisdiction of the dīwān-u'l-qaḍā.[1]

The jurists recognized from the beginning that there were spheres of human rights that needed protection and yet they did not come strictly within the definition of qaḍāyā. For instance, if a public servant, through cupidity, selfishness or neglect was responsible for the infringement of the rights of a citizen, it called for investigation and disciplinary action by the caliph or his nominee. The public servants were the agents of the caliph and it was his duty to keep them in order and to ensure that the administration functioned impartially and efficiently. This branch of justice was called naẓar fi'l-maẓālim, or simply maẓālim.

If an individual could suffer at the hands of the state through its employees, the state could also have occasion of complaint against an individual. This should not be confused with the injuries sustained by society through the criminal activities of individuals. Broadly speaking all criminal activity directed against the state is also injurious to the society, hence the justification of punishment for such activities. Ordinary crimes were, however, left within the jurisdiction of the dīwān-u'l-qaḍā; only political crimes were looked upon as crimes against the state. As political considerations were dominant in the adjudication of such cases, it came to be called siyāsat.

The Mughul Empire did not deviate from these traditions. They, as will appear from the following discussion, had become so deep rooted in the world of Islam that it was natural for the Mughuls to accept them almost in their entirety. Indeed they had come to be regarded as a part of the Muslim law, the shar'. Besides, they did not come into conflict with the popular notion of the monarch being the fountain-head of justice. Through the dīwān-u'l-qaḍā, he indirectly dispensed justice and in cases of miscarriage of justice,

[1] Muḥammad Murtaḍā al-Ḥusainī, Part X, p. 296.

his intervention was sought by the aggrieved; as head of the administration he heard complaints against his servants and agents and as defender of the realm he tried rebels and prisoners of war.

The diwān-u'l-qaḍā has a long history. In the lifetime of the Prophet, he dispensed justice in person. This tradition continued in the early days of the Caliphate and even later, at least in theory, the caliph remained the chief guarantor of justice in the realm. The Sultans of Dehlī, as the representatives of the caliph, held the same position through the theory of delegation. The Mughuls, as has been mentioned earlier, believed in their own caliphate.

However, with the expansion of the territories of Islam, the Prophet himself had found it necessary to appoint men in different areas to dispense justice.[2] At Medina itself he does not seem to have delegated the function of dispensing justice to anyone,[3] though 'Umar was considered to be an authority on law and was approached for legal opinions even in the lifetime of the Prophet.[4] Abū Bakr was also consulted occasionally.[5] After the death of the Prophet, Abū Bakr appointed 'Umar as the qāḍī at Medina,[6] probably because his hands were full with the suppression of the revolt of the tribes. When 'Umar became the caliph, he also appointed a qāḍī at Medina,[7] and then the tradition of appointing a qāḍī to dispense justice at the capital became well established. This statement is, however, not free from controversy. Several authors hold that 'Umar was the first to appoint a qāḍī.[8] The argument generally advanced is that it was under him that the frontiers of the Caliphate expanded to an extent that the appointment of a qāḍī at Medina was considered necessary. This is a fallacious argument because Abū Bakr had even more pressing reasons. Besides these authorities depend upon a tradition ascribed to Ẓuhrī to the effect that the Prophet, Abū Bakr and 'Umar

[2] Ibn Sa'd, ii, p. 337.

[3] A'n-Nakdī, p. 7.

[4] Ibn Sa'd, p. 336.

[5] *Ibid.*, p. 335. Also, A'n-Nakdī, p. 7.

[6] Ṭabrī, Part IV, p. 50; Ḥayyān, Part I, p. 104; Al-Qurṭubī, ii, p. 417.

[7] A'n-Nakdī, p. 8; Jurjī Zaidān, Part, I, p 184.

[8] *Ibid.*

did not appoint a qāḍi.[9] This tradition can be accepted neither on the basis of probability for reasons given above, nor in face of repeated and stronger traditions to the contrary on which the statement is based.

Imām Abū Yūsuf was the first qāḍī who was given the title of qāḍī-u'l-quḍāt by the Abbasid caliph Hārūn-a'r-Rashīd (786-809).[10] This was not an empty title; the Imām was first given the right to appoint qāḍis in the city of Baghdād and later in the entire realm.[11] This established the pattern of judicial organization in Muslim countries, because Rashid's example was followed in Spain and Egypt.[12] In the Mughul Empire as well, the provincial and local qāḍīs were appointed by the chief qāḍī of the empire.[13]

The delegation of judicial authority to the qāḍī-u'l-quḍāt would, in any case, have been necessary with the rise of non-Arab rulers who were not familiar with the Arabic language, in which the basic information about Muslim law was contained. With the growth and development of Muslim jurisprudence, its complexities and subtleties were multiplied and unless the ruler was a competent lawyer himself, he could not adequately act as a judge. The Muslim jurists and judges built up for themselves, through their erudition, piety and impartiality, a position of almost unassailable independence and dignity. Through their influence with the people, they became immune from interference by the government.[14]

The dīwān-u'l-qaḍā was an important institution of the Sultanate of Dehlī and its organization generally conformed to the pattern evolved in the rest of the Muslim world, especially in the Abbasid caliphate.[15]

[9] Ḥayyān, Part I, p. 105.

[10] Jurjī Zaidān, Part I, p. 185; A'n-Nakdī, p. 9.

[11] *Ibid.*; Jurjī Zaidān Part I, p. 185.

[12] *Ibid.*

[13] 'Alī Muḥammad Khān, *Supplement*, p. 250.

[14] There are many instances, *e.g.*, Shaikh 'Abd-u'llah Ajodhanī, see 'Abd-u'llah, B.M. ms. or 197, f. 19.

[15] I.H. Qureshi, *The Administration of the Sultanate of Dehli*, pp. 159-161.

The Mug͟huls inherited the system. In the beginning of his reign Akbar displayed profound regard for 'Abd-u'n-Nabī, who held the posts of the ṣadr-u'ṣ-ṣudūr and qāḍī-u'l-quḍāt, but later a conflict developed between the Emperor and the S͟haik͟h. The reason of the conflict is interesting. The qāḍī of Mathura had ordered the construction of a mosque. A wealthy Brahmin, out of hostility to Islam, removed the building material. Thereupon the Brahmin was summoned to the qāḍī's court. The Brahmin not only disobeyed the summons but he also used abusive language for the Prophet. On the qāḍī's report the Brahmin was summoned to the capital and 'Abd-u'n-Nabī, in view of the Brahmin's contumacy and continued use of abusive language against the Prophet, sentenced him to death. As all sentences of capital punishment had to be approved by the emperor, 'Abd-u'n-Nabī submitted the case to Akbar for orders. Akbar had, by now, turned away from orthodoxy and he did not like the idea of executing the Brahmin. Besides, the Hindu ladies of the imperial household and others opposed to th orthodox group in the court interceded with Akbar on behalf of the Brahmin. Akbar first of all tried to find out a flaw in the case, therefore he ordered a secret inquiry into the facts, entrusting some of the leading opponents of 'Abd-u'n-Nabī with the responsibility. The inquiry, however, confirmed the facts on which the sentence was based. Akbar, even then, did not like to confirm the sentence, but he was too circumspect to take upon himself the responsibility of setting aside the sentence. He had really wanted 'Abd-u'n-Nabī to take the responsibility of saving the Brahmin, but the S͟haik͟h refused to take the hint and continued to press for orders. At last Akbar, instead of giving any clear orders, left the matter in the hands of the S͟haik͟h who executed the Brahmin.[16] This incident brings into relief the position of the chief judge of the empire. Akbar with all his might and heterodoxy did not consider it politic to overrule the qāḍī-u'l-quḍāt. The latter also, in spite of his awareness of the monarch's wishes in

[16] Bada'ūnī, iii, pp. 80-83. The Ḥanafī fiqh does not prescribe any punishment for abusing the Prophet. The S͟haik͟h, however, could base his decision on the rulings of other schools if he thought that the interests of Islam and the realm were thus served better.

the matter, did not swerve from what he considered to be his duty.

Akbar's imperious nature and the promptings of those in whose interest it was to turn him away from orthodoxy did not leave matters there. They embarked upon a well organized campaign of calumny against the orthodox ulema of the court that has found its way into the writings of Abū-'l-Faḍl. Even Badā'ūnī has clouded the issues, because, contrary to popular belief, he was no friend of the orthodox party.[17]

It is, however, obvious that Akbar wanted to break the power of the ulema. An independent judiciary administering a law in the formulation of which he had no say irked him. The heterodox group found in Shaikh Mubārak—a man of undoubted ability and the father of Akbar's trusted counsellor, Abū-'l-Faḍl—a scholar who was willing to oblige Akbar by offering a plausible solution. He drew up a document[18] to which the leading theologians of the court were forced to affix their signatures. Its main purport was to lay it down that if the jurists differed on any point of the law, Akbar could decide which interpretation he would accept and enforce. Armed with this authority, it seems, Akbar hoped to instigate his supporters to raise a controversy regarding any legal ruling that came into conflict with his views and then to give his own judgment, thus securing to himself the highest legal authority in the state. The general principle enunciated in the maḥḍar (as the document was called) was sound and in accordance with the principles of Islamic law, because if the jurists cannot agree on a point, the monarch has to choose some interpretation and enforce it. But then there should be no doubt about the bona fides of the monarch, and, what is equally important, he should possess sufficient knowledge and legal acumen to arrive at a sound decision.[19] It is obvious that Akbar was not acting in good faith, because he

[17] Badā'ūnī was, to say the least, tinged with Mahdawism. This creed was strict in its adherence to the shar, but it had come into conflict with orthodoxy.

Badā'ūnī shows his devotion to the letter of the shar' and hostility to the orthodox simultaneously.

[18] Badā'ūnī, ii, pp. 271, 272 gives the text, which is preceded by a narration of the circumstances in which it was produced and signed.

[19] Jurjī Zaidān, Part I, p. 88; Māwardī, p. 4.

was motivated really by the desire of subverting the established law; besides, being virtually illiterate, he was not capable of understanding the niceties of jurisprudence. Even learned monarchs had relied in legal matters upon the advice of some qualified jurist who was appointed as the head of the departments of religious affairs and justice.

It is interesting, however, that the plan did not succeed, because history does not record a single instance in which Akbar openly interfered in judicial proceedings or set aside a judgment. He had to take recourse to the well known method of having a pliant judiciary. The *Ā'īn-i-Akbarī*[20] prescribes as one of the conditions of appointment to the highest judicial and religious post adherence to Akbar's religious philosophy. This policy seems to have been pursued with great thoroughness.[21] We read in Badā'ūnī's pages how scandalous, from the point of view of Islam, was the behaviour of many judicial officers.[22] Even allowing for exaggeration and Badā'ūnī's hostility to Akbar's religious views, it is obvious that Akbar's nominees were models neither of rectitude nor of independence.[23] Such appointments in direct contravention of the traditions of Muslim judiciary created a sense of horror which is reflected in the orthodox literature of the period.

The situation began to improve towards the end of the reign when Akbar lost interest in religious innovations. With the coming of Jahāngīr, there took place a significant change in the policies of the state[24] and Akbar's heresies having died with him, the

[20] Abū-'l-Faḍl, *Ā'īn-i-Akbarī*, ii, Ā'īn 19 lays it down that the ṣadr-u's-ṣudūr should be "a right thinking man, from the forehead of whose words and deeds should shine the mark of peace with all, general kindness and everlasting greatness." "Peace with all"—a term borrowed from the ṣūfīs who used it for the tolerance and appreciation of all creeds—was applied by Akbar to his eclectic philosophy.

[21] The Ā'īn cited above gives only an inkling how the emoluments and grants of religious men were cut down and gradually old recipients of grants were totally eliminated. All qāḍīs appointed before the time of the pliant Sulṭān Khwājah were dismissed on a general charge of corruption.

[22] Badā'ūnī, ii, p. 309. For general opinion about the highest judicial and religious official see *ibid.*, iii, p. 141.

[23] Shaikh Aḥmad Sarhindī has letters in the *Maktūbāt-i-Imām-i-Rabbānī* (e.g.v.i, letters 53, 65, 194, 195 etc.) which show that the evil was not limited to the capital.

[24] *Ibid.*, letter 194.

main temptation to interfere in the judicial administration was removed. The prestige and power of the qāḍis and especially of the qāḍi-u'l-quḍāt reached their pinnacle under 'Ālamgir I[25]. Indeed the independence of the courts became proverbial[26] and the wishes of the monarchs received little consideration, as is illustrated by the fact that once 'Ālamgir I instructed his agent to ask for capital punishment in a case, but the court refused to accept the plea.[27] This incident seems to have been so characteristic that the Muslim historians have ignored it. It finds a place in the gossipping account of a foreigner to whom it must have struck as remarkable.

In view of the basic philosophy of social and political organization in Islam the qāḍi's position, qualifications and functions have received detailed consideration from Muslim writers on jurisprudence. It is the duty of the society to provide for the adjudication of disputes;[28] the appointment of a judicial officer is an organized form of discharging this duty. The tradition of appointing judicial officers was established by the Prophet himself;[29] and was followed by his successors.[30] The office of the qāḍi is, therefore, well enshrined in the sunnah. It was inconceivable for any Muslim community not to be within the jurisdiction of some qāḍi; every township possessing a sizable Muslim population had a qāḍi attached to it.[31] The system was well rooted in the subcontinent when the Mughuls established their empire.[32] The Mughuls

[25] Khawāfī Khān, ii, p. 216. The Emperor himself said, "There is no function greater than qaḍā", Ashraf Khān, f. 97a.

[26] Manucci, ii, p. 254.

[27] The accused was Qāḍī Mir, Manucci, iv, p. 119.

[28] It is farḍ 'ala-'l-kifāyah. A'sh-Shīrāzī, ii, p. 289. A farḍ 'ala-'l-kifāyah is a duty which must be discharged by some members of the society, otherwise the entire society remains in default. In other words, it is a duty imposed upon the society which must be discharged on its behalf by some individuals, A's-Sarkhasī, Part XVI, p.60. Also Al-Kāsānī, Part VII., pp. 2-3.

[29] A'sh-Shīrāzī, ii, p. 289

[30] *Ibid.*

[31] 'Alī Muḥammad Khān, *Supplement*, pp. 173, 250; Shākir Khān, f. 141a.

[32] For details see I.H. Qureshi, *The Administration of the Sultanate of Dehlī*, pp. 160-161.

did not bring about any significant changes.[33] Akbar's innovations affected the spirit but not the forms of the institution and after his death, even the spirit was restored.

The qāḍī's functions have been defined carefully by the jurists. In the beginning he was concerned only with civil and criminal justice. In the course of time his functions expanded. He was entrusted with the guardianship of certain beneficent activities of the Muslim society. For instance he supervised the management of the property of the insane, the insolvent, orphans and idiots. He kept an eye upon the execution of testamentary dispositions and the administration of endowments. He arranged the marriages of widows who had no guardians to safeguard their interests. Later on he began to look after the maintenance of streets and public buildings. He inquired into the honesty and trustworthiness of trustees, agents and notaries.[34]

The jurists have also gone into great details regarding the qualifications of a qāḍī.[35] He must be a free adult Muslim male. Insane, blind and mute persons are disqualified. Some go so far as to lay it down that the qāḍī must be capable of independent ijtihād, but this condition has not been considered to be binding by the Ḥanafis.[36] Piety and erudition, however, have always been considered necessary, but the ruling given by a qāḍī does not become invalid by the fact of his lack of piety, provided that the ruling itself is in accordance with the shar'.[37] A qāḍī's impartiality should be above question and he should not permit himself to be prejudiced against a party because of his religion, nation or race.[38] The presence of learned jurists in a court to assist the qāḍī was encouraged.[39] It was, however, not considered necessary.

[33] The Mughuls attached a qāḍī to the imperial court, who accompanied the emperor on his marches. He was called qāḍī-i-'askar; Kāẓim, p. 1102. There was also a mir 'adl attached to the court called mir 'adl-i-'askar; 'Abd-u'l-Ḥamid, ii, p. 311.

[34] Jurji Zaidān, p. 185. Māwardī, pp. 67-69.

[35] Al-Kāsānī, vii, p. 3.

[36] *Ibid.*, pp. 4, 5.

[37] *Ibid.*, p. 3.

[38] A's-Sarkhasī, xvi, p. 61.

[39] *Ibid.*, p. 79.

When the Prophet sent Ma'ādh to Yemen, he asked, "How will you decide disputes?" Ma'ādh replied "I will decide disputes in accordance with what is in the Book of God." "If it is not in the Book of God?", asked the Prophet. "In accordance with the sunnah of the Prophet of God.", replied Ma'ādh. "If it is not in the sunnah of the Prophet of God?", once again asked the Prophet. Ma'ādh replied "Then I will use my reason." The Prophet at this praised God for guiding Ma'ādh aright.[40] On this tradition of the Prophet is based the entire structure of the shar'. The Qur'ān provides the immutable basis; the authentic traditions of the Prophet come next in importance; and in the application of these to human affairs, human reason inevitably plays an important, albeit a subsidiary, role. When there was unanimity of understanding among the companions of the Prophet on the interpretation of a verse of the Qur'ān or a ḥadīth, it was considered authoritative, because they could not be unanimous unless they found the tradition in accordance with the established sunnah.[41] In the course of time learned jurists built up such an imposing structure of well integrated, consistent and logical interpretation that it was difficult for the qāḍis and the people not to accept its authority and ijmā' came to embrace the consensus of later authorities as well. Gradually the four leading schools of jurisprudence established themselves in the different parts of the Muslim world. The subcontinent was overwhelmingly Ḥanafī, and the courts under the Sultans of Dehlī as well as the Mughuls administered the Ḥanafī system of law. Where there was no clear guidance from the shar', the qāḍī applied 'ādah, the customary law.

The Mughul Empire had large numbers of non-Muslims as its subjects, hence, in accordance with the shar' itself, the Muslim law could be applied to the non-Muslims only within certain well defined limits. The Hindus had their own personal law and the provisions of the shar' regarding marriage, divorce and inheritance did not apply to them. The principles of the shar' were applied, in so far as it was feasible without injustice, to disputes arising

[40] Tirmidhi, ii, pp. 275, 276.

[41] Imām Shāfi'ī, p. 671,

between Muslims and non-Muslims. Cases between non-Muslims, if they belonged to a group with common customs were decided in the light of those customs, 'ādah. Those cases where neither the principles of shar' nor 'ādah could be applied were decided on the basis of equity. A large number of cases were decided by the panchāyats and were never brought to the court of the qāḍī.

The criminal code was based upon the shar' according to the Ḥanafī interpretation.[42] According to the shar' itself, whereas it is necessary to punish criminals in the interest of the society, the criminal code of Islam cannot be applied fully to the non-believers, because it does not accord with their moral sense. Some provisions do not apply to them at all, others should be enforced with leniency.[43] No one in the realm was permitted to inflict capital punishment and all cases where such punishment was recommended were referred to the emperor.[44] All recommendations for capital punishment were scrutinized carefully and they were accepted only when there was complete justification for executing the offender.[45]

The governors of provinces and officers in charge of smaller units were required to render all assistance to the qāḍī.[46] In addition there was an affiliated department for discharging the executive duties of the court. Under the Sultans of Dehli it was under the dādbek or amīr-i-dād.[47] The Mughuls called this officer mīr 'adl, but there was no significant change in his functions. The *Ā'īn-i-Akbarī* has put the relationship between the qāḍī and the mīr 'adl in a nutshell where it says: "One finds out, the other puts (the finding) into effect."[48] He was, however, empowered to draw the attention of the qāḍī to a miscarriage of justice and to delay

[42] A number of regulations are contained in a farmān of 'Ālamgīr I issued in the 15th regnal year. It has been reproduced by Muḥammad 'Alī Khān, i, pp. 277-282.

[43] Al-Andulūsī, Part xi, pp. 158-180 gives the points of view of the various schools on this point.

[44] Kāẓim p. 1078.

[45] 'Abd-u'l-Ḥamīd, i, p. 140.

[46] For the Mughul Empire, Kāẓim, pp. 1075, 1076.

[47] I.H. Qureshi, *The Administration of the Sultanate of Dehli*, pp. 161, 162.

[48] Abū-'l-Faḍl, *Ā'īn-ī-Akbarī*, iii, Ā'īn 4.

the execution of some decisions pending trial by a higher court.[49]

This shows that the qāḍī was concerned with the hearing of the case and after recording and assessing evidence he was to give his ruling and decision. In this he was often assisted by a faqīh or a muftī, who was a trained jurist.[50] For such matters as ensuring the attendance of parties and witnesses and the execution of his decrees he was dependent on the mīr 'adl. Besides, the mīr 'adl was responsible for presenting the accused for trial at the court of the qāḍī. Thus the mīr 'adl looked after the executive branch of justice, the qāḍī being responsible for the hearing of cases and giving decisions.

We find the office of the mīr 'adl well established before the Mughuls[51] but its earlier origins are a little obscure. There is a passage in Māwardī's *Al-aḥkām-u's-sulṭāniyah* which seems to give a clue.[52] While discussing naẓar-fi'l-maẓālim it lays down that the person in charge of it must be sufficiently powerful to enforce his orders, but in case he is given the limited jurisdiction of "enforcing what the qāḍī is unable to enforce" he need not be an officer of such a high rank.[53] The importance of this passage lies in its envisaging an officer for enforcing the decrees of the qāḍī and assisting him in summoning to his presence those who otherwise might not have attended. These in essence are the duties of the mīr 'adl. As Māwardī is well known for basing his book on the practices of his times, it is not unlikely that such an officer was actually appointed, probably when either the nature or the quality of work justified his appointment.

The *Ā'īn* also implies that the primary appointment was that of the qāḍī, if knowledge and capacity to enforce decisions were not found in one man, a mīr 'adl also was to be appointed. In actual practice the mīr 'adl was appointed in most of the important cities.[54]

[49] Fakhr-i-Mudabbir, ff. 45b-46b.

[50] Al-Sarkhasī, Part xvi, p. 61.

[51] I.H. Qureshi, *The Administration of the Sultanate of Dehlī*, pp. 161, 162.

[52] Māwardī, p. 73.

[53] There is an identical passage in Farra. The two authors, Māwardī and Farra were contemporaries.

[54] 'Alī Muḥammad Khān, i, 263.

Next in importance to qaḍā came maẓālim. The institution is said to have come into existence before the beginning of the Prophet's mission. It is reported that there had been instances where some powerful residents of Mecca had seized the goods of strangers who had come for a pilgrimage when Abū Sufiyān and 'Abbās bin 'Abd-u'l-Muṭṭalib persuaded the Quraish to enter into a covenent to prevent such highhandedness.[55] The Prophet who was twentyfive at that time was present. "A deed of the days of ignorance that had been dictated by political necessity, became, because of the presence of the Prophet and through his insistence, an act of the Prophet and an injunction of the shar'.[56] It is reported that the Prophet himself sat to hear cases of maẓālim.[57] There can be little doubt that with the growth of the Muslim empire, the caliphs must have attended to complaints against their officials, but the institution does not seem to have been well defined until towards the end of 'Alī's tenure of office, when, because of the growing tensions within the body politic, cases of highhanded-ness began to engage the caliph's attention, even though they were not frequent enough to make it necessary for him to set aside any definite time for maẓālim.[58] It is said that 'Abd-u'l-Malik bin Marwān was the first caliph to set aside a day for sitting as a court of maẓālim, though he assigned the duties of inquiry and judgment to his qāḍī. It was, however, understood that the qāḍī was acting on behalf of and under the direct supervision of the caliph who kept himself informed about the case at all stages of the procedure. 'Umar ibn 'Abd-u'l-'Azīz took the entire procedure in his hands. Thus was established the tradition of a separate court of māẓalim, either presided over by the monarch himself or by his nominee who was a high official of the state.[59] By the time of the Mughul conquest it had become customary in the subcontinent for the monarch to set aside a day for sitting as a court of maẓalim.[60]

[55] Māwardī, p. 75.

[56] *Ibid.*, p. 76.

[57] a'n-Nuwairī, vi, pp. 268, 269.

[58] Māwardī, pp. 73, 74.

[59] *Ibid.*, p. 74.

[60] I.H. Qureshi, *The Administration of the Sultanate of Dehlī*, p. 158.

The Mughul emperors, like their predecessors took pains to keep in touch with their subjects. Akbar showed himself every morning to his subjects, where any one could draw the attention of the monarch by raising his hand holding a petition.[61] He was then escorted by mace-bearers to the imperial audience in the dawlat-khānah-i-khāṣ where the hearing took place. If the case required an inquiry, it was ordered. Cases were decided in accordance with the shar'.[62] Where the shar' did not apply, customary law, principles of equity or the regulations of the state were applied.[63] Later 'Ālamgīr I abolished the jharokah-i-darshan because it smacked of the deification of the monarch in his view,[64] but steps were taken to ensure the access of complainants to the monarch. The emperors maintained the custom of earmarking a day of the week for the purpose of holding a court of maẓālim.[65] It was attended by the officers of the court, the qāḍī-i-'askar, jurists and others learned in law.[66]

The jurists have discussed at length the constitution of a court of maẓālim. It must contain men well versed in inquiry and the assessment of evidence as well as learned lawyers for a proper application of the law.[67] The jurisdiction of such courts embraced, above all, complaints of high-handedness or injustice against the servants of the state. It also took cognizance of cases arising out of disobedience to a qaḍā court. Sometimes such cases as could not be tried in the qāḍī's court under the normal procedures of law were dealt with by the courts of maẓālim because they did not consider themselves bound by all the niceties of legal procedure, if the ends of justice could be better obtained by following a different method.[68] A qaḍā court limited itself to legal obligations, but

[61] The jharokah-i-darshan, Abū'l-Faḍl, *Ā'īn-i-Akbari*, i, Ā'īn 73; *Dastūr-u'l-'amal-i-āgāhī* f. 7a; Kāẓim, p. 1098.

[62] 'Abd-u'l-Ḥamīd, i, p. 145, Kāẓim, pp. 1097, 1098.

[63] *Ibid.*

[64] Khawāfī Khān, p. 213.

[65] 'Abd-u'l-Ḥamīd, i, p. 150; Chandra Bhān Brahman, *Qawā'id-i-salṭanat-i-Shāh Jahān*, p. 60; Kazim, p. 1102.

[66] *Ibid.*

[67] Māwardī, pp. 76-80.

[68] *Ibid.*, p. 79.

a maẓālim court had wider authority because it could take cognizance of extra-juridical matters in public interest, if such action was legally permissible.[69] A comparatively modern statement that maẓālim constituted courts of appeal is only partially correct,[70] because there were only two categories of cases which could be taken to a court of maẓālim from the court of the qāḍī. One of these has already been mentioned. If the qāḍī could not enforce his orders, the monarch or his nominee undertook to do so. The other consisted of cases where a qāḍī's bonafides were questioned. This obviously came under maẓālim because such cases concerned the behaviour of a public official. If the qāḍī had failed, because of his limited powers, to get at the facts, the case could be taken up by the maẓālim, because certain methods of investigation were available to rulers which the qāḍī could not employ in collecting or sifting evidence.[71]

In the beginning there was no distinction between ordinary and political crimes and both were tried by the qāḍīs, but soon considerations of state led to a special treatment of crimes committed for political reasons. The murderers of the caliph 'Uthmān were never tried. In course of time, especially under the Abbasids, the tradition grew up of placing political crimes under the special jurisdiction of the monarch. It was, however, understood that the monarch should not transgress the shar'.[72]

Under the Sultans of Dehlī there were instances of the execution of rebels and prisoners of war at the instance of the monarch. With his characteristic thoroughness Muḥammad bin Tughluq organized a department called dīwān-i-siyāsat for inquiry into political crimes. This department included jurists, who were asked to make it certain that no one should be punished against the law.[73]

The Mughul emperors considered themselves authorized to exe-

69 *Ibid.*, Al-Farrā has parallel passages for most of these references.

70 Jurjī Zaidān, part i, p. 187.

71 Māwardī, p. 79.

72 al-Kalabī, pp. 6-62.

73 I.H. Qureshi. *The Administration of the Sultanate of Dehlī*, pp. 157, 158.

cute refractory and rebellious persons. There were occasions, albeit rare, when a monarch ordered the execution of some one without adequate reasons, having been overcome with sudden anger. For instance Akbar executed a poor wretch who was found asleep in the palace when he should have been lighting the candles.[74] More justified was his execution of Adham Khān who was not only guilty of the assassination of Atgah Khān but whose intentions about Akbar as well were in all probability criminal.[75] Despite such aberrations, the Mughuls were normally lenient rulers and rebels and enemies were more often pardoned than treated harshly. There is the classic example of Humāyūn who was so tolerant of the rebellious activities of his brothers that they lost all fear of punishment. Ultimately, Kāmrān, who had given no peace to Humāyūn was punished at the instance of Humāyūn's generals who were tired of fighting fruitless battles for their forgiving master.[76] In spite of this his life was spared. Similarly Khusraw was not dealt with severely until Jahāngīr's officers insisted upon proper punishment being meted out to the prince.[77]

'Ālamgīr is reported to have been so averse to inflicting capital punishment that his administration suffered in consequence.[78] Even then he realized that political exigencies sometimes demanded extra legal measures.[79] His predilections are apparent from the punishments that he prescribed for rebellion.[80] He laid it down that if a group of persons were rebellious and were

[74] Vincent Smith, *Akbar*, p. 118.
Akbar perhaps thought the person to be deliberately disrespectful to light and fire which the emperor considered to be sacred.

[75] Abū-'l-Faḍl, *Akbarnāmah*, ii, pp. 174-176.

[76] Gulbadan Begam, pp. 95, 96.

[77] Beni Prasad, p. 165.

[78] Khawāfī Khān, ii, p. 550.

[79] He wrote, "It is my desire that I should eschew all sin, especially the sin of injustice. However, because empire cannot endure without political punishment, sometimes orders are issued on the basis of exigencies. In these, consciously or unconsciously, my own desires play a part. I consulted the learned on this point: (they gave the opinion that) through the grace of God (my) intentions are sincere, therefore, perhaps, there may be no blame. 'Verily all actions are subservient to intentions' is a true hadith and has been repeated by various chains of narrators." Ashraf Khān, f. 21b.

[80] *Ibid.*

engaged in warlike preparations and equipping themselves for hostilities, but if they still had not taken up positions, they should be seized and imprisoned until they repented. In case actual hostilities had started, military action had to be taken against them. If the rebels repented, all their belongings were to be restored to them.[81]

We, however, do not hear of any special department having been organized for dealing with political crimes. The sentence was pronounced by the monarch in consultation with his officials. Legal opinion regarding the propriety of the punishment was generally obtained.[82] The emperor and his chief advisers may be said to have constituted a court martial when they tried political crimes. These powers were delegated for minor rebellions to governors and generals,[83] though all cases where capital punishment was recommended had to be referred to the emperor for final orders.[84] ʻĀlamgīr I appointed a group of jurists to try Dārā Shikūh. It is obvious that this was a political trial. Dārā Shikūh had been the leader of the heterodox group and an opponent of orthodoxy. Indeed he was likely to be a second Akbar and would have proved more effective because he was learned.[85] The trial by learned jurists was meant to demonstrate to the orthodox that the empire had been saved from a revival of heresy by Awrangzīb's success in coming to the throne. Besides ʻĀlamgīr I wanted to demonstrate that his treatment of his father was justified. His subjects in whom feelings of filial piety were deeply engrained would understand his action better if the issue were clearly brought out and adjudicated by prominent doctors of the sharʻ. Their pronouncement that Dārā Shikūh's religious opinions amounted to apostasy was of considerable importance. If Dārā Shikūh was an apostate, ʻĀlamgīr I had fought for a cause, not for himself; if in that process Shāh Jahān had to be deposed,

[81] *Ibid.*

[82] Kāẓim, p. 1078.

[83] Kewal Rām, f. 165b.

[84] *Ibid.*

[85] For Dārā Shikūh's views and learning see Ḥasrat.

it was not an act of filial impiety, but a necessary sacrifice for a higher cause. Hence the case had to be referred to a special tribunal consisting of theologians and jurists. This was tantamount to the handing over of a case to a civil court because it was thought that the Emperor being a party himself should not try the case.

The existence of the courts of maẓālim and the prerogative of the sovereign to decide what treatment should be meted out to criminals and rebels has caused considerable confusion in the writings of later writers who give the impression that the emperor concerned himself with all kinds of cases. It is true that in accordance with the Islamic theory of law, the caliph is the enforcer of the shar' which also includes the functions of the supreme arbiter in the realm. In this sense the Mughul emperor was the fountain of justice; but there were well defined institutions through which it was dispensed and there were only two categories of cases—siyāsat and maẓālim—that formed part of the monarch's personal jurisdiction. Only a small proportion of cases fell under these categories.

A large number of cases were never referred to the courts instituted by the government. The villages, in accordance with hoary traditions of self-government, had panchāyats, or councils of the leading inhabitants, who decided most disputes. As they were fully cognizant of happenings in their small communities, the chances of a miscarriage of justice were meagre. In the towns as well the guild and caste panchāyats were active. They not only acted as arbitrators but also as courts to try petty offences. The punishments took the forms of public humiliation, fines and ostracism for periods conforming to the seriousness of the offence. Disobedience always was punished with ostracism until the offender submitted. Ostracism had grave social and economic consequences, especially in a caste ridden society, hence the order of the panchāyats were invariably obeyed. In cases of grave offences, like murder or robbery, the matter was taken out of the hands of the panchāyats and the issues were decided by a court of law.

A judicial system depends for its utility on the spirit that animates it. The Muslim tradition has been to look upon dispensing justice as an act of worship.[86] A tradition of the Prophet in which he is reported to have said that a moment spent in the dispensation of justice is better than seventy years of devotion was held in high esteem and widely quoted.[87] "Dominion can subsist in spite of misbelief", says the *Siyāsatnāmah*, "but it cannot endure with the existence of injustice."[88] The Mughuls had a high sense of justice. They did not like their sons or the high officials of the state to act as tyrants. "If I were guilty of an unjust act, I would rise in judgment against myself", said Akbar, "what shall I say then of my sons, my kindred and others?"[89] 'Ālamgīr I saw to it that the highest in the land obeyed the orders of the courts, even though they were summoned to answer the complaint of a beggar.[90] Jahāngīr punished a noble of the standing of Muqarrab Khān on the complaint of an old woman.[91] This emperor took pride in the fact that the first order of his reign was to construct "a chain of justice" which anyone seeking the protection of the monarch against the injustice of any of his officials could pull to raise an alarm in the palace.[92] He was so scrupulous that even illness did not prevent him from attending to his public duties; he appeared regularly in the jharokhah-i-darshan and the dīwān-i-khāṣ wa 'ām.[93] Shāh Jahān's historian considered it the chief purpose of monarchy that the weak should be protected against the oppression of the mighty and "in ordering the affairs of his fellow beings, the monarch should be a friend and a helper through justice and (the imposition of) equality (before law)."[94] The sin for which 'Ālamgīr I had the greatest

[86] a'n-Nuwairī, vi, al-Jarrāḥī, ii, p. 58.

[87] *e.g.*, Māhrū, Letter xix.

[88] Niẓām-u'l-mulk, p. 8.

[89] Abū-'l-Faḍl, "*Ā'īn-i-Akbarī*", v, p. 234.

[90] Kāẓim, pp. 1075, 1076.

[91] Jahāngīr, p. 83.

[92] *Ibid.*, p. 3. The chain was made of gold. It was 30 yards long and 60 bells were attached to it.

[93] *Ibid.*, p. 130.

[94] 'Abd-u'l-Ḥamīd, i, p. 143.

horror was injustice.[95] The sayings of the monarchs and their efforts to realize their ideals, even the sentiments of their historians, cannot be dismissed lightly as being mere cant, because they have not been accused by their contemporaries of injustice. Besides, it was natural that they should say what was expected of them, which is a sure indication of the ideals of monarchy during the period.

An important adjunct of the judicial administration was the department of hisbah. It was subordinate to the dīwān-i-qāḍā and worked under its general supervision. The functions of the muḥtasib were, however, distinct from those of the qāḍī. The muḥtasib was theoretically responsible for the maintenance of the Islamic code of morals and behaviour.[96] It was his duty to ensure the smooth working of the Muslim society and to remove causes of public inconvenience and infringement of undisputed rights. Māwardī points out that ḥisbah stands between qāḍā and maẓālim.[97] The qādī's duty was to adjudicate on disputes and he could not take cognizance of any matter that was not brought before him. The muhtasib's jurisdiction extended only to disputes relating to weights and measures, adulteration or fraud in merchandize and loans that were not disputed and yet which were not paid despite the debtor's capacity to meet his obligation. Such cases were within the jurisdiction of the muhtasib because they fell in the category of obvious misdemeanours.[98] Besides the maintenance of proper standards of probity in trade is an important factor in the smooth functioning of society. Ḥisbah was distinct from maẓālim because the latter dealt with matters where the qāḍī was incapable of enforcing his orders, whereas the qāḍī's jurisdiction was purposely restricted in matters which were dealt with by the muḥtasib.[99] Even in the matters where the muḥtasib normally had jurisdiction, if the facts were in dispute

[95] Ashraf Khān, f. 21b.
[96] Māwardī p. 228.
[97] *Ibid.*
[98] *Ibid.*
[99] *Ibid.*, p. 229.

and needed judicial trial, he had no power.[100] For instance if the debtor denied the debt, the case had to go to the qāḍī. Similarly if the facts regarding short measure, adulteration or fraud in transactions were disputed the matter had to be decided by the qāḍī.[101] The main difference between qāḍā, maẓālim and iḥtisāb was that the qāḍī was a judge; the president of a maẓālim court was an executive officer endowed with certain judicial functions; the muḥtasib was purely an executive officer.

The muḥtasib was expected to perform a number of humanitarian duties. He was not to permit maltreatment of slaves and servants.[102] He was to prevent cruelty to animals, so that they were not overloaded, made to work beyond their capacity or otherwise ill-used.[103] He was to arrange for the care of foundlings and orphans.[104] Schoolmasters were not to be immoderate in inflicting punishment upon children.[105] He was responsible for the proper maintenance of the public utilities. He was to see that the water supply, the city walls, the public thoroughfares, the markets, hospices and inns were all maintained properly. The amenities existing for travellers were in his care. Areas earmarked for the encampment of caravans were not only to be maintained but if too many caravans arrived at the same time, priorities for the use of these areas were to be fixed by him.[106] He was to see that river and seaports were kept in good condition and that boats were sea worthy and not overloaded.[107] In the city itself it was his duty to prevent encroachments on public thoroughfares and squares,[108] to order the demolition of structures which were likely to collapse and endanger life.[109] He was to forbid the use of high buildings if

100 Māwardī, p. 229.

101 *Ibid.*, Ibn Khaldūn, i, p. 406.

102 Māwardī, pp. 234, 243, 244.

103 *Ibid.*

104 Von Kraemer, pp. 292-296.

105 Māwardī, pp. 233, 234, 240, 241; Ibn Khaldūn, i, p. 406.

106 Māwardī, p. 178.

107 Ibn Khaldūn, i, p. 406; Māwardī, p. 244.

108 *Ibid.*

109 Ibn Khaldūn, i, p. 406.

they interfered with the privacy of the neighbours.[110] In short he discharged many of the duties of modern municipal government. He dealt with "matters arising out of the continuous transaction among the inhabitants of a city without which civilization cannot find fulfilment or maintain itself in accordance with the principles of justice."[111]

The muḥtasib has sometimes been called the censor of public morals. This title is justified only to the extent that it was his duty not to permit any public violation of the law or decencies. It was not within his province to pry into the affairs of the people or break into their privacy.[112] In purely religious matters he was to prohibit the dissemination of heretical opinions among the Muslims, though this did not involve the suppression of opinions held valid by the different orthodox schools of Islam.[113] He most definitely had no jurisdiction over the religions of the dhimmis. It was, however, his concern to ensure the observance of public decencies by the dhimmis.[114] He was also expected to see that the public prayers were organized.[115] As a corollary it was his duty to maintain the mosques in a proper state of repairs. Where the mosque was under the management of a local community he was to use persuasion to induce it to undertake repairs or reconstruction; where state aid was necessary he was to approach the government for help.[116]

The most important section of the muḥtasib's duties was the supervision of the markets. The Prophet laid great emphasis upon fair dealings and he took a stern view of any attempt on the part of the vendor to defraud the buyer. He is reported to have said, "Those guilty of adulteration do not belong to us"[117] The Prophet

[110] Māwardī, p. 243.

[111] Ḥājī Khalifah, i, column 15.

[112] Māwardī, pp. 238, 239. Hence the Persian saying: محتسب را درون خانه چه کار

[113] Māwardī, pp. 228, 236.

[114] *Ibid.*, pp. 237, 238.

[115] *Ibid.*, pp. 230-232.

[116] *Ibid.*, pp. 232, 233.

[117] Quoted by Māwardī, p. 240, also from Tirmidhi by 'Abd-u'l-Ḥayy, i, p. 285. Also vide Tirmidhi, p. 169.

took personal interest in the maintenance of standards of fair dealing and honesty in the market.[118] After the conquest of Mecca, he appointed a supervisor of its market.[119] Under 'Umar the muḥ asib emerged with many duties which have generally been associated with his office ever since.[120] Māwardī has gone into details about the muḥtasib's duties in connection with the control of the market. He prescribes the use of weights and measures bearing the imprint of the seal of the muḥtasib and holds the opinion that those using unauthorized weights and measures should be punished. In case a person forges the seal, he should be treated in the same manner as those who forge currency.[121] Though the muḥtasib was responsible for seeing that no one charged excessive prices, it was not within his province to control prices artificially, because any undue interference with economic factors would be injurious to society. Some jurists, however, permit the control of the prices of essential commodities in case of scarcity.[122] Māwardī is of opinion that the muḥtasib should not only keep an eye on merchants and craftsmen, but also on certain professions that are of public importance. For instance it was necessary to see that teachers and physicians were adequately qualified and possessed the necessary qualities of character for these important professions.[123]

The duties of the muḥtasib having been incorporated into the s̲h̲ar', his post became a part of the organization of the departments of justice and religious affairs. With the establishment of Muslim rule in the subcontinent of India and Pakistan, the office of the muḥtasib came into existence in accordance with tradition and the s̲h̲ar', though the duty of controlling prices was vested in a different officer.[124] This was done probably because of the doubtful validity of price control according to the Ḥanafī school.

[118] *Ibid.*

[119] *Ibid.*, p. 285.

[120] *Ibid.*, pp. 285, 286.

[121] Māwardī, p. 240.

[122] *Ibid.*, p. 243.

[123] *Ibid.*, p. 242.

[124] I.H. Qureshi. *The Administration of the Sultanate of Dehlī*, pp. 164-173.

The organization of these departments did not undergo any drastic change and it seems that the muḥtasibs continued to be appointed. The earlier histories do not throw much light on the problem and the *Ā'īn-i-Akbarī* does not even mention the office and the duties of the muḥtasib. This is, however, no indication of the office having fallen into disuse, because the histories mention only the changes effected by the various monarchs in the administration, and the *Ā'īn* also, does not go into the details of the organization of several departments. The departments of religious affairs and justice receive but cursory mention in the *Ā'īn*.

It is, however, quite possible that Akbar did not appoint muḥtasibs because of his aversion to orthodoxy. The *Ā'īn* assigns to the kotwāl some of the functions of the muḥtasib. This is not conclusive evidence because Badā'ūnī, who is generally critical of Akbar's measures, would, in all probability, have mentioned such a drastic step. Besides, if Akbar continued with the appointment of the ṣadr it is less likely that he should have discontinued the appointment of the muḥtasibs. The later authorities however mention the office and make it clear that important cities and townships had muḥtasibs posted in them whose appointment orders were issued by the ṣadr-u'ṣ-ṣudur.[125] Officers posted in the cities were given the rank of 250 dhāt and 10 sawārs. The governor of the province assigned to the muḥtasib a posse of cavalrymen to assist him in his duties, which included the supervision of weights and measures. The muḥtasibs posted in small townships were paid suitable salaries in cash or given assignments in land.[126] Some authorities also mention parganah muḥtasibs[127] which would imply a rural jurisdiction as well. It is more likely, however, that they were posted at the parganah headquarters.

The silence of the earlier authorities on the topic of iḥtisāb can be further explained by the fact that there was no chief muḥtasib, either for the entire empire or the provinces. The appointment and supervision of the local muḥtasibs was the duty of the ṣadr-

[125] 'Alī Muḥammad Khān, *Supplement*, p. 250.

[126] *Ibid.*, p. 251.

[127] Shākir Khān, p. 145b.

u'ṣ-ṣudur and the provincial ṣūbahdārs. 'Ālamgīr I, however, thought it necessary to appoint a learned and pious theologian as the chief muḥtasib of the empire to ensure the observance of the moral code of Islam. The person selected was Mullā Wajīh of Tūrān who was given the rank of 1000 dhāt and 100 sawār with a salary of fifteen thousand rupees per annum. A body of manṣabdārs and aḥadis was attached to him so that his orders could be enforced.[128]

The Mughuls calculated the cash value of the state demand on agricultural produce on the basis of the prices of the various commodities prevalent in a locality. For this purpose it was necessary to provide for regular reports of the rates prevalent in the local market. This duty was assigned to an official called karorah.[129] He seems to have been posted at the capital. There were nirkhīs posted at various places to keep an eye on the prices.[130] When he found that because of a temporary shortage or hoarding, the price of a commodity had been unreasonably increased, he interfered and fixed a proper price. It is obvious that this was done with circumspection and due regard to economic factors otherwise the system could not have worked. 'Ālamgīr I, however, abolished price control because it was pointed out to him by the 'ulamā that it was not permitted by the shar' as the vendor had the legal right to sell his property at any price that he liked.[131] This view was based on the ruling of the Ḥanafī school of jurisprudence; the Mālikīs do not subscribe to it. The department of price control does not seem to have been under the muḥtasib under the Mughuls and appears to have functioned under the supervision of the kotwāl.[132] Some of the duties of the muḥtasib have been assigned to the kotwāl in the *Ā'īn*. For instance he is required to keep an eye on weights and measures, to forbid the manufacture and sale of intoxicating drinks and to provide for separate access to wells and rivers to

[128] Kāẓim, p. 392.

[129] Khwājah Yāsīn, f. 76b.

[130] Khawāfī Khān, ii, p. 395. Nirkhī is from nirkh, price rate.

[131] *Ibid.*, p 396.

[132] Abū-'l-Faḍl, *Ā'īn-i-Akbarī*, iii Ā'īn 6.

women.[133] It is not clear whether these duties were performed by the kotwāl in cooperation with the muḥtasib or independently; nor, as has been mentioned, can it be determined with certainty whether Akbar did appoint muḥtasibs at all.

The institution of police like so many administrative organs of Muslim polities can be traced to the days of the Prophet in whose days Sa'd bin Abī Waqāṣ is said to have taken upon himself the duty of night watchman. Later it seems that the Prophet appointed several persons to guard Medina at night. Abū Bakr appointed 'Umar as the police chief of Medina and when 'Umar became the caliph he himself took up the duties of the chief police officer.[134] In the earlier period the police was called 'asas. Later it seems to be called shurṭah. It was subordinate to the qāḍī, because its main purpose was to execute the decrees of the qāḍī and to bring criminals before him for trial.

In the Sultanate of Dehlī and the Mughul Empire, the duties of the head of the police, the ṣāḥib-i-shurṭah were performed by an officer known as kotwāl.[135] Originally the word was probably used for the commandant of a fort, when he had some police duties attached to his office as well. Under the Sultans of Dehli, however, he had become a police officer.[136]

The *Ā'īn-i-Akbarī* has a full description of his duties under Akbar. If the duties assigned to him in connection with Akbar's religious measures are taken out of this account, they correspond reasonably well with the duties of the kotwāl under the sultans. Apart from the special duties assigned to him because of Dīn-ī-Ilāhī which will be discussed later, the kotwāl was expected to guard streets of the city during the night. It was his duty to keep a census of the houses and to organize them into muḥallahs, the inhabitants of which had to give a written undertaking of helping one another in all emergencies. A leading citizen was appointed the head of the locality, who was to keep a record of all new-

[133] *Ibid.*

[134] 'Abd-u'l-Ḥayy, pp. 292, 293.

[135] Originally a word of Hindu origin. Kot-fort, wāl-keeper. The *t* in kot is hard, but because of its adoption by the Turks, in kotwal, it is soft.

[136] I.H. Qureshi, *The Administration of the Sultanate of Dehlī*, p. 173.

comers and of those who left. This record was regularly handed over to the office of the kotwāl. In addition, the kotwāl had to keep a number of spies and informers who kept him informed of all illegal and criminal activities. He was also to organize the guilds of different categories of craftsmen and professions and recognize some honest person as the head of each guild, so that he could ensure honesty of transactions. He was to maintain a separate inn for strangers whose record was to be kept carefully. After a part of the night was over, he was to stop the movement of the citizens. He was responsible for catching thiefs and finding out stolen property. If he failed in finding and restoring the stolen property to its rightful owner, he was held responsible for the loss and had to pay the damages out of his own pocket. It has already been mentioned that under Akbar he was assigned some of the duties of the muḥtasib, like the supervision of weights and measures and seeing that people were not defrauded through faulty or unauthorized coins. He was also to see that there was no encroachment on the public streets and that they were kept clean. As the muḥtasib was entrusted with the enforcement of the public morality of Islam, under Akbar the kotwāl was expected to enforce the tenets of Dīn-i-Ilāhī. For instance he was to see that butchers, bird trappers, washers of dead bodies and sweepers lived in separate quarters and did not mix with others, that people did not mix with executioners, that animals were not slaughtered on certain days held holy by the followers of Dīn-i-Ilāhī and that cows, buffaloes, horses and camels were not slaughtered at all.[137] With the cancellation of such regulations on the accession of Jahāngīr (and perhaps earlier), these duties also died a natural death. The later authorities do not assign to the kotwāl any of the traditional duties of the muḥtasib, though it was his duty to cooperate with the muḥtasib in the enforcement of public morality.[138] The prisons were under the kotwāl. Orders for imprisonment and release were passed by the qāḍī.[139] Police duties in the rural areas were in charge of the fawjdārs whose functions will be mentioned later.

137 Abū-l'-Faḍl, *Ā'in-i-Akbari*, iii, Ā'īn 6.

138 This is apparent from the description of the kotwal's duties under 'Ālamgir I as mentioned in *Kaifiyat-i-ṣūbajāt-i-mumālik-i-maḥrūsah-i-Hindustān*, f. 224a.

139 *Ibid*.

CHAPTER X

Religious Affairs, Education and the Patronage of Culture

THE Department of Religious Affairs was under the ṣadr-u'ṣ-ṣudūr. The offices of the qāḍī-u'l-quḍāt, the chief judge of the empire, and of the ṣadr-u'ṣ-ṣudūr were generally combined. In case they were kept separate, the ṣadr-u'ṣ-ṣudūr took precedence and was responsible for the judicial administration and religious affairs of the realm[1] and the qāḍī-u'l-quḍāt simply held court as the chief judge./ The office of the ṣadr-u'ṣ-ṣudūr originated with the institution of the post of the qāḍī-u'l-quḍāt under the Abbasids when Imām Abū Yūsuf was given the authority to appoint the qāḍīs outside the capital.[2] In the Sultanate of Dehlī, however, the office existed from the beginning.[3] The Mughuls not only continued it but, in the beginning, they also attached the same importance to it as had been by the sultans. Abū-'l-Faḍl writing of the appointment of Shaikh 'Abdu'n-Nabī in the 10th regnal year says that it is important that "a

[1] Abū-'l-Faḍl, *Ā'in-i-Akbarī*, ii, Ā'in 19.

[2] Ā'n-Nakdī, p. 9.

[3] I.H. Qureshi, *The Administration of the Sultanate of Dehlī*, pp. 175, 176.

person distinguished for his wisdom, foresight, truthfulness, integrity and understanding should be appointed to the exalted post of the ṣadr. He should be one who has the virtues of faith, sincerity and kindness, so that through him the poor, the deserving and the needy may attain the good fortune of kissing the sublime threshold and receive, in accordance with their condition and talent, stipends and grants from the emperor.[4] Four categories of persons were considered deserving to get aid from the state through the ṣadr-u'ṣ-ṣudūr. The first were "the seekers of wisdom who do not distinguish the night from the day in acquiring true knowledge" and "who have withdrawn their hand from everything else".[5] The second consisted of persons "who had declared war on their own desires" and in search of spiritual advancement had "turned their faces away from the people of the world." The third were helpless persons who did not have the capacity of earning a livelihood. The fourth were people of good birth "who through their shortsightedness had not learnt a profession."[6] Thus the learned, the religious recluses, those incapable of work and persons of good birth lacking the necessary training for earning the means of sustenance were the concern of the ṣadr-u'ṣ-ṣudūr.

As the head of the Department of Religious Affairs, he was responsible for the appointment of the qāḍis and the muḥtasibs, because these offices were considered to be of a religious nature. In areas where the local community was not able to maintain a mosque, the ṣadr appointed the staff and provided for the expenses.[7] It was open to any group of Muslims to appoint an imām of their choice in a mosque, but if the imām asked for a grant from the state, his case was dealt with by the Department of Religious Affairs, where his qualifications were scrutinized and a suitable grant was made. Thus the ṣadr's department had a say in the choice of imāms. To some big mosques khaṭibs, or preachers also were attached. The imāms and khaṭibs were graduates of colleges

[4] Abū-'l-Faḍl, *Akbarnāmah*, ii, p. 247.

[5] Abū-'l-Faḍl, *Ā'in-i-Akbarī*, ii, Ā'in 19.

[6] *Ibid.*

[7] Kāẓim, p. 1085.

who had specialized in theology and sometimes in tajwīd, or the skill of reciting the Qur'ān correctly in accordance with Arab accent and pronunciation.

Akbar's quarrel with 'Abd-u'n-Nabī has been already discussed. Its repercussions on the general policies of the state and the position of the monarchy have also been mentioned.[8] It was inevitable that the Department of Religious Affairs which hitherto had been the stronghold of orthodoxy, also should be affected. Abū-'l-Faḍl would have us believe that even before the appointment of 'Abd-u'n-Nabī as the ṣadr-u'ṣ-ṣudūr, there were complaints of corruption against the department. It was for this reason that 'Abd-u'n-Nabī was appointed. "The land grants given to the Afghans and the chaudharīs" were annulled and other grantees were subjected to the new ṣadr's scrutiny. It seems that the purpose was to deprive those who had been classified by the Afghans under the category of "men of noble birth who, through lack of foresight, had not learnt a profession", because it was not considered politic to give such support to the scions of the defeated race. The reason for scrutinizing the grants of others also seems to have been to eliminate the notion that the beneficiaries owed their means of livelihood to the munificence of the previous dynasty. Those who were found deserving after the scrutiny were confirmed in their grants. Their holdings were, however, scattered, and, therefore, orders were given to consolidate the holdings. The reason was that the grants given by the Department of Religious Affairs were mostly small and the grantees could not deal with the powerful jāgīrdārs or the officers of the government. To save the grantees from difficulties separate areas were marked for the suyūrghāl grants, as they were known under the Mughuls. Then Abū-'l-Faḍl goes on to say that "stories began to reach the ears" regarding 'Abd-u'n-Nabī as well. This statement may be dismissed as a part of the general campaign to vilify the orthodox ulema, because we have seen that 'Abd-u'n-Nabī was a man of courage and convictions. As Akbar was determined to break the power of orthodoxy, he first victimized the more prominent ulema

[8] Vide supra Chapters II and IX.

who had grants of five hundred bighas or more. Their grants were suspended pending inquiry by the Emperor himself. As this did not produce the desired effect, it was ordered that every grant of more than a hundred bighas, that had not already been scrutinized, should be split up into five parts, three of which were to be resumed. Thus these grantees were deprived of sixty per cent of their income—only Irānī and Tūrānī ladies were left alone. If a person requested for a transfer of his grant from one place to another, a reduction of twentyfive per cent was made. It seems that all these measures did not break the spirit of the judiciary and the orthodox religious leaders, therefore, Akbar took the extraordinary step of dismissing all the qādīs who had been appointed before the time of Sultan Khwājah, who was a member of Dīn-i-Ilāhī.[9] Thus orthodoxy had received a mortal blow, but Akbar was still not satisfied. It seems that the subsequent ṣadrs who were all members of his Dīn-i-Ilāhī did not show the same enthusiasm in persecuting the orthodox grant holders as Akbar had desired, therefore there was a fresh scrutiny under Ṣadr Jahān who worked under the supervision of Abū-'l-Faḍl.

These facts have been taken from the *Ā'īn-i-Akbarī*[10] and, therefore, may be considered to be the official record of what transpired. They find confirmation in the pages of Badā'ūnī as well. As all the grantees "from the eastern districts upto Bhakkar on the Indus" had been asked to get their grants scrutinized, it is obvious that they were put to great hardship. The subordinate officials and others in the Department found an opportunity for corruption, but Badā'ūnī, who was no friend of 'Abd-u'n-Nabī and is critical of his arrogance, does not even hint that the Shaikh was corrupt. His main grouse is that 'Abd-u'n-nabī was niggardly in his grants. This was because he had to carry out the Emperor's directive that too much land should not be given away.[11] Badā'ūnī says that ultimately, under the influence of Abū-'l-Faḍl and Shaikh Mubārak many Muslim families were ruined.[12] This must have happened to

9 Badā'ūnī, ii, p. 340.
10 Abū-'l-Faḍl, *Ā'īn-i-Akbarī*, ii, Ā'īn 19.
11 Badā'ūnī, ii, pp. 204-205.
12 *Ibid.*, p. 199.

the families of all the dismissed qāḍīs. Gradually there was so little left for the ṣadr to do that the office sank into insignificance, even though the succeeding ṣadrs were members of the Dīn-i-Ilāhī.[13] This is also a commentary on the failure of Akbar's policy of persecuting the orthodox ulema. Except for some flattering courtiers, who perhaps were employed at the capital, few seem to have come forward in the countryside to ask for fresh grants, because Badā'ūnī informs us that the areas which had been allocated for suyūrghāls now ran waste.[14] This shows that people were willing to starve but not to compromise with their principles. In view of these facts it is obvious that Akbar's measures were not dictated by the corruption of the earlier ṣadrs or the frauds of the grantees, as Abu-'l-Faḍl would have us believe, but they were enforced in a vain attempt to break the spirit of the grantees and to force them to subscribe to his views. The fault of the grantees was that "the practices of these grant-holders did not come up to the wise counsels of His Majesty."[15] A good deal has been written on Akbar's religious views, but few facts are as revealing as his measures dealing with the suyūrghāls.

The grants were given in various forms. If given in cash, they were called waẓīfah; if a grant of land was made it was called suyūrghāl, though the older names of milk and madad-i-ma'āsh were used more often. These lands were hereditary and the grants were not conditional upon service, hence they come to be called milk or property, unlike jāgīrs which were assignments on revenue and represented only a method of the payment of the salary attached to the rank or the office. Madad-i-ma'āsh described the real purpose of the grant, because the term means "assistance in subsistence." These lands were also called īmah and the grantees were known īmahdārs, holders of grants.[16] Akbar laid it down that half the land in every grant should be uncultivated and if in previous grants some one had been given all cultivated land, one

[13] *Ibid.*, p. 343.

[14] *Ibid.*

[15] Abū-'l-Faḍl, *Ā'īn-i-Akbarī*, ii, Ā'īn 19.

[16] *Imāh* is a variant of the more correct *Yūmah*, which is a Turkish word meaning daily rations or allowance, *Ghiyāth-u'l-lughāt*.

fourth of the total grant should be taken and a new grant be made for the remainder. In this way the grantee would be left with only three eighths of the original area of cultivated land which was in his possession. The waẓīfah could be paid at daily rates or after specified periods. The ṣadr was assisted by a financial administrator who was styled dīwān-i-sa'ādat.[17]

Shāh Jahān dealt with the affairs of the Department of Religious Affairs in the Dawlat-khānah-i-khāṣ wa 'ām, where the ṣadr-u'ṣ-ṣudūr (also styled as ṣadr-i-kul) read out the recommendations of the provincial ṣadrs (also styled as ṣadr-i-juzw) after having scrutinized them himself and obtained the emperor's orders regarding the grants to be made to them. In the same meeting he made his own recommendations and obtained orders on them as well.[18] Under 'Ālamgīr I as well the same procedure was followed. The main difference was that he dealt with the question of grants in the Dawlat-khānah-i-khāṣ.[19]

The Department of Religious Affairs dealt with only one aspect of charity. It has been mentioned that stipends and land were given through it to men of learning and persons of gentle birth who were incapable of earning a livelihood; in particular ladies left without support were considered deserving of such help. The Mughuls, however, found other ways and means of helping the poor and the destitute.

All the money raised from zakāt on commercial goods for the Muslims was kept in a separate treasury and was earmarked for charitable purposes. The stipends paid to the deserving poor came from this treasury.[20] Under 'Ālamgīr I when jiziyah was reimposed, it was also kept in a separate treasury and was spent on charitable purposes.[21] In important centres a taḥwīldār was appointed to provide for langars or free kitchens which were maintained at important shrines and educational institutions.[22] Cooked food

17 Abū-'l-Faḍl, *Āi'n-i-Akbarī*, ii, Ā'īn 19.

18 'Abd-u'l-Ḥamīd. i, p. 147.

19 Kāẓim, p. 1102.

20 'Alī Muḥammad Khān, *Supplement*, p. 228.

21 *Ibid.*

22 *Ibid.*, p. 186.

was also distributed to the poor, some of whom were given uncooked food instead, presumably because the caste Hindus would not eat anything touched by Muslims.[23] Akbar is reported to have said that it was his desire that mendicancy should disappear from his dominions. He, however, adopted the wrong method of giving alms for this purpose. "Many people were plentifully supplied with means, but because of the malady of avarice, it proved of no avail."[24] Indeed this was not only Akbar's experience. Throughout the period of Muslim rule this kind of charity built up an army of parasites and worthless beggars.

A method of pleasing the monarch was nit͟hār. A sum of money was put into a tray which was brought before the emperor and was then distributed among the poor. It was by no means an imperial prerogative, because nit͟hār was performed for private individuals as well. As charity has been enjoined and highly praised in the Qur'ān, it was believed that it could fight ill fortune of every kind and was an insurance of continued good fortune. When the emperor visited any of his female relations, this ceremony was performed and even the austere 'Ālamgīr I did not frown at it.[25] Sometimes the money was scattered over the head and then collected for distribution among the poor,[26] in processions it was thrown in handfuls into the crowd. It was also customary to perform nit͟hār in absentia[27]. It also was the custom for well to do citizens to make endowments as nit͟hār for the monarch. One interesting incident is the assignment of land to a Hindu by the chaudharīs and qānūngūs of a parganah.[28] This was a Hindu religious grant made as an offering to ward off evil and calamities from the Emperor' 'Ālamgīr I.[29] It is obvious

[23] Brahman, *Qawā'id-i-salṭanat-i-S͟hāh Jahān*, p. 57.

[24] Abū-'l-Faḍl, *Ā'īn-i-Akbarī*, v, p. 231.

[25] Kāẓim, p. 449.

[26] *Ibid.*, 154.

[27] *Ibid.*, p. 365.

[28] *Dastūr-u'l-'amal Awrangzīb 'Ālamgīr Pād͟shāh G͟hāzī*, B.M. f. 198b.

[29] The text runs: "We chaudharīs and qānūngūs in view of the fact that Koklānand Adhikārī has no means of livelihood take into consideration his straitened circumstances and of our free will and inclination transfer to him one bānī of land...in the way of Brāhmotra as a sacrifice for the sacred person (literally, head) of His Imperial Majesty." Brāhmotra is land given in charity in the name of Brahmā.

that such deeds must have won the approbation of the monarch.

The funeral expenses of the destitute were paid out of the funds for charities which were placed in the custody of the qāḍiṣ in all important centres.[30]

Another form of charity was the establishment of hospitals,[31] but this does not seem to have been within the jurisdiction of the Department of Religious Affairs. Under Shāh Jahān and 'Ālamgīr I it became customary for the empress to make recommendations for grants and allowances to deserving women.[32] The emperor passed suitable orders. The orders for regular grants must have been sent to the Department of Religious Affairs and the donations for specific purposes were in all probability paid from the Household funds. In this category would fall the sums of money donated for the dowries and wedding expenses of poor maidens, whose parents, otherwise, would have found it difficult to marry them off.[33] Similarly, if because of famine conditions it was found necessary to give relief to the population, the Department of Religious Affairs does not seem to come into the picture. The state maintained granaries in various parts of the empire, and stocks were released in times of scarcity. The cultivators were required to pay ten seers per bīgah in kind as part of the state demand on agricultural produce, the rest being payable in cash.[34] The government made suitable concessions to the peasants whose crops suffered, sometimes even foregoing the entire revenue. The peasants were helped with loans, called taqāwī.[35]

It was customary every year to appoint a man as Mīr Hājj to lead the pilgrimage to the Hijaz and to send money to the guardians of the sacred shrines,[36] but this also seems to have been done directly by the monarch without any reference to the Department of Religious Affairs.

30 'Alī Muḥammad Khān, i, 338.

31 *e.g.*, Jahāngīr, p. 4.

32 Kāẓim, p. 1104; 'Abd-u'l-Ḥamīd, i, p. 153.

33 *Ibid.*, i, p. 153.

34 Abū-'l-Faḍl, *Ā'īn-i-Akbarī*, ii, Ā'īn 21.

35 *e.g.*, Muḥammad Ṣāliḥ, *'Amal-i-ṣāliḥ*, i, p. 422.

36 *e.g.*, Abū-'l-Faḍl, *Akbarnāmah*, iii, p. 264; Kāẓim, pp. 449, 450.

The Department, however, exercised considerable influence upon education. In all Muslim countries education was not controlled by the state and any person who was qualified and felt the urge could set himself up as a teacher. The jurists have laid it down that the muḥtasib should not permit ill-qualified or disreputable persons to act as teachers.[37] Beyond this there seems to have been no interference by the government. Every educational institution recruited its own teaching staff and ran its affairs as it liked. Many of these institutions were run by private donations or pious endowments. Quite a few, however, received aid in one form or another. Some were given suyūrg͟hāl or grants in land, others were given cash. Very often the institution as such received only a modest grant, but the members of its teaching faculty were given grants in their individual capacity and could, therefore, devote themselves to teaching and academic pursuits.[38] In all Muslim educational institutions no fees were charged and deserving students were supplied not only with books but also with all means of sustenance. The Department of Religious Affairs provided grants for the maintenance of such institutions if an endowment did not exist already for the purpose.[39]

Grants were not made exclusively to Muslim institutions and scholars. A large number of Hindu temples, priests and scholars were recipients of such grants. 'Ālamgīr I is generally accused by non-Muslim authors of discriminating against non-Muslims and even persecuting them. The large number of documents found all over the subcontinent recording grants of land and money to Hindu temples, priests and others, belies the accusation.[40] The schools teaching Sanskrit and Hindu religion were thus benefited. Abū-'l-Faḍl gives a list of the leading spiritual leaders and scholars who received grants from the Department of Religious Affairs. He divides them into five categories. The first includes those whom

[37] Māwardī, p. 242.

[38] Kāẓim, p. 1085.

[39] *Ibid.*

[40] Series of articles by Jnan Chand in *Journal of Pakistan Historical Society*, January 1958, April 1958, July 1958, October 1958, January 1959 and April 1959.

Abū-'l-Faḍl considered to be well versed in matters spiritual as well as intellectual. It includes twenty one persons of whom nine are Hindus. Among those who were considered eminent in the field of spiritual attainments he mentions fifteen, of whom four are Hindus. Among intellectuals who were learned both in religious and profane sciences, he mentions twelve, of whom none is a Hindu. Among those who were eminent philosophers he mentions twenty-two, of whom fifteen are Hindus, of physicians twenty-nine find mention of whom four are Hindus, of those who knew the religious sciences, he mentions fortythree of whom two are Hindus. It is difficult to draw any conclusions from this list because it is not complete. Besides, it cannot be a safe guide even for the reign of Akbar, because all the men mentioned did not necessarily get the grants at the same time.[41] Some included in the list had obviously died or incurred Akbar's hostility at the time the list was drawn.

The Mughul Empire has rightly been called a 'culture state'. Its patronage of learning and education drew scholars from the neighbouring Muslim countries. The patronage was not limited to religious education. Abū-'l-Faḍl mentions the subjects that were taught in schools during Akbar's reign. They include ethics, arithmetic, accounting, agriculture, mensuration, engineering, astronomy, domestic science, civics and politics, medicine, logic, higher mathematics, history, the physical and mechanical sciences and theology.[42] It is true that in the sixteenth century the sciences had not made the rapid strides of the subsequent centuries, but the education imparted was liberal and comprehensive. Religion provided a strong base for this education, but it would be a mistake to think that the entire content of education was religious. The secular sciences and rational disciplines received considerable impetus in the reign of Akbar by the arrival of Mīr Fath-u'llah Shirāzī who introduced the study of the works of the later Muslim philosophers like Muḥaqqiq Dawwānī, Mīr Ṣadr-u'd-dīn, Mīr Ghiyāth-u'd-dīn Manṣūr and Mirzā Jān Mīr. These

[41] Abū-'l-Faḍl, *Ā'īn-i-Akbarī*, ii, pp. 232-235.

[42] Abū-'l-Faḍl, *Ā'īn-i-Akbarī*, ii, Ā'īn 25.

works were introduced in the syllabus giving a great impetus to the study of philosophy.[43] The tradition has persisted even to this day of the inclusion of philosophy, logic and even mathematics in the syllabus of the old fashioned Muslim seminaries in the subcontinent, though the utility of teaching philosophy has suffered because no cognizance has been taken of recent developments in the subjects. Mathematics has suffered for the same reason and also because its practical aspects are ignored.

Education made rapid strides under the continued patronage of the state. 'Ālamgīr I in particular made such liberal grants for educational purposes that even the smaller townships began to produce scholars of great eminence.[44]

Apart from the patronage extended to formal education, the Mughul emperors paid large sums of money to men who devoted themselves to literature or poetry. Abū'l-Faḍl gives the list of the prominent poets who were subsidized by Akbar. Their number reaches the high figure of fiftynine, in spite of the fact that the monarch did "not care for poets" and attached "no weight to a handful of imagination."[45] Among the poets who thrived during the heyday of Mughul rule, some achieved immortality and have been recognized as masters wherever Persian literature has been appreciated. Of these Faidi, 'Urfī, Naẓīrī, Ṣā'ib, and Bedil deserve special mention.

As a vehicle of literary expression prose did not attract the same attention. Even then the period produced a number of good writers. Abū-'l-Fadl, Faiḍī, Badā'ūni and Ni'mat Khān 'Āli were the better known prose writers. 'Ālamgīr I perhaps wrote the best prose of the age. His style was simple, straightforward and terse; yet it achieved an unequalled elegance. The most significant fact about his style is that it was a revolt against the meaningless artificiality of the professional writers of the age. Among other persons of royal lineage, the princess Zib-u'n-nisā distinguished herself as a poetess and Dārā Shikūh as a writer on religious, mystic

[43] Mīr Āzād Bilgrāmī, p. 238.

[44] Nadwi, Saiyyid Sulaimān, *Hayāt-i-Shibli*, p. 1, gives details about the progress made in the eastern districts of modern Uttar Pradesh in India.

[45] Abū-'l-Faḍl, *Ā'īn-i-Akbari*, ii, Ā'īn 30, section relating to poets.

and philosophical subjects. Akbar showed great interest in the translation of the Hindu classics into Persian. The *Mahābhārata*, the *Rāmāyana*, the *Singhāsan Batīsī*, the *Atharva Veda*, the *Harvansha* and the *Rāj Tarangini* were translated under his orders. Dārā Shikūh is well known for his translation of the Upanishad which he called *Sirr-i-Akbar*. A translation of the *Bhagvad Gītā* is also ascribed to him.

The Mughul Empire has earned universal praise for its architectural achievements. Its buildings combine strength with refinement and delicacy; it has been rightly said of the Mughuls that they built like Titans and finished like jewellers. The subcontinent had already developed traditions of Muslim architecture that had produced great buildings like the Quṭb Mīnār and 'Alā'ī Darwāzah at Delhi, the screen in the Masjid Qubbat-u'l-Islām, Sher Shah's tomb at Sasseram and his mosque in the Old Fort of Delhi before Akbar started with his building programme. Bābur and Humāyūn had little time to create any masterpieces, though both of them constructed a number of buildings. Akbar was a great builder and his department for the construction of buildings seems to have been well organized and extensive. Abū-'l-Faḍl talks of the construction of fortresses, palaces, sarā'is, tanks, wells, schools and places of worship. The emperor took a personal interest in the department. Abū-'l-Faḍl emphasises that architecture depicts the ideals of the builder, and says about Akbar that he "gives an expression to his heart and soul in the garment of water and clay".[46] Akbar's greatest buildings were built at Fathpur Sikrī, his capital near Agra, which was abandoned after having been occupied for fifteen years only. Here the buildings fall into two broad categories. The main mosque and Baland Darwāzah are Muslim in style and execution. The palaces have many more features of Hindu architecture. The main reason seems to have been that the Muslim builders had to concentrate on the mosque and its appendage the Baland Darwāzah whereas Hindu craftsmen had to be utilized for the lesser buildings. In these beams,

[46] Abū-'l-Faḍl, *Ā'in-i-Akbari*, i, Ā'īn, 85. The translation is mine. Blochmann's translation is neither literal, nor does it catch the spirit of the original in this instance.

brackets and pillars are much more in evidence. The medium used is red sandstone with some marble ornamentation. The surface decoration carved on the stone is exquisite and justifies Abū-'l-Faḍl's remark that "clever workmen chisel it so skilfully as no turner could do with wood."[47] Abū-'l-Faḍl is reminded of wood because Hindu workmen had a habit of thinking in terms of wood even when they built in stone. The buildings of Fatpḥur Sikrī where Hindu features dominate are no exception.

With Akbar's death the style of architecture took a turn. The Islamic elements began to dominate and arches, domes and vaulted roofs came into greater use than pillars, beams and brackets; the silhouette became more calligraphic with the flowing lines of minarets and domes. Jahāngīr was not a great builder, but under Shāh Jahān Mughul architecture reached the apogee of its development. Red sandstone gave place to marble and tessellation to pietra dura. Shāh Jahān's reign produced mosques like the Motī Masjid of Agra and the Jāmi' Masjid of Delhī, a mausoleum like the Tāj Maḥal, palaces like the Dīwān-i-khāṣ of Delhi and cities like Shāhjahānābād. Under 'Ālamgīr I the Deccan wars did not permit any extensive building programme. Besides, it was difficult to excel the Tāj Maḥal and the Jāmi' Masjid. Yet the Pādshāhī mosque of Lahore and the Motī Masjid of Delhī are not insignificant contributions to architecture

The Mughul emperors are also well known for their patronage of miniature painting. Humāyūn found time in the midst of his exile to visit Tabrīz to meet some of the renowned calligraphists and painters there. He extended an invitation to Mir Sayyid 'Alī of Tabrīz and Khwājah 'Abd-u'ṣ-Ṣamad who paid his respects to Humāyūn at Tabrīz. They later came and joined Humāyūn. Akbar organized a regular department where under the guidance of these two masters others were trained and experiments were made in the use of new materials. The colours were especially improved considerably. The earlier paintings were on cloth but soon paper of very high quality and treated especially came into use. A good number of Hindu artists also received training in the

[47] *Ibid.*, Ā'īn, 86.

new techniques. They were particularly useful in illustrating the Persian translations of the Hindu epics, the *Mahābhārata* and the *Rāmāyana*. Abū-'l-Faḍl gives a good account of the department in which, he says, many manṣabdārs, ahadīs and others held appointments. Humāyūn and Akbar themselves had taken lessons. Akbar personally saw the work of the painters and rewarded them in accordance with the quality of the picture.[48] Akbar's successors continued their interest in painting. The school reached its zenith under Jahāngīr who was not only a great patron but also a connoisseur. His eye was so sharp that he could point out the work of each single artist in a composite work. The school maintained its excellence under Shāh Jahān, though critics are prone to discern weaknesses in the excessive use of gold and elaborate ornamental margins. There was, however, no deterioration in the qualities of composition, delineation or portraiture of character. The artists were still able to depict the very soul of the subject in their painting of the face. Like his predecessors Shāh Jahān himself inspected the paintings of artists like Nādir-u'z-Zamānī.[49] It is generally believed that 'Ālamgīr I's puritanism led to the withdrawal of imperial patronage from the painters which resulted in the decline of the school. This is not true, because 'Ālamgīr I did employ painters. It is a remarkable tribute to his painters that when his son was imprisoned for a while, a portrait of the prince was sent regularly to the Emperor along with the report of the physicians to reassure the imperial father that this son was in good health. There are paintings extant not only of 'Ālamgīr's youth, but also of his old age. There are several in which he is shown directing seiges of famous strongholds of the Deccan or in the midst of other military engagements. The school declined because of over ripeness; it had achieved what it could within its rigidly defined objects. After 'Ālamgīr I's death the empire was so beset with difficulties that it was no longer in a position to extend patronage to the art.

The allied art of calligraphy also received liberal patronage.

[48] Abū-'l-Faḍl, *Ā'īn-i-Akbarī*, ii, Ā'īn, 24.

[49] Brahman, *Qawā'id-i-Salṭanat-i-Shāh Jahān*, p. 54.

Despite Akbar's lack of proper education, he took a personal interest in the work of the calligraphists. The most famous calligraphist of his court was Muḥammad Husain of Kāshmīr, who was given the title of zarrīnqalam,[50] He excelled in the nasta'līq type of characters. The calligraphists were attached to the library, because the monarchs desired to have the best specimens of book production in their collections. This meant not only the employment of excellent calligraphists but also of illuminators, which craft ultimately invaded paintings as well, because the decorations of the margins of books were transferred to the borders of paintings also. Miniature painters also were employed to illustrate the books and some of the best miniatures were produced as illustrations. Just as miniatures were painted separately as well and were kept singly or in albums, pieces of calligraphy also were kept on specially prepared boards (waşlīs) or in albums. Sometimes the obverse of a waşlī would have a painting and the reverse a piece of calligraphy. Calligraphy was extensively used for ornamentation on cloth and buildings. In the latter it lent itself extremely well to surface decoration. Murals had a limited use in palaces and buildings; except for Akbar who decorated one or two buildings with murals, their use was not popular with the Mughuls. Calligraphy, however, was used extensively. The Arabic characters are remarkably suitable for calligraphy. It maintained its vigour much longer than other fine arts encouraged by the Mughuls. The most famous calligraphists of the Mughul period was Yāqūt who was attached to Shāh Jahān's court. Shah Jahān himself was an excellent calligraphist.[51] Though other styles were practised, the most popular was nasta'liq.

Music had reached its high level mark under the Sūrs. Sultan 'Ādil Shāh was himself a great musician: he had two eminent pupils, Bāz Bahādur, the ruler of Mālwah and Miyān Tān Sen. About the latter Abū-'l-Faḍl says, "A singer like him has not been in India for the last thousand years.[52] Judging from the fact that

[50] Abū-'l-Faḍl, *Ā'īn-i-Akbarī*, i, Ā'in, 34.

[51] Brahman, *Qawā'id-i-Salṭanat-i-Shāh Jahān*, p. 52.

[52] Abū-'l-Faḍl, *Ā'īn-i-Akbarī*, ii, Ā'īn, 30.

the populace has forgotten both 'Ādil Shāh Sūr and Bāz Bahādur and Miyān Tān Sen's reputation lives even today as the greatest musician that this subcontinent has produced, Miyān Tān Sen must have deserved the praise bestowed upon him by Abū-'l-Faḍl, who was not lavish in his praise for any one except his patron Akbar and the members of his own family. Tān Sen's grave at Gwalior is visited even today by the musicians of the subcontinent, who mention his name with great respect. It is significant that the three greatest names in music in the subcontinent of that period should all be Muslim. Abū-'l-Faḍl considers thirty-six persons worthy of being mentioned in his list of court musicians; of these no more than three are Hindu. Music had thus become almost a Muslim monopoly who contributed greatly to its development. Tān Sen, so highly revered that his name has become a by-word in the subcontinent, is accused by some recent Hindu students of music of corrupting the ancient Indian tradition by the introduction of new features. It is forgotten that if all the "corruptions" introduced by Miyān Tān Sen and other Muslim musicians since the days of Amīr Khusraw are taken away, very little will be left of Indian music. It is also significant that in Abū-'l-Faḍl's list no less than twelve musicians belong to Gwalior. It would not be unreasonable to surmise that Gwalior as the seat of Tān Sen's school of musicians played an important role in the development of music in that area. Bāz Bahādur also has received his share of praise from Abū-'l-Faḍl who calls him "a singer without rival." Ten of the musicians mentioned by Abū-'l-Faḍl are from Muslim countries outside the subcontinent, which shows that the Mughuls had not abjured their love of Central Asian music. The part played by Central Asian tradition in the development of Indian music needs investigation. The musicians were divided into seven groups, one for each day of the week, so that they might hold themselves in readiness if summoned for a performance.[53] Under Jahāngīr as well, the leading court musicians were Muslims. Under Shāh Jahān out of the three outstanding musicians, two have Muslim names. Lāl Khān, son-in-law to

[53] *Ibid.*

Bilās (who was Tān Sen's son and like him a Muslim) was given the title of gunsamundar (the ocean of excellence). He had acquired the knowledge of music from Tān Sen's pupils and did not have a peer in singing dhurpad. His four sons provided the accompaniment. One of his sons Khushḥāl was a good composer. The best composer and writer of songs, however, was Jagannāth, who was, on this account, given the title of Kab Rā'i.[54] Shāh Jahān himself had a good knowledge of music. He was particularly conversant with the techniques of Indian music.[55] Jagannāth dedicated twelve of his compositions in dhurpad to Shāh Jahān in the eighth year of his reign. The emperor was so pleased that the musician was weighed against silver rupees which were given to him as a reward.[56]

'Ālamgīr I only tolerated music on occasions when traditionally it had become a part of the court ceremonial, especially on the occasion of certain celebrations.[57] On such occasions the musicians were rewarded in the usual manner.[58] But it seems that gradually he gave up the patronage of the art. The musicians attached to the court were given other duties to perform at enhanced salaries, and music was discontinued at imperial functions. The musicians were disheartened and took out a procession with a mock coffin and loud lamentations when the monarch was in the jharokah. The Emperor inquired whose funeral it was and being told that it was music they were going to bury, the Emperor remarked, "Bury it deep so that no sound or echo of it is heard again."[59] Music, however, was not buried and was resurrected by 'Ālamgīr's successors with a vengeance.

The Mughul emperors encouraged craftsmen to produce the finest textiles and gold and silver wares. Anyone who achieved distinction in an art or craft and produced wares of beauty and

[54] 'Abd-u'l-Ḥamīd, ii, p. 5. He gives a short history of the developments in Indian music towards the beginning of Akbar's reign (*ibid.*, pp. 6, 7). Kab Rā'i is a Persian corruption of Kavi (poet) rā'i (prince or chief).

[55] *Ibid.*, i, p. 152.

[56] *Ibid.*, ii, p. 56.

[57] Kāẓim, p. 1072.

[58] *e.g.*, Kāẓim, p. 448.

[59] Khawāfī Khān, ii, p. 252.

good workmanship could hope for patronage. Indeed the monarchs found time to inspect and admire pieces worthy of eliciting praise. They admitted to their company men of learning as well as skill; their parties included calligraphists, painters, architects, engineers, poets, physicians, astronomers and musicians. Muslim divines and Hindu pandits, writers and scholars all were invited. Discussions were encouraged and the emperor displayed great qualities of appreciation and criticism.[60]

The nobles followed the example of their sovereign and every officer of high rank was a patron of learning and crafts. A good portion of the salaries paid to these officers was spent on the patronage of learning and culture. With such patronage the general cultural level was high. About one of the cities of the empire, Lahore, a Hindu author says that poets from various countries would congregate every Friday in Masjid Wazīr Khān and recite their poetry. Books on different topics and in different languages were on sale on these occasions. Paintings and pieces of calligraphy were available for purchase. Young students and old men of learning jostled one another in the crowd, looking at books and examining paintings and calligraphy.[61]

In the remarkable cultural achievements of the Mughul Empire the Hindus participated fully. The architectural styles developed at the capitals were adopted by Hindu potentates. The visitor to Amber finds himself in the midst of a complex of buildings which were no different in style or spirit from the palaces of Agra and Shāhjahānabād. Hindu nobles began to imitate the Mughuls even in the construction of tombs. Though there was no tradition of the burial of the dead among the caste Hindus, yet the nobles began to build memorials to the dead, called samādhīs, which borrowed freely from the tomb architecture of the Mughuls. The Mughul style even penetrated some of the temples. Its influence was even more marked in Jain temples. Many of the miniature painters at the court were Hindus. A parallel school, called the

[60] Brahman, *Qawā'id-i-Salṭanat-i-Shāh Jahān*, p. 54 gives a good description of Shāh Jahān's association with men of distinction in various spheres of life.

[61] Brahman, *Chahār Chaman*, f. 49a.

Rajput style, was developed by the Hindus who applied the techniques of the Mughul school to Hindu themes. Religious and mythological lore provided a rich source of inspiration to these artists. There were Hindu calligraphists and some of their work has been preserved for posterity. An album preserved in the National Museum of Pakistan at Karachi has pieces by a Hindu calligraphist who impartially has put into beautiful nasta'līq script phrases and couplets borrowed from Hindu and Muslim sources. Though the leading masters of music during this period were Muslims, yet the Hindus also achieved eminence. In the realm of Persian literature the Hindus soon came to the forefront. Akbar's abolition of Hindi as an official language for agrarian records was in all probability dictated by the fact that by then the knowledge of Persian had become quite common. It seems to have given a further impetus to the spread of the knowledge of Persian among the Hindus. We find many Hindus among the ranks of those who wrote History, poetry and elegant prose in Persian. Some were competent lexicographists. Quite a few achieved eminance.[62]

In Hindi itself there was a continuation of the renaissance begun by the great Bhaktī poets. In this period one of the greatest Hindi poets was 'Abd-u'r-Raḥīm Khān Khānān, whose writings are part of the classics of Hindi. In the reign of Akbar and Jahāngīr lived the immortal Hindi poet, Tulsī Dāsa who was one of the greatest poets of any time or any language. His version of the *Rāmāyana* is so full of compassion and feelings of devotion that it soon captured the imagination of the Hindu masses, so that it became almost the Bible of the Hindus of the areas where Hindi was spoken or understood.

The Mughul influence penetrated into the manners and mores of the upper classes of the Hindus, until in polite behaviour and gracious living the Mughul ways became the norms. This remained true until the Mughul influence was replaced by the British or uprooted by Hindu revivalism. Among the Muslims there grew up a sympathy and understanding of Hinduism which was

[62] Saiyid Sulaimān Nadwī, *Hindu'on ki ta'līm Musalmānon ke 'ahd men,* has listed many Hindu historians, poets, prose writers, lexicographers, translators and writers on rational disciplines.

not limited to writers like Abū-'l-Faḍl who has left an excellent account of Hindu philosophy and religion. Some far more orthodox Muslims have recorded their appreciation of Hinduism. The famous Muslim divine and mystic Mirzā Maẓhar Jān Jānān says about the Hindus in one of his letters:

"All their sects are unanimous regarding monotheism and look upon the world as created by God and contingent in its nature . . . They are greatly advanced in rational and traditional knowledge, in mystic disciplines and practices and in inquiries into gnosticism and spiritual experience. Their libraries are extant even today. Their idol worship is not based in polytheism but has a different significance . . . Prophets have been sent to India as well and their sayings are preserved in the books of the Hindus."[63]

[63] Mirzā Maẓhar Jān Jānān Shahīd, Letter XIV, pp. 25, 26.

CHAPTER XI

Provincial and Local Government

THE Mughul Empire was divided into provinces, called ṣūbahs. Each ṣūbah consisted of several sarkārs further subdivided into maḥāls or parganahs. A convenient number of villages called mawḍa'ṣ or dihs were included in each maḥāl.[1] In Mughul administrative jargon a village was not only the conglomeration of houses where the peasants lived but also the land surrounding it. Hence the boundary of each mawḍa' was clearly demarcated. Each one of these was an administrative unit. Smaller hamlets called naglahṣ were included in mawḍa'ṣ. Under Shāh Jahān his wazīr Sa'd-u'llah Khān established a new unit called a chaklah,[2] which included a number of parganahs. The sarkar was not abolished, so that the chaklah did not replace it.

A province was under a governor who, in the beginning, was called a sipahsālār or commander of armed forces.[3] As his title

[1] Lachhmī Narāyan Shafīq f. 80 b.

[2] *Dastūr-u'l-'amal*, B.M. ms. or 2026, f. 34 a.

[3] Abū-'l-Faḍl, *Ā'īn-i-Akbarī*, iii, Ā'īn 3.

signifies his main duty was the defence of the area and the maintenance of peace and order. However, from the very beginning, he was also the head of the civil administration. The *Ā'in* says that "the forces of the province and its inhabitants are under his order". On the civil side his duty was to encourage and expand cultivation. He was required to extend all help to the peasants and to appoint the 'āmils and keep himself informed about their work. He was also to undertake the construction of tanks, wells, canals, sarā'is and other buildings of public utility. He was also to interest himself in laying orchards and gardens.[4]

This description of functions is remarkably similar to the instructions given by Quṭb-u'd-dīn Aibak to one of his governors. Similar instructions were given by Fīrūz Shāh to Fath Khān when the latter was appointed as governor.[5]

Thus the functions of the governors do not seem to have changed during all the centuries of Muslim rule in the subcontinent. These functions were really based in the classical traditions of Muslim administration.

The use of the word sipahsālār as the title of the provincial governor seems soon to have fallen into disuse and in the literature of the later reigns it gave place to the terms ṣūbahdār and, some times even, nāẓim-i-ṣūbah.[6]

Four provinces of the Deccan were grouped into a viceroyalty, which was generally conferred upon a son of the emperor. The charge was termed ayālat.[7] Sometimes the provincial governor was assigned a nā'ib. This was done if a minor prince was appointed as governor. In such instances the prince was really in training

[4] *Ibid.*, Sarā'i, a caravanserai, an inn.

[5] I. H. Qureshi, *The Administration of the Sultanate of Dehli*, pp. 198, 199.

[6] *e.g.*, *Kaifiyat-i-ṣūbajāt-i-mumālik-i-maḥrūsah-i-Hindustān*, f. 239 a, 'Ali Muḥammad Khān, *Supplement*, p. 149 etc.

[7] In a letter to Shāh Jahān's minister Sa'd-u'llah Khān, Awrangzīb writes, "His Majesty has conferred upon me the ayālat of these four provinces (ṣūbahs) which form a large wilāyat and because it is contiguous to the frontiers of rulers in possession of financial resources and armies, it cannot be compared with the provinces (ṣūb ths) of Bengal and Ahmadābād"; Qābil Khān and Muḥammad Ṣādiq, f. 131b. Though Awrangzib calls Bengal a ṣūbah, Bengal is called an *ayālat* by Abū'-l-Faḍl, *Akbarnāmah*, iii, p. 266. In *Ā'in-i-Akbari*, however, the word ṣūbah is used.

and the nāi'b carried out all the duties of a governor.[8]

The Mughul governors were all appointed with defined powers. Only the hereditary tributary chiefs had a different status. According to the classical Muslim definition the Mughul governorships were imārat-ul-khāṣṣah or imārat-u'l-tanfīdh. A governor with defined powers was traditionally entrusted with the supervision of the troops, the punishment of criminals and rebels and home defence. He was not allowed to intervene in the administration of justice or the levy of taxes. Nor was he given the right to lead prayers or act as the spiritual leader of the people.[9] The Mughuls believed in a centralized system of government and were generally averse to delegating too much authority. Even hereditary Hindu rulers like the rulers of Rajputana states found that their traditional independence was being circumscribed in many ways. One method was to enrol them as manṣabdārs and treat them like ordinary servants of the state. However, their autonomy within their states was not seriously affected. The rulers of Golconda and Bijapur were in a different category. They had been independent sultans before the Mughul encroachment began. Even when they became tributaries and accepted a subordinate status, their territories did not become provinces and continued, so long as they were permitted to exist, as semi-independent states with separate fiscal and military establishments. They had their own services and, though the Mughuls ceased to refer to them as monarchs,[10] they continued to be styled as sultans within their territories. Their administration was in no sense amalgamated into the Mughul system.

The government of the province was organized on the same lines as the government at the centre. Apart from the governor, every province had its own dīwān, bakhshī, mīr 'adl, ṣadr (who was also the provincial qāḍī), kotwāl, mīr baḥr and waqā'i'nawīs.[11]

The dīwān was the head of the department of finance in the

[8] The duties of a nā' ib ṣūbahdār have been mentioned in *Kaifiyat-i-ṣūbajāt-i-mumālik-i-maḥrūsah-i-Hindustān*, f. 215b.

[9] Māwardī, pp. 30, 31; Farrā, p. 20.

[10] The Mughuls called them dunyādārs, an euphemism implying that they were not monarchs in the true sense.

[11] Abū'-l-Faḍl, *Akbarnāmah*, iii, p. 282 Waqā'i'nawīs was also called wāqi'ahnawīs.

province and his main duty was to see that the agrarian administration in his charge was kept upto the mark. For this purpose he was to be in constant communication with the revenue staff in the parganahs. It was in his office that all the returns of assessment and realization from the parganahs were audited and then consolidated into abstracts for transmission to the central ministry of finance. The original returns were transmitted to the central ministry after a harvest for further auditing. He also kept a record of īmah lands and the documents under which they had been issued.[12] Similarly all data necessary for the assessment of the state demand were kept in his office. He was especially instructed to ensure that the peasants were dealt with fairly and that every legitimate encouragement was given to cultivators.[13]

The provincial ba<u>kh</u>s<u>h</u>ī was responsible for issuing certificates to the manṣabdārs that the conditions of their manṣab had been fulfilled. Only on the production of this certificate was the salary paid by the dīwān. In case the payment was made in the form of jāgīr, an account was maintained by the dīwān of any deductions that had had to be made because of his failure to fulfil any of the terms of the manṣab. In case of the manṣabdār's death it was the provincial ba<u>kh</u>s<u>h</u>ī's duty to take over his jāgīr. A manṣabdār could not leave the station where he was posted without the provincial ba<u>kh</u>s<u>h</u>ī's permission. He was also responsible for the transmission of the reports of the waqā'i'nawīs to the central government.[14]

The provincial ṣadr made recommendations of grants to the ṣadr-u'ṣ-ṣudūr. The provincial mīr 'adl performed the same functions in the province as the central mīr 'adl at the centre. The kotwāl's duties were limited to the provincial capital and he had no jurisdiction over the kotwāls of other areas. The provincial mīr baḥr was responsible for the maintenance of the river and sea ports within his jurisdiction in good condition, to guard and

[12] *Kaifiyat-i-ṣūbajāt-i-mumālik-i-maḥrūsah-i-Hindustān*, ff. 216, 217; *Dastūr-u'l-'amal*, B.M. ms. or. 2026, ff. 18-20 gives an interesting list of the registers maintained at the office of the provincial dīwān.

[13] *Kaifiyat-i-ṣūbajāt-i-mumālik-i-maḥrūsah-i-Hindustān*, ff. 216, 217.

[14] 'Alī Muḥammad <u>Kh</u>ān, *Supplement*, p. 175.

supervise river communications and to keep the nawwārah in good order.[15] The waqā'i'nawis kept the central government informed of the happenings in the province.[16] Later a sawāniḥnawis was added to send intelligence reports. He worked unknown to the officials and the public. He was, therefore, styled khufiyahnawis or the secret reporter.

The provincial officers worked under the general supervision of the governor, but they were really responsible to their counterparts at the centre.

The sarkārs were under fawjdārs.[17] The fawjdār of a sarkār was subordinate to the ṣūbahdār and his primary duty was to maintain peace.[18] He, however, had the permission to write directly to the imperial court.[19] Sher Shāh had an officer called munṣif-i-munṣifān stationed in each sarkār. He was required to supervise the assessment staff in the various parganahs included in the sarkār.[20] The Mughuls did not have any assessment staff attached to the sarkār. The reason seems to be that the Mughul administration at the provincial level was so well organized that there was little justification for duplicating the inspecting staff at the level of the sarkār. The administration of a chaklah will be described later.

The parganah was the hub of rural administration under the Muslim rulers of the subcontinent. It was as important as the district under the British. The staff for the assessment and realization of the state demand on agricultural produce was centred in the parganah. The administrative machinery of the parganah did not undergo any remarkable change when the Mughuls established their rule; the institutions developed by the Sultans continued to function with minor changes in nomenclature and organization.[21]

The head of the parganah administration under the Mughuls

[15] nawwārah, from Hindi nāw, a boat, was river navy.

[16] 'Alī Muḥammad Khān, *Supplement*, p. 175.

[17] *Dastūr-u'l-'amal*, B.M. ms. or. 2026 f. 34a.

[18] Abū-'l-Faḍl, *Ā'in-i-Akbarī*, iii, Ā'īn 4.

[19] This is borne out by the fact that communications from the fawjdārs were read out before the emperor, 'Abd-u'l-Ḥamīd. i, p. 147.

[20] I.H. Qureshi. *The Administration of the Sultanate of Dehli*, pp. 210, 260.

[21] For the administration of a parganah under the Sultans see *ibid.*, pp. 208, 209, 259, 260.

was the ʻāmil. It was his duty to see that all the procedures regarding the assessment and realization of the state dues were followed honestly and that the system ran smoothly and efficiently. He was particularly enjoined to expand the area under cultivation and it was realized that this could not be achieved without ensuring the well-being of the peasant. The ʻāmil, therefore, was to keep a strict watch over his staff to see that no injustice was committed and only the dues prescribed by the state were realized from the cultivator. All cultivators were to have direct access to him to ensure fair dealing.[22] During Akbar's reign the assessment also was the direct responsibility of the ʻāmil; for this reason the Ā'īn does not mention a separate assessment officer. The assessment staff is mentioned in the same Ā'īn as the ʻāmil and the duties of assessment are clearly assigned to him.[23] If there occurred a partial or complete failure of the crops, the amīn, who had his headquarters at the provincial capital, came down to assess the extent of the damage and to recommend remission of the state demand.[24] Thus in Akbar's days the ʻāmil had considerable authority because in his hands were concentrated the powers of general administration and the assessment and realization of the state demand on agricultural produce.[25] It was in the reign of Shāh Jahān that his minister Islām Khān revived the traditions of the Sultanate and appointed an amīn in every parganah. He was made responsible for assessment. The ʻāmil was left with police duties and the realization of the state demand.[26]

The Ā'īn mentions the police duties of the ʻāmil and makes him responsible for punishing contumacy and rebellion.[27] When a separate assessment officer called amīn, was appointed in the parganah, police duties gained more importance among the functions of the ʻāmil and he came to be called a fawjdār as well. Thus there are extant a number of documents in which fawjdārs of

22 Abū-'l-Faḍl, *Ā'īn-i-Akbari*, iii, Ā'īn. 7.

23 *Ibid.*

24 *Dastūr-u'l-ʻamal*, B.M. ms. or. 2026. f. 33.

25 *Ibid.*

26 *Ibid.*

27 Abū-'l-Faḍl, *Ā'īn-i-Akbari*, iii, Ā'īn 7.

parganahs have been mentioned.[28] The duties of the fawjdār of a parganah have been described clearly in a letter of Prince Awrangzib. He says that the fawjdār was expected to increase the revenue of the parganah, to ensure that none was treated unjustly and no village was left uncultivated, and to create conditions of peace and security within his charge so that travellers might move about without any anxiety or fear of highwaymen.[29] It seems that in some smaller parganahs the duties of the fawjdār and the amīn were combined.[30]

It seems that there was not sufficient work in the parganahs to keep both the 'āmil and the amīn busy. This is not unlikely because after the Ā'īn-i-dahsālah had been promulgated and the ḍabṭī system had worked for some time, the work of the assessment must have become lighter and Islām Khān's experiment could not have had much justification from the very beginning. This must be the reason why in many parganahs the offices of the 'āmil and amīn were combined. The main reason for Islām Khān's action must have been the inconvenience caused to the peasants as well as the parganah revenue staff by the delay in the arrival of the amīn from the provincial headquarters, who must have been kept busy because of requisitions from various parganahs and the slow means of communication available in those days.

These seem to have been the reasons which prompted Sa'd-u'llah Khān to create a new unit of chaklah. He withdrew the amīn from each parganah and posted him in the chaklah which consisted of a number of parganahs. The duties of assessment and collection of revenue were considered sufficient for him. It was then thought desirable to have another officer stationed at the headquarters of the chaklah as well for the punishment of rebels and keeping the roads safe for travellers. The chaklah, therefore, also came to have a fawjdār. The 'āmil of the parganah was made subordinate to the fawjdār and the amīn of the chaklah.[31]

[28] *e.g., Kaifiyat-i-ṣūbajāt-i-mumālik-i-maḥrūsah-i-Hindustān*, ff. 217a, 227a.

[29] Ashraf Khān, f. 7a.

[30] *Ibid.*

[31] *Dastūr-u'l-'amal*, B.M. or 2026, f. 34a.

The multiplicity of terms for the single office of the 'āmil has caused considerable confusion. Abū-'l-Faḍl himself has used the word 'amalguzār, a variant somewhat more consistent with his anxiety to write as pure Persian as possible.[32] In subsequent literature the word 'amalguzār is seldom used. Another title for the same office is karorī. In the 19th year of his reign, Akbar divided the khāliṣah lands into one hundred eighty two units. It was expected that each one of these units, if fully cultivated, would produce a crore (ten million) dām. Hence the officers in charge of these units were called karorīs.[33] It is obvious that this was but a fancy of the emperor because it was an impossible task to carve out units on the basis of income which was in any case not constant from year to year. The parganahs must have been based upon geographical considerations. The term karorī, however, persisted. Another title of the same office was shiqqdār.[34] which had come down from the days of the Afghāns. The last of the series was fawjdār, which came into use for reasons already mentioned. As it caused confusion because of the appointment of a fawjdār in every chaklah and the continuance of a fawjdār in the sarkār, the title fell into disuse so far as the head of the parganah administration was concerned.

Except for the period when an amīn was appointed for the parganah the assessment staff worked under the supervision of the 'āmil.[35] It consisted of officials who measured the land, assessed the yield and kept a record of the figures. The *Ā'īn* mentions the designations of the officers but does not give details of their functions.[36] It, however, seems reasonable to conclude from the dictionary meanings of the terms used that the ḍābiṭ

[32] Abū-'l-Faḍl, *Ā'īn-i-Akbarī*, iii, Ā'īn 8, In *Akbarnāmah* (*e.g.*, iii, p. 117) Abū'l-Faḍl uses the word 'āmil as well.

[33] Abu-'l-Faḍl, *Akbarnāmah*, iii, p. 117. Badā'ūnī has scathing comments upon this measure, Badā'ūnī, ii, pp. 189, 190. The measure did not succeed because all the waste land could not be brought under cultivation.

[34] For details how shiqqdār came to be used for an 'āmil, see. I. H. Qureshi, *The Administration of the Sultanate of Dehli*, pp. 209, 259, 260. For the use of the term under the Mughuls, *Dastūr-u'l-'amal-i-Haḍrat Awrangzib 'Ālamgir Padshāh Ghāzī*, B.M. ms. Addl. 6599, f. 186b.

[35] Abū-'l-Faḍl, *Ā'īn-i-Akbarī*, iii, Ā'īn 7.

[36] *Ibid.*, Ā'īns 7 and 8.

was the chief assessment officer, the paimāyindah and the jarīb-kash measured the land and probably assessed the crops, the bitikchī (who should not be confused with the bitikchī of the parganah) prepared and maintained the record of the figures arrived at and the thāpahdār marked off the lands already measured and, if an actual division of the crops was demanded under the system of sharing, put seals on the grain and took steps to guard it so that no one removed any portion of it before the division.[37]

Next to the 'āmil in the parganah administration came the bitikchī. He may roughly be defined as the chief accountant and registrar of the parganah, because it was in his office that all the accounts were maintained and the documents signed by the various officials and the peasants were kept. The old title of kārkun, common in the days of the Sultanate[38], did not go out of use even under 'Ālamgir.[39] Instead of the two kārkuns in each parganah, one for keeping the records in Persian and the other in Hindi, Akbar kept only one bitikchī who kept the records in Persian.[40]

Each parganah had a treasury which was in the charge of a khazānahdār also called a foṭahdār or a khazīnahdār.[41] This officer dates back to the days of the Sultanate.[42] Because of the very nature of the office there was no significant change in his functions.

[37] Ḍābiṭ is obviously one who enforces the ḍābiṭāh or regulations, hence the head of the staff. Jarīb-kash: jarīb was used to measure the land, kash, literally "the drawer of"- jarīb-kash, the man who "drew" the jarīb; Paimāyindah: one who measures or computes (Paimūdan = measure or estimate, *Bahār-i-'Ajam*). Thāpahdār = one who puts a thāpah. (Thāpah was a mark, mostly of the hand, put on kneaded wet clay on the door of a barn or enclosure, to seal it from intruders, *Farhang-i-Āṣafiyah*). Ḍābiṭ also refers to ḍabṭī, assessment in accordance with the Ā'īn-i-dahsālah.

[38] I.H. Qureshi, *The Administration of the Sultanate of Dehlī*, pp. 209, 259, 260.

[39] *Dastūr-u'l-'amal-i-Haḍrat Awrangzīb 'Ālamgīr Pādshah Ghāzī*, f. 187b.

[40] Kewal Rām, f. 164b. The non-technical word nawīsindah is also used occasionally, *e.g.*, Abū-'l-Faḍl, *Akbarnāmah*, iii, p, 117.

[41] Abū-'l-Faḍl, *A'īn-i-Akbari*, iii, Ā'īn 9.

[42] I.H. Qureshi, *The Administration of the Sultanate of Dehlī*, pp. 209, 259, 260.

The use of the term amīn in different senses has caused some confusion. Khwājah Yāsin has clarified the different uses of the word. He says that:

(i) an amīn was a person resident at the court who inquired into any matter entrusted to him so that he might make a full and impartial report to the monarch;

(ii) the term was also applied to a person who was stationed in a province by the emperor so that he might hold in trust the royal treasury located there, inform the emperor of any lapse on behalf of the governor and keep all records (relating to revenue) under his control;

(iii) the term also applied to a commissioner appointed to look into any special matter needing investigation; and

(iv) it also referred to an assessment officer.[43]

This list is, however, not exhaustive because amīns were assigned other duties as well.

An important factor in the parganah administration was the qānūngū who prepared statements showing in detail the area cultivated, the crops grown and the expected or actual yield, copies of which were sent, after certification by the 'āmil, the chaudharī and the qānūngū to the provincial dīwān. He gave to each assessee a document called a pattah which contained all data relating to the assessment of his holding. The assessee executed a deed confirming his acceptance of the assessment. This document, called a qabūliyat, was retained by him, but copies were sent to the office of the provincial dīwān.[44] In case the crops were damaged by some unforeseen circumstances, he had to assess the extent of the damage and recommend appropriate reduction in the state demand.[45] Each parganah had several qānūngūs[46] who kept the records of the annual medium yield of the area on the basis of which the decennial average was calculated in accordance with the Ā'īn-i-dahsālah. Copies of these records were deposited in the

[43] Khwājah Yāsin. f. 46a.

[44] *Dastūr-u'l-'amal*, B.M. ms. or 2026. f. 22b.

[45] *Ibid.*, f. 24b.

[46] *Ibid.*

office of the provincial as well as the central diwān.[47] In certain areas the duties of a qānūngū were combined with those of the chaudharī, who was also associated with the parganah administration as a person cognizant of the conditions in the parganah. The chaudhari was especially required to report to the 'āmil's office all land brought under cultivation.[48] He was punished if he suppressed any information about cultivated areas.

In smaller parganahs the duties of the 'āmil and amīn were sometimes combined.[49] It is interesting to note that the word mushrif was not completely discarded even under Mughul rule.[50] It was in common use under the Turkish sultāns; later, under the Afghāns, it tended to be replaced by munṣif and amīn.[51] The word munṣif, literally a judge, is an index to the ideals of Indo-Muslim agrarian administration. Similarly an amīn is a trustee who is expected to discharge his duties impartially. He was expected to act as an impartial judge in adjudicating the shares of the state and the cultivator.[52]

These administrative terms were used throughout the empire except in the province of Kabul where, "like Samarqand and Bukhārā, a parganah consisting of tappajāt and villages, is called a tūmān."[53] The chief administrative officer of a tūmān was called an irmān.[54] The irmān of Peshawar was expected to pay into the treasury at Kabul a fixed sum of money which, in the eighteenth century, was fixed at five thousand rupees per annum. This would indicate that the elaborate system of assessment and realization in force in settled areas did not apply to the difficult areas of the tribal north-west.[55]

When an area was assigned as a jāgīr, there was no change in

[47] *Kaifiyat-i-ṣūbajāt-i-mumālik-i-maḥrūsah-i-Hindustān*, f. 220b.

[48] Shākīr Khān, f. 154a.

[49] *Kaifiyat-i-ṣūbajāt-i-mumālik-i-maḥrūsah-i-Hindustān*, f. 227.

[50] *Ibid.*, f. 236b.

[51] I.H. Qureshi, *The Administration of the Sultanate of Dehli*, pp. 208-209.

[52] *Dastūr-u'l-'amal*, B.M. ms. or 2026 ff. 21, 22.

[53] Abū-'l-Faḍl, *Ā'in-i-Akbarī*, i, p. 592 (in the information relating to the ṣūbah of Kābul).

[54] *Kaifiyat-i-ṣūbajāt-i-mumālik-i-maḥrūsah-i-Hindustān*, f. 232a.

[55] *Ibid.*

its administrative organization. The officials were appointed by the jāgīrdārs, but he contended himself by posting his nominees to one or two key positions. The rest of the staff was permitted to continue functioning, because this was in the interest of the jāgīrdār as the local officials were conversant with the conditions in the area. If the central government found any deterioration in the administration, it cancelled the assignment.[56] The usual records and registers were maintained and copies were submitted to the provincial and central dīwāns.[57] Special care was taken to ensure that the decennial tables of medium yield were kept up-to-date. The state took pains to ensure that officers treated the peasants with consideration and observed all the rules and regulations laid down by the government. The various abstracts, statements and reports submitted by the jāgīrdārs as well as the intelligence service kept the government informed of all significant happenings. Persons coming from Iran or Central Asia and employed by the government were not assigned jāgīrs until they had gained experience and become familiar with local customs and the temperament of the people.[58] When an area was taken out of the assignment of a jāgīrdār, pending final decision whether it would be reassigned to some one else or brought into khāliṣah, it was termed pā'ibāqī and the 'āmil and amīn were entrusted with the task of seeing that assessment, collection and administration did not suffer in any manner.[59] When an 'āmil was removed, a barāmadnawīs was appointed who drew up a statement of all accounts and, after getting it authenticated by other officials, submitted it to the central office for final clearance.[60]

The collection of urban taxes was entrusted to another set of officials who were directly under the control of the dīwān. In case such revenue was assigned to a jāgīrdār, he controlled the staff subject to the general supervision of the provincial and central dīwāns. Whether the taxes were assigned to a jāgīrdār or levied

[56] Qābil Khān and Muḥammad Ṣādiq, f. 50a.

[57] *Dastūr-u'l-'amal*, B.M. ms. or 2026, f. 21.

[58] Khawāfī Khān, ii, p. 187. This rule was laid down by Shāh Jahān.

[59] *Kaifiyat-i-ṣubajāt-i-mumālik-i-maḥrūsah-i-Hindustān* ff. 229a.

[60] *Ibid.*, f. 221a.

directly, the administration at the local level was not affected. An amīn was at the head, assisted by chaudharīs selected from amongst the taxpayers.[61] There were separate amīns and chaudharīs for the cattle markets. If the volume of the collections justified it, other trades also were given a separate set of officials.[62] The cash was kept in the custody of a dārog͟hah also called a foṭahdār or a taḥwīldār.[63] The mints, which were scattered in different parts of the empire, also had the same set up.[64]

The maintenance of internal peace and order was an important function of the provincial governor. The duties of the heads of the administration in the sarkār and the parganah have already been discussed and it has been mentioned that they were responsible for the security of their respective charges. So far as the urban areas were concerned, every city of some proportions had a kotwāl,[65] whose duties have been discussed in a previous chapter.[66] It was essential for an extensive empire to provide for the maintenance of law and order in the rural areas. The governor and the fawjdārs were entrusted with this duty. To them may be added, the qilʿahdārs who were the commandants of garrisons stationed at strategic points,[67] and the thānahdārs who were in charge of police units stationed at various places for guarding communications and maintaining peace.[68] However, such units were like small islands in the midst of a vast countryside studded with villages and hamlets. Quite often the terrain was difficult or covered with deep forests making it easy for robbers to ply their trade. In such areas the villagers themselves were not averse to waylaying travellers or banding themselves together to terrorize the countryside. Whenever it became unsafe for peaceful peasants to cultivate their holdings, they would give up their lands and

[61] *Ibid.*, f. 222a.

[62] *Ibid.*, *e g.*, the jewellers had their own amīns and chaudharīs.

[63] *Ibid.*, f. 222b.

[64] *Ibid*, ff. 223a,b.

[65] *Ibid.*, f. 224b.

[66] vide *supra*, Chapter IX.

[67] *Kaifiyat-i-ṣūbajāt-i-mumālik-i-maḥrūsah-i-Hindustān*, f. 216b.

[68] *Ibid.*, p. 217b.

crowd into towns for shelter. When this happened, the economy of the area was disrupted and the finances of the state suffered. A system, therefore, had to be devised to stop infringement of the common peace.

The first step in this direction was to take stringent measures against refractory elements who thrived on robbery. The parganah officials and jāgirdārs were alike instructed to root out any defiance of authority and to punish rebels and robbers. Loyal cultivators were to be compensated for any loss inflicted upon them by robbers and rebels. In case the parganah officials found it beyond their resources to deal with the situation, they were instructed to seek help from the neighbouring parganahs.[69] They were also required to guard the roads and in case of robbery or theft, were enjoined to make every effort to recover the goods and to restore them to their owners. In case they failed to recover the goods, they were to pay compensation out of their own pockets.[70] Officers responsible for the maintenance of peace were assigned detachments of cavalry and infantry according to the requirements of the area.[71]

There were a number of Hindu chiefs, who had exercised authority in their areas since times immemorial.[72] They had been left alone by successive Hindu and Muslim dynasties. Their outlook was insular and they did not show much inclination to combine themselves into formidable groups. Within their own areas, however, they were powerful, because their authority was based on traditional loyalties of their followers and the rural heirarchy. Sometimes these loyalties were tribal which made them even stronger. The relations of these chiefs with the ruling dynasties depended on the vigour and strength of their government. The Hindu dynasties were often content to receive formal allegiance and some cooperation in times of need. The Muslim conquest was made

[69] Kewal Rām. f. 165.

[70] *Kaifiyat-i-ṣūbajāt-i-mumālik-i-maḥrūsah-i-Hindustān*, B.M. ms. or 1779 f. 217.

[71] Interesting details are available regarding the strength of these detachments in 'Alī Muḥammad Khān, *Supplement*, pp. 170-172.

[72] For a fuller discussion see I. H. Qureshi, *The Administration of the Sultanate of Dehli*, pp. 210, 211.

easier because of the indifference of a large number of chiefs towards the fate of the ruling dynasty. The Sultans pursued a three-pronged policy of winning over the peasants through enlightened agrarian administration; entrusting the chiefs, who were willing to cooperate with responsibility and a share in rural administration for which there were adequate perquisites; and punishing those who proved refractory or rebellious. This policy succeeded remarkably well, but it had one inherent weakness. It left the chiefs very much in positions of influence and authority and whenever the power of the state waned, the chiefs quietly assumed all powers until they were again brought under control by a resuscitated central or provincial authority. By the time the Mug͟hul Empire was established, they had learnt the value of cooperating with a strong government and the Mug͟huls had less spade work to do than the Sultans. The problem was, however, perennial. The Marathas demonstrated that local chieftains could set government authority at nought by combining together in rebellion. Indeed the ills of the eighteenth century, when the subcontinent sank into anarchy, primarily arose out of the consciousness that central authority had weakened to an extent that it could be defied with impunity. The infection was so potent that even Muslim officials who ought to have known better participated in the general scramble for power.

It has been mentioned that the local chieftains were entitled to certain perquisites and concessions. They were often excused from paying the state demand on lands cultivated by them directly. They were, however, when this concession was not given to them. forbidden to make the peasants pay for them. The Sultans and the Mug͟huls were equally anxious to see that the burden of the chiefs was not passed on to the peasants.[73] The Maratha demand for chauth, which was a fourth of the revenue collected as state demand on agricultural produce, had its basis in the perquisites of the local chieftains. The *Mir'at-i-Aḥmadī*,[74] throws interesting light on the origin of the institution. It says that "when the sultans

[73] Baranī, p. 287, also *supra*, Chapter VIII.

[74] 'Alī Muḥammad K͟hān, *Supplement*. pp. 228, 229.

of Gujrat's brought the country under their control, a number of Rajputs and Kolis who had lived in the area for several generations raised their heads everywhere in turbulence and caused disturbances in every direction. To pacify them, it was decided that a fourth of the lands of their settlements were to be left to them for cultivation without any state demand. They were required (in return) to maintain peace and security in the area". It is doubtful if this was a new measure. It is not improbable that the rebellion was for the restoration of an ancient right. Some old families of Gujrat possess documents which prove the existence of chauth before the rise of the Marathas in a different form. The chieftain was promised a commission of a fourth of the state demand if he maintained order and helped in the proper assessment and collection of government dues in his area.[75] The *Mir'at* goes on to say that out of the produce of the lands left in the hands of the chiefs, they were required to pay a salāmī (tribute) which was fixed in accordance with the area and productivity of their holdings. Those who had entire parganahs as their holdings were required to serve the state, especially in emergencies when they were required to join the army with their followers. In course of time this also was commuted for a fixed tribute.[76]

In the beginning the state must have contented itself with allegiance and tribute. As the control and strength of the government increased, it was able to impose certain responsibilities on the chiefs. The Sultans had been able to evolve a pattern of relationship with chiefs of different categories. The k͟hūṭs and muqaddams had been reduced to the position of village headmen and the larger princedoms were treated as tributaries with varying degrees of autonomy. This pattern of relationship survived the Muslim empire and the bewildering variety in legal and political status can be studied even in the treaties and sanads collected by Aitchison.[77] In view of the complexity of these relations it would be futile to arrive at any generalization, but it would be correct to

[75] The author has described one such document in *Proceedings of Indian Historical Records Commission*, 1946.

[76] 'Alī Muḥammad K͟hān, *Supplement*, p. 229.

[77] Aitchison.

say that the relations between the Mughul government and the chieftains embraced all the shades of difference between the tributary ruler and the village headman. History had taken a major hand in the determination of the status of each chieftain. The terms obtained by some ancestor at the time of his submission to the Mughul or a previous supreme authority had almost been sanctified by tradition and unless there was some need to change the relationship, the chiefs were left alone. Even though the Mughul theory about some tributaries changed because of their enrolment in the manṣabdāri system, the tradition of assigning them their own territories in lieu of salary acted as a deterrent to any profound change in the system. If a petty chieftain rose high, his patrimony was not taken away, but the increase in the salary brought him either additional cash or assignment.

The term zamīndār was applied to some tributaries. It was in use under the sultans, and had gained some popularity by the time of the Lodīs,[78] but it came into more frequent use under the Mughuls. They issued regular letters of appointment to the zamīndārs prescribing the amount of tribute they had to pay and assigning them their duties. These were "to treat the people well and to make all efforts to suppress refractory and rebellious trouble makers and bring them to the path of rectitude, especially to root out completely thieves and robbers . . . to increase cultivation and . . . to guard the communications so that travellers could move about without difficulty." If any theft or robbery did take place within the territory assigned to a zamīndār, he was to seize the culprits and to restore the property to its proper owners. In case he failed to do so, he was to compensate them for their losses.[79] The khūṭs and muqaddams of the Sultanate[80] changed into the chaudharīs of the Mughul period.[81] The word khūṭ seems to have fallen into disuse, and though the term muqaddam seems to have been discarded in official records, it continued to be used in the country-

[78] e g., Khusraw used the word Zamīndārī in *Diwalrāni Khiḍr Khān*, p. 70; I. H. Qureshi, *The Administration of the Sultanate of Dehli*, p. 211.

[79] *Kaifiyat-i-ṣūbajāt-i-mumālik-i-maḥrūsah-i-Hindustān*, f. 221a.

[80] I.H. Qureshi, *The Administration of the Sultanate of Dehli*, pp. 210, 211.

[81] *Kaifiyat-i-ṣūbajāt-i-mumālik-i-maḥrūsah-i-Hindustān*, f. 220.

side of certain provinces during the first two decades of the twentieth century for addressing an important villager.[82] The term chaudharī dates back to the Sultans and perhaps even earlier,[83] but it was not used so frequently. The chaudharīs were village headmen and it was their duty to help the officials in the assessment and collection of state demand in their areas. Sometimes the office of the chaudharī was combined with that of the qānūngū, whose main duty was the maintenance of the schedules of produce.[84]

One of the main problems of a large empire in an age when fast means of transport were not available was that of the maintenance of the means of communications. It was fully realized that roads and rivers were the arteries of the empire. The grand trunk road from Bengal to Attock had existed since the days of the Sultanate, and had been maintained and improved by successive rulers.[85] Jahāngīr mentions that there existed a shaded "avenue" between Bengal and Agra and between Agra and Attock. He put kroh minārs between Agra and Lahore to mark the distance, and, every five krohs he built a well.[86] Communications between the capital and the Deccan had also been maintained similarly. New roads were built to open up the country. In case an old alignment was found defective, new diversions were created.[87] Attock was connected with Kabul by a good road[88]. New inns of solid masonry complete with mosques and baths were constructed. New bridges were built and old ones repaired. The jāgīrdārs and local officers were asked by Jahāngīr to build inns along the roads in their areas.[89]

82 The author of this treatise found it in use in Western districts of the United Provinces.

83 I. H. Qureshi, *The Administration of the Sultanate of Dehlī*, p. 208.

84 *Kaifiyat-i-ṣūbajāt-i-mumālik-i-maḥrūsah-i-Hindustān*, f. 220.

85 I.H. Qureshi, *The Administration of the Sultanate of Dehlī*, pp. 213, 214.

86 Jahāngīr, p. 227. Kroh = a distance of about 2½ miles. The Kroh minārs were plastered masonry pillars about ten feet high. Some of them can be seen even today. Jahāngīr uses 'khiyābān' for avenue.

87 *e.g.*, Qābil Khān and Muḥammad Ṣādiq, f. 29b.

88 Kāẓim, p. 1085.

89 Jahāngīr, p. 3.

The security of the roads was not neglected. In a vast empire which embraced within its borders mountains, plateaus, deserts and forests and where there were still fairly extensive uninhabitated tracts, it was impossible to root out highway robbery, but every effort was made to protect travellers and to promote the safe transit of merchandise. Some European travellers have exaggerated the risks they ran in undertaking long journeys within the Mughul Empire. In this they have mainly succumbed to the weakness of all early travellers who were fond of embellishing their adventures with such stories. More trustworthy evidence is provided by the fact that European traders considered it worth their while to establish factories hundreds of miles away from seaports and found such enterprize lucrative.

It has been mentioned how local officials and Hindu chieftains were entrusted with the duty of guarding the communications. They were held responsible for any theft or robbery in their charge and were made to compensate the aggrieved party if they failed to recover the property. If the terrain was difficult, special appointments were made to guard the area.[90] In case the person appointed did not discharge his duties properly he was punished. At suitable distances police posts were established which were known as thānahs and nākahs.[91] The latter was established to guard a place where a caravan could be surprised and waylaid.

The sultans had established an excellent system for the transmission of letters and messages. The post was of two kinds: one carried by horsemen and the other by runners. The latter was faster.[92] The Mughuls maintained the system with minor changes. Pelsaert was impressed with the remarkable speed at which letters were carried.[93] He says that a distance of seven hundred krohs was covered in as short a time as ten days.[94] Jahāngīr received

[90] *e.g.*, Mahdī Khān, f. 17a

[91] 'Alī Muḥammad Khān, *Supplement*, pp. 170-172.

[92] For details vide I. H. Qureshi, *The Administration of the Sultanate of Dehlī*, pp. 211, 212.

[93] Moreland, *Jahāngīr's India*, p. 58.

[94] A kroh=200 jarībs=5000 yards of Shāh Jahān (which roughly come to a little over 2½ modern miles), 'Alī Muḥammad Khān, *Supplement*, p. 176.

melons from Afghānistān and mangoes from Bengal in good condition through the post.[95] The speed at which post had to travel was prescribed, and if there was any delay, those responsible for it were punished.[96] There was a net work of dāk chowkīs, each one of which had mewrahs who carried the letters packed in nalwahs to the next post. The person who collected the post for despatch and distributed it when received was called harkārah.[97]

Like the Sultans the Mughuls had a good system of intelligence. The waqā'i'nawīs was stationed at the provincial capital and reported all matters of importance to the royal court. He had his agents in the parganahs as well as in all important offices of the provincial capital. When it was discovered that some waqā'i' nawīses had not been faithful in their reports, a parallel set of officers was appointed to make secret reports. Thus every provincial capital came to have a sawāniḥnawīs who was also called khufiyahnawīs.[98] He also had his agents posted at different places. They were given an independent status, so that they were not under the control of the local authorities,[99] against whom sometimes they had to report. The reports of the sawāniḥnawīses were scrutinized and all important items were read out to the emperor.[100] If some sawāniḥnawis failed to report a matter to the court or concealed any information, he was censured or punished."[101]

'At the provincial level the provincial bakhshī was responsible for ensuring the prompt transmission of all correspondence with

95 *Islamic Culture*, Hyderabad Deccan, 1944 p. 278.

96 'Alī Muḥammad Khān, *Supplement*. p. 176.

97 *Ibid.*, p. 175. Dāk is an old Hindi word, still in use for post. Like the word 'post' it also originally meant a station, from which new terms like dāk bungalows are derived. Nalwah was a cylindrical light container for papers. Harkārah, [Har=every: kār=work; kārah=of work or use] originally a general utility person, doing miscellaneous work, came in course of time to be identified with a person who collected and distributed mail. The word is now falling into disuse, but until recently was used for a mail carrier and also a postman.

98 *Ibid.*, Waqā'i'=events; sawāniḥ, originally untoward events, loosely used for happenings; khufiyah=secret.

99 Khawāfī Khān, ii, p. 4.

100 Kāẓim, p. 1102.

101 Ashraf Khān, f. 21a.

the imperial court.[102] Sealed reports and letters, however, were not opened and were sent intact to the centre. The system seems to have worked efficiently and the emperor was kept well informed about the affairs of his realm. As the emperor travelled extensively and complainants were encouraged to bring their grievances to him, the officials came to cultivate a feeling that they could not hide their shortcomings for any length of time, which acted as a deterrent during the palmy days of the empire.

This was the broad structure of the provincial and local government. In addition there were a large number of officers styled variously as mushrifs, mutaṣaddīs, amins, even fawjdārs who were assigned especial duties, like the administration of ports and prisons whose detailed functions would be too tedious to describe. The general pattern was that in accordance with the volume and nature of work, superintendents, administrators and clerks were appointed to see that the interests of the state and the people did not suffer.

[102] 'Ali Muḥammad Khān, *Supplement*, p. 175.

CHAPTER XII

The Ideals of Mughul Government

THE description of the administrative institutions of a state remains incomplete unless an effort is made to understand its ideals and the spirit of its government. It is, therefore, necessary to try to discover the guiding principles of Mughul statecraft and policies. Fortunately there is ample material available to the student to arrive at reasonably sound conclusions in this regard.

Perhaps the most revealing evidence is provided by the image that the Mughuls were able to create of the position and functions of the emperor in the popular mind, an image which stands out clearly not only in historical and other literature of the period, but also in folklore which exists even today in the form of popular stories, narrated in the villages of the areas that constituted the Mughul's vast dominions when his power had not declined. The emperor was looked upon as the father of the people whose function it was to protect the weak and avenge the persecuted. It is true that sometimes there were rebellions that had to be punished and there were wars of conquest or reprisal, but these did not succeed in obliterating the image among the large mass of people. The emperor's person and office inspired such respect that a group of Hindus would not go about their daily work or even touch food until they had seen the emperor early in the morning when he appeared at the jharokah to receive the petitions of his subjects.[1] The feelings of devotion that prompted such a rite could not have come into existence without a belief that the emperor was benevolent and just. The fashion of decrying Muslim rule and painting it in lurid colours started quite late. The contemporaries of the Mughuls were strangers to the sentiments displayed by these later writers, because even the Hindu writers of that period write enthusiastically about the Mughul monarchs and their institutions.[2] Indeed it irked the early British writers to see that the Hindus cherished the memory of their erstwhile Muslim rulers with affection and nostalgia.[3] Hence they set themselves the task of educating the Hindus in looking at their history from a different angle.[4] These mentors succeeded only too well in their mission. For quite a long time it was almost an article of faith with Hindu intellectuals that the establishment of Muslim rule was an unparalleled disaster for the Hindu races. It is, however, significant that when Hindu scholars made themselves familiar with original sources, they reached reasonably sound conclusions.[5] And even more significant is the fact that the Hindu masses remained unaffected by British promptings until they were affected

[1] This sect was called Darshaniyah, from Hindi darshan, to behold some one sacred or venerable, Khawāfī Khān, i, p. 213; Ashraf Khān, f. 34b.

[2] *e.g.*, Sujān Rā'i Munshi, the author of *Khulāṣat-u't-tawārikh*, Rā'i Bindrāban the author of *Lubb-u't-tawārikh-i-Hind*, Chandra Bhan Brahman, the author of *Chahār Chaman*, to name only a few.

[3] vide Elliot and Dowson, pp. xii and xiii; also Elliot's original preface which was published with the *Bibliographical Index to the Historians of Mohammadan India* in 1849. Through his work Elliot hoped that the British "should no longer hear bombastic Babus..... rant about patriotism and the degradation of their present position". He sought to cure these "Babus" of nostalgia for Muslim rule. Bābū was a term of contempt used by the British for educated Hindus.

[4] *Ibid.*

[5] *e.g.*, Beni Prasad in his *Jahāngir:* Banarsi Prasad Saksena in his *Shāhjahān of Dihli*.

by the propaganda of virulent Hindu communal organisations.

In an age when media of mass publicity were not available to the government, the creation of a favourable image could be achieved only through sustained solid effort and the constant pursuit of benevolent and just policies. There was hardly ever an occasion when instructions were issued to subordinate officials that the benevolent feelings of the emperor were not reiterated.[6] In all books dealing with administration one finds a constant theme of emphasis upon a just and benevolent administration. The basic book on Mughul administration, the *Ā'īn-i-Akbarī*, and the numerous *dastūr-u'l-'amals* are alike in this respect. There are innumerable farmāns and other documents scattered all over the subcontinent and also preserved in various collections of the world where the anxiety of the Mughul government to dispense justice and look after the interests of the people finds constant expression. Indeed the evidence in favour of the benevolent character of the Mughul government is overwhelming. No sane monarch would again and again express his desire to act as the father of his people and direct his servants to be mindful of the interests of the population, if he were not sincerely benevolent, because otherwise he would be drawing constant attention to his own shortcomings and lack of public spirit. Furthermore, if the Mughul government had not been benevolent, the prestige of the Mughul emperor would not have been so high as to impel the destroyers of his authority like the Marathas and the British to clothe themselves with legal authority derived from him.[7]

The Mughul emperors possessed a high sense of responsibility. So much depended upon their character that the government would have collapsed if they had faltered or shown laxity. They had to be constantly vigilant to ensure compliance with their orders. They spent a good deal of time in listening to the reports from far flung parts of their empire and took pains to maintain

[6] There are too many examples to be given here. One selected at random is from the famous Muḥammad Hāshim farmān which says that the Emperor's mind is everguided by "affection and kindness towards the great and the small." *Oriental Miscellany*, 1789, p. 50.

[7] Vide *supra* Chapter II.

their news service and intelligence in proper gear. Their own life had to be rigorously disciplined, because their duties were heavy and exacting. They had little leisure. The greater part of their day was spent in the transaction of public business. Only men with an iron will and a strong sense of duty could have subjected themselves to such a rigorous schedule of duties. And when the dynasty failed to produce men of calibre it did collapse. No man can pay such a heavy price for the sake of power alone, if through that power he does not seek to attain some higher goal. This goal was the desire to earn the pleasure of God through the service of human beings. The Mughuls looked upon a proper discharge of their duties as worship.[8] Even if they had approached their duties with purely mundane desires, the object could have been only the achievement of glory. They were conscious of the fact that real glory could not be won with tyranny. The Mughuls knew it well that their power could be sustained only through the gratitude of their subjects. And they were deeply conscious that destiny had vested them with power and authority so that they could look after those who had been placed under them.[9] The emperors were sustained by such thoughts in the discharge of their onerous duties.

A corollary of this attitude was the endeavour to dispense justice. A screen in the Red Fort at Delhi has an emblem, a balance with even scales. It represents justice and embodies the Mughul ideal of dealing evenly with all. The Mughuls did not take into consideration the high position or power of the persecutor or the lowly status or weakness of the persecuted. Their courts were expected to dispense justice without fear or favour and they themselves were available for hearing the complaints of their subjects who might have felt deprived of some right or due. They devised methods of maintaining direct contacts with their subjects. They permitted no one to deny the poor and the lowly access if they sought justice. All servants of the state were instructed to prevent injustice and persecution and to punish those who were guilty of

[8] *e.g.*, Akbar said, "For rulers worship consists in the dispensation of justice and the improvement of the realm", Abū-'l-Faḍl, *Ā'īn-i-Akbarī*, v, p. 244.

[9] This is a familiar theme in all Mughul literature on administration.

transgressing the limits of their authority. The reporters scattered all over the empire were enjoined to report any lapse on the part of the officials. The Mughuls firmly believed in the text-book maxim found in all treatises on Muslim statecraft that "a polity can endure despite disbelief but it cannot last without justice".[10] The Prophet's saying that a moment spent in the dispensation of justice is better than seventy years of worship was widely quoted.[11] The Mughul government was, therefore, firmly established in justice. It had a well established system of courts which enforced widely accepted notions of right and wrong. The systems of law enforced by the Mughuls were civilized, generally accepted and conducive to orderly social life.

The Mughuls established a high standard of religious tolerance. Akbar's eclecticism led him to the extreme of weakening the hold of Islam upon the polity. Jahāngīr restored the rites and institutions of Islam that had come under eclipse because of Akbar's heterodoxy. Shah Jahān and 'Ālamgīr I were both orthodox in their approach to religious matters. Both of them have been criticized for their policies in the Deccan, but it can be easily demonstrated that they were guided by political considerations. As a matter of fact Shāh Jahān's policy was vacillating to a degree that the determination usually engendered by religious feelings was completely absent.[12] 'Ālamgīr I had no choice left but that of fighting to the bitter end the forces of anarchy and disorder let loose on his southern frontiers.[13] 'Ālamgīr's efforts to reintroduce the orthodox laws of Islam in relation to non-Muslims created resentment among the Hindus, but they did not result in any large scale persecution.[14] Hindus continued to occupy high positions and man revenue administration. There are extant a large number of documents recording grants of land and stipends to Hindu

[10] Niẓām-u'l-mulk, p. 8.

[11] The saying is quoted in a'n-Nuwairī, p. 33.

[12] For a fuller discussion vide *History of Freedom Movement*, i, pp. 24, 25.

[13] *Ibid.*, Also I.H. Qureshi, *The Muslim Community of the Indo-Pakistan Subcontinent*. pp. 165-167.

[14] *Ibid.*, pp. 161, 162.

temples and priests.[15] This shows that the charges of intolerance levelled against this monarch are grossly exaggerated. Whatever impact the emperor's measures had on the Hindus was limited to small sections of their population and to a short period of time. Even then 'Ālamgir's policies were far more tolerant than those of any non-Muslim monarch of those days. Intrinsically as well, these policies were neither comprehensive nor ruthlessly enforced.[16] Indeed they were often frustrated because of the lack of cooperation from Hindu civil servants. Even an effort to associate Muslims with Hindu officials did not succeed,[17] because it was not easy to find so many trained Muslims within such a short time. The reimposition of jiziyah did not bring much money to the coffers of the state because there were so many exemptions and the assessment was not too strict.[18] If 'Ālamgir I had been the tyrant to the Hindus that some later writers try to make him out, we should not have come across records of Hindu village communities granting lands in charity to the indigent among their coreligionists "to ward off evil from the head" of the Emperor.[19]

The Mughuls were great believers in merit. They prided themselves on being good judges of men. Akbar is reported to have said, "Kingship is in fact the understanding of men's worth."[20] Recruitment to the services was strictly on the basis of merit. Even friendship with the monarch did not result in rapid promotion. Akbar was distraught with grief when Abū-'l-Faḍl was waylaid and killed, but in spite of his undoubted literary talent, he did not rise too high either in his rank or his emoluments. Monarchs did not permit their personal likes and dislikes to affect the prospects of a public servant. They were even willing to ignore serious lapses in loyalty in able generals and administrators. So

[15] Jnan Chandra, "Aurangzib and Hindu Temples", *Journal of the Pakistan Historical Society*, Karachi, October 1957, pp. 247-254.

[16] Khawāfi Khan, ii, p. 252.

[17] *Ibid.*

[18] The entire province of Gujrat produced five hundred thousand rupees 'Alī Muḥammad Khān, i, p. 297.

[19] *Dastūr-u'l-'amal Awrangzib 'Ālamgir Pādshāh Ghāzi*, BM ms. Addl. 6599 f. 158b.

[20] Abū-'l-Faḍl, *Ā'in-i-Akbari*, v. p. 243.

genuine was the recognition of merit that men were drawn from various parts of the Muslim world and if they showed any talent or capacity, they received patronage and encouragement. Some of them, like I'timād-u'd-dawlah and Chīn Qilīch Khān rose to occupy important positions. Any person who showed talent for military or civil service could enter the Mughul services and, if he proved capable, earn promotions. At the time of recruitment sons of important officials received appointments in accordance with their merit.

The Mughuls had a progressive outlook. They were always willing to listen to new ideas and to try them out. They were on the look out for improving their arms. In the beginning they welcomed Ottoman engineers to improve their artillery. When they discovered that the Europeans had begun to manufacture better guns, they began to employ them. There was a gradual improvement in Mughul artillery as a result of this policy. Akbar sent a special envoy to the Portuguese to find out what new articles were available in their possessions. European paintings were welcome and were successfully imitated.

The Mughuls, however, were no blind imitators. They adopted whatever they thought was useful to them. They were circumscribed by their confidence in their resources and power. They failed to realize the danger of an expanding Europe. They do not seem to have awakened to the perilous importance of the problem posed by an aggressive sea power establishing a hold on the sea washing the shores of their dominions. However, it has to be conceded that so long as the Mughuls remained strong, they were capable of dealing with the Western intruders within the empire. 'Ālamgīr I taught the English a good lesson which led them to forget for some time their dreams of an Indian Empire. Earlier, Shāh Jahān had dealt effectively with the Portuguese pirates in Bengal despite the difficulty of the delta terrain for land forces. The Mughul Empire was sufficiently strong to deal with the smaller states within the subcontinent and to quell rebellions if they did not become general conflagrations. Even the Marathas received sharp blows and if 'Ālamgīr's successors had shown the same vigour and foresight, perhaps the end would not have been so dismal.

Intrinsically, however, the Mughul armies were weak. The manṣabdārī system had its strong points, but it weakened the military organisation. It mixed up civil and military matters and sometimes officers with reasonably good civilian capabilities were entrusted with difficult military campaigns which resulted in disasters. Bīr Bal's handling of the campaign against the North-western tribes illustrates the point. The Mughuls were not able to hold their own against the neighbouring empires. They lost Qandahar to Irān and Shāh Jahān's dream of bringing Central Asia under Mughul influence was shattered because of military weakness. It is obvious, therefore, that the empire could not be sustained by military strength. It had to earn the affection and the cooperation of the people, which it succeeded in doing through benevolence, justice and good government.

The Mughul Empire has rightly been called a culture state. It encouraged cultural endeavour through lavish patronage. It produced a galaxy of poets, historians, scholars, painters, calligraphists, architects, musicians and craftsmen. Its achievements in culture have received high praise, even from those who are otherwise critical of Mughul achievements and policies. The Mughuls brought about a renaissance in which, helped by good government and patronage, genius found a scope for blossoming into masterpieces. The emperors set a noble example which was followed by many great officials of rearing and rewarding talent. Some great men like Tulsīdāsa, the author of the *Rāmāyana*, preferred to live in obscurity, unknown to the court or the officials, only to become famous through popular acclaim. Others like Tānsen lived in the limelight of full official recognition. All, however, found their genius quickened by the great forces which this renaissance liberated. Behind every man who gained immortality there were many who, through interest and diligence, set standards that had to be excelled before recognition could come. Poplars grow tall only in forests, trees standing on bleak and barren land seldom survive the winds or drought. We have it on good authority that for every painter who was employed by the court or a noble there were many who practised their art in the bazar sustained by the interest of the common people. The same is true of poets, architects, craftsmen and musicians. Thus the appreciation of art in its various forms was widespread and culture was by no means the monopoly of the few.

Culture was sustained by tradition as well as by prosperity. The population of the subcontinent under the Mughuls has been estimated at a hundred million. There was no shortage of cultivable land. Indeed the anxiety of the state to ensure the expansion of cultivation shows that there was comparatively a shortage of peasants. This is readily understood if it is remembered that the empire was self-sufficient in all its needs and exported not only raw produce but finished materials as well.

In textiles alone, it clothed practically all the countries whose shores are washed by the Indian Ocean. Then it also exported cloth to Europe. At a later date even distant America felt the competition of the Indian looms.[21] Every township in the subcontinent has even now a number of weavers who still work on handlooms or have taken to other trades, mostly agriculture. This gives an indication how many were employed in the manufacture of cloth. Shipbuilding was another important industry. The forests of India provided the cheapest material for shipbuilding. The Arabs used ships built in India for their trade in the Indian Ocean.[22] Shipbuilding continued to be a thriving industry throughout the Muslim period. In the fourteenth century Friar Oderic crossed the Indian Ocean in an Indian ship manned by Indian seamen.[23] In 1670 East India Company's factor at Balasore wrote to the Court of Directors at London: "Many English merchants and others have their ships and vessels yearly built. Here is the best and well grown timber in sufficient plenty, the best iron upon the coast. Any sort of iron work is here ingeniously performed by the natives, as spikes, bolts, anchors and the

21 In 1816-17, "the cotton merchants of Massachusetts, Connecticut and Pennsylvania petitioned for protection against the low-priced goods from England and India". E.L. Bogart and D.L. Kemmerer, p. 391.

22 Barbosa, ii, pp. 76, 93, 107.

23 Mill, iii, p. 129.

like. Very expert master builders there are several here, they build very well and launch with as much discretion as I have seen in any part of the world. They have an excellent way of working shrouds, stays, and any other rigging for the ships."[24] Shipping remained an important industry upto the end of the eighteenth century. Wellesly wrote in 1800, "The port of Calcutta contains about 10,000 tons of shipping built in India of a description calculated for the conveyance of cargo to England."[25] This industry was destroyed because the ship builders of the port of London raised such a storm of protest that the Court of Directors forbade the use of Indian ships and sailors. England had to ban Indian built ships from carrying goods to her ports to save its own shipbuilding industry from competition.

There were several other articles like leather goods and candied fruit which found a ready market in other countries. Indian sugar found mention in the literature of other countries.[26] It was customary for men to wear arms and therefore there was a thriving industry for manufacturing swords, daggers, shields, armours, arrows, bows, spears and matchlocks. Indian knowledge of metallurgy made swords manufactured in the country famous in the world.[27] All this industry was sustained through manual work and needed a large number of workers.

There was a thriving community of traders, quite a few of them being merchant princes with wide connections and large investments. Some of them were richer than the East India Company in the seventeenth century.[28]

[24] Quoted in Mookerji, p. 333.

[25] *Ibid*., p. 182.

[26] *e.g.*, Ḥāfiẓ.

شکر شکن شوند همه طوطیان هند   زین قند پارسی که به بنگاله می رود

[27] A good example of Indian knowledge of metallurgy is provided by the iron pillar at Quṭb near Delhi which is the purest iron in existence and it does not rust because of its purity.

[28] Manrique, ii, p. 140 says that Patna possessed six hundred brokers and a large number of traders. Fryer, i, p. 289 speaks of many brokers carrying on business on behalf of principals in upcountry "that drive as great a trade as the Company". Manrique. (i. 44) says that Khatri merchants of Dacca possessed such vast quantities of money "that being difficult to count, it used commonly to be weighed". About Dehlī he says that its houses of merchants had "such vast sums of money piled up that if they had been covered over they would have struck the ordinary gaze as being merely heaps of grain rather than piles of anything so very unusual". Thevenot, p. 29, mentions that Shīvāji took from one house of a bania "30,000,000 francs".

There was a middle class in the towns which consisted of civil and military personnel of the government, merchants, artisans, teachers, physicians and others. The Mughul government was a complicated bureaucracy which needed a large number of public servants. There was a standing army that absorbed even larger members. There was little pressure on cultivable land and there was a comparative scarcity of peasants. This is borne out by the fact that throughout the period the government found it necessary to maintain production of agricultural commodities at a satisfactory level to feed the people and supply several industries with raw materials which it was able to do only by encouraging cultivation.

Throughout the period there was an active trade between the Empire and the littoral areas of the Indian Ocean and beyond to Europe in the West and China in the East in many manufactured and raw commodities.[29] All travellers testify to the low prices of commodities,[30] an impression that is confirmed by the data in the *Ā'īn-i-Akbarī* and other local authorities. Prices were not low because of any scarcity of species. There is incontrovertible evidence of abundance of coins and precious metals.[31] Abundance of species and low prices cannot exist together for any length of time without abundance of production. No customary regime of prices can last without a scientific basis. The only conclusion that can be drawn is that there was abundance of production which means prosperity. And this conclusion is supported by all other evidence that we possess.

Moreland has been led away by the writings of some travellers who were struck by the simplicity of the furniture in rural homes

29 Some of the articles that find mention are: textiles, wheat, millets, rice, pulses, oilseeds, scents, ginger, sugar, fish, precious stones, indigo, hides, opium, leather goods, saltpetre, beads, borax, lac, drugs etc.

30 Nikitin lived on 2/3 farthing a day in India; Vasco da Gama could buy for a penny bread that could sustain a man for a day in an area where wheat was not plentiful; he could buy a shirt for 1/10 of the price he would have paid in Portugal. (Girdlamo Seringi's letter on Vasco da Gama's first voyage.)

31 One reads of large sums of money hoarded in forts, temples and in the houses of merchants and private persons. The sums of money that fell into the hands of conquerors time and again sound fabulous. For merchants vide supra. Hoarding and use of silver and gold jewellery has been a common practice.

and the custom among the Hindus of certain areas of dressing scantily.[32] These factors were based in climate and social mores and had to do nothing with poverty.[33] In a climate where it is more pleasant outdoors, too many rooms and heavy furniture are not necessary. The oriental custom of sitting upon the floor obviates most of the furniture used in the West.

A wealthy state can exist only among a prosperous people. A poor people could not have sustained the most splendorous empire of the age. Prosperity cannot exist without good government and enlightened policies.

Travellers from Europe and Asia were alike struck by the magnificence of the imperial and gubernatorial courts, the establishments of high officials and merchant princes and of state functions. The architectural remains tell but a part of the story of the splendour that was the Mughul Empire. Only people with refined tastes and a sense of proportion and beauty could have built mausoleums like the Taj Mahal and I'timād-u'd-dawlah, mosques like the Jāmi' Masjid and the Pearl Mosque and palaces like the forts of Agra and Shāhjahānābād. Under the Mughuls the art of living attained an incomparable grace, polite behaviour received an unsurpassed polish and good taste achieved a rare refinement.

[32] Moreland, *India at the Death of Akbar*, pp. 274 ff.

[33] Compare Tavernier, ii, p. 63 who says, "In this country one pays no attention to dress and a person who has but a miserable ell of calico about his loins may some times have a good parcel of diamonds concealed." Also, Nicolo di Conti who says "The style of dress is different in different regions. Wool is very little used. There is great abundance of flax and silk, and of these they make their garments. Almost all, both men and women, wear a linen cloth bound round the body so as to cover the front of the person and descending as low as the knees and over this a garment of linen or silk, which, with the men descends to just below the knees, and with the women, to the ankles. They cannot wear more clothing on account of great heat, and for the same reason they only wear sandals with purple and golden ties, as we see in ancient statues. In some places, the women have shoes made of leather, and ornaments of gold on their arms and on their hands, also around their necks and legs, of the weight of three pounds and studded with gems. The manner of adorning the head is various, but for the most part the head is covered with a cloth embroidered with gold, the hair being bound up with a silken cord." Major, *India in the XV century* pp. 22, 23. This evidence can be multiplied. 'Abd-u'r-Razzāq speaks of Hindus in Malabar going about only with loin cloths, but then "the king and beggars both go in this fashion" 'Abd-u'r-Razzāq (v. ii, f. 239b). When he had audience with the Zamorin he "saw a man with his body naked like the other Hindus". *Ibid.* The Zamorin was not naked because he could not afford clothes.

For more than two centuries the standards set by them were accepted as ideals by the cultured sectors of the society and they began to lose their validity only when the prestige of the West dimmed the memories of the past and introduced new norms and mores. Such lasting victories could be won only through good administration and high ideals of government and meticulous care for the welfare of the people.

APPENDIX A

The Ā'īn-i-dahsālah

THE translation of this Ā'īn in Blochmann and Jarrett's work is full of errors; it has caused a number of scholars to go astray in understanding the true significance of Akbar's measures. Vincent Smith and others jumped to the conclusion that the settlement was decennial and was revised every 10 years. This conclusion is completely unwarranted. Moreland has laid students of Indian History under obligation by publishing a new translation with an illuminating commentary in his book *The Agrarian System of Moslem India*. He has removed a number of misunderstandings, yet his translation is not free from errors and his commentary, in spite of its success in throwing welcome light on the nature of Akbar's reforms, fails to remove all the misconceptions. The study of the problem has been carried a little further in this appendix.

It is necessary to begin with a new translation. For the sake of convenience Moreland's version has been maintained, except where the needs of accurate understanding demand otherwise.

Translation

1. From the beginning of this eternal reign, every year unavaricious and high minded experts used to ascertain prices and lay them before the royal court,
2. and taking the schedule of crop yields and the prices thereof, used to fix the schedule of demand rates (dastūr),
3. and this caused great vexation.
4. During the time when Khwājah 'Abd-u'l-Majīd Āṣaf Khān held the exalted post of the wazīr, the jam' of the realm was raqamī,
5. and whatever entered the minds (of the officials) was added (to the valuation just) with the pen and (then) given in assignment,
6. As the empire was not extensive, and such servants as rendered (meritorious) services were promoted frequently,
7. there used to be increase and decrease from bribe taking and self interest.
8. And when this supreme office (*i.e.*, the wizārat) came to Muẓaffar Khān and Rājah Todar Mal in the 15th Ilāhi year, they took the taqsīmāt-i-mulk from the qānūngūs,
9. (and) the maḥṣūl having been determined by conjecture and estimate, a new jam' was put into force.
10. Ten qānūngūs were nominated who received statements from the local qānūngūs and deposited them in the record office.
11. Although (the new jam') fell somewhat below the former, yet there was great distance between it (*i.e.*, the new jam') and the ḥāṣil.
12. And when, through the wisdom of the sovereign, the empire was greatly extended, every year there used to be great trouble in ascertaining prices,
13. and various difficulties used to arise from delay. Sometimes the peasant would have to complain of excess demand, and sometimes the assignee would have to lament arrears.
14. His Majesty proposed a remedy and established the jam'-i-dahsālah (which gave general satisfaction).

15. From the 15th to the 24th year they added up the maḥṣūl for ten years and took 1/10th of that as harsālah;
16. But "they" took the ascertained figures for the 20th to the 24th years, and (those) for the previous five years from the statements of upright men,
17. and the harsāl of the jins-i-kāmil was thus ascertained;
18. And the year which was superfluous was taken out; as is given in the following tables.

It is necessary at the outset to explain the reasons for differing from Moreland's translation where I have done so materially. In the first sentence Moreland has "throne" whereas I have used the phrase "royal court." The phrase used in the original is wālā dargāh and obviously refers to the Ministry. Abū-'l-Faḍl would not even dream of suggesting that the Emperor looked personally into the matter and yet the system did not work, because it is a historical fact that Akbar was not interested in the administration at the beginning of the reign. In the second sentence Moreland uses the phrase "the schedule of cash rates" whereas I have used the phrase "the schedule of demand rates." The original uses dastūr and it is obvious from the context that the purpose was to fix a demand-rate in cash. Land was grouped together on this basis into dastūrs which is additional evidence for my conclusion. The fifth sentence is translated by Moreland in the following words "and they used to show whatever they pleased with the pen of enhanced salary." This does not make sense. Actually tan numūdan is a technical term and means the award of an assignment or fixing a salary. Qalam should be read without an iḍāfah. Moreland has been misled by Blochmann who has put an iḍāfah on qalam in his text. The sentence should simply read "ānchih ba khāṭir mi rasid ba qalam afzūdah tan mī numūdand". The sense would be clear if the reader pauses a little after rasid and then after afzūdah. Qalam-i-afzūdah is contrary to Persian idiom and a purist like Abū-'l-Faḍl could not be guilty of its perpetration. The significance of mī should be kept in view. It denotes māḍī istimrārī and implies continuity. The officials continued arbitrary inflation without any method as individual cases of assignment came before them. In the eleventh sentence it is obvious that Abū-'l-Faḍl is referring to the difference between the new jam' and the actual yield and I do not think that Moreland's conjecture that the reference is to the former jam' is logical. My translation of the 17th and 18th sentences is entirely different from Moreland for reasons which I will discuss in greater detail a little later.

As must have been noticed, the translation is full of technical terms and, therefore, it is necessary to interpret it further. Moreland in the commentary on his translation, has raised a number of points which will also require discussion. The first sentence, as Moreland also says, is fairly clear. Here we are told that at the beginning of the reign experts used to ascertain prices and report them to the Ministry of Finance. On the basis of these reports the schedules of crop yields which had been maintained for some time were converted into cash schedules. The results were unsatisfactory because of delay. This perhaps implies that the older method of permitting the local officials to commute the state demand into cash had been discarded and the court laid down the rates for all cash payments. This, of course, would result in difficulties. Next we are told that when 'Abd-u'l-Majid Āṣaf Khān was the wazīr the jam' of the realm was raqami. Moreland has raised the question whether the word jam' means demand or valuation. In my opinion there can be little doubt that jam' refers to valuation and not to demand. It is obvious that it would be impossible without serious consequences to fix the demand rate arbitrarily without any reference to the actual yield because the peasant would neither be willing nor able to pay an arbitrarily inflated demand. Raqamī, which simply means written, would mean that the jam' was arbitrary and not based on actual yields. Moreland himself dismisses the possibility of jam' being demand for valid reasons. The more important of these are—

(1) That the figures in Ā'īn-i-Nūzdahsālah would become meaningless and fictitious; this would mean a double process of seasonal calculation of assessment rates not intended to be used and arbitrary fixing of demand without any reference to these rates;

(2) This would further imply a lump assessment which is opposed to the entire spirit of Akbar's measures from the beginning; and

(3) The purpose for which this was done has been mentioned in the next sentence which was the artificial increase in the salaries of the high officials which was paid by assignment. An inflated demand would not have required inflation in the value of the assignments though the *Ā'īn* clearly mentions that it was the assignments which were inflated in their valuation. Besides, we are also told in *Akbarnāmah* (ii, 270) that Akbar turned his attention to the artificial valuation which had been nominally increased for the sake of appearances owing to a large number of high officials and the smallness of the realm. Here also the words used are jam'-i-raqami-i-qalamī and this inflation in valuation was the cause of corruption. Musta'id Khān (on page 213) mentions the same fact in more clear language and calls the valuation of the assignments a pillar of snow which figuratively meant that the assignment offered seemed to be substantial, but the first warmth of reality melted it away. It is also obvious that the peasants would not be in a position to offer bribes to the officials of the Ministry and, therefore, corruption could increase and decrease only the valuation of the assignment.

Thus it is clearly valuation alone which is the subject of these sentences. A uniform inflation of valuation can give the government some insight into the real state of affairs, but because of corruption the inflation had not been uniform and, therefore, the entire record of the state, so far as the yield and valuation were concerned, had been thrown into confusion. It was, therefore, necessary that something should be done to find out the real state of affairs. We are, therefore, told that when Muzaffar Khān and Rājah Todar Mal were appointed in the Ministry, an effort was made to find out the real facts. Taqsīmāt-i-mulk clearly refers to the schedules of produce because Barani used the phrase qismāt-i-būd-wa-nābūd and it is obvious that taqsīmāt is another version of that phrase. Qismāt-i-būd-wa-nābūd means schedules of yield and the failure of crops. It is obvious that the new ministers appointed qānūngūs to collect the schedules from the various areas. This is yet another proof of the fact that the demand was not inflated. It was only the valuation which had beer tampered with, because the local officials maintained a record of the actual produce irrespective of what was shown in the official records for the purpose of deceiving either the assignee or the world. As the result of this measure a new jam' was produced. This jam' was clearly a new valuation and not a new assessment of the demand rate.

The Ā'īn then goes on to the question of assessment and does not mention the fact of the new valuation. But this information is supplied by *Akbarnāmah* (iii, p. 170) which tells us that this valuation was also unsatisfactory and, therefore, the officers were put upon a cash salary so that valuation might not be required. The rest of the Ā'īn is devoted to the formulation of a new method by which a new demand rate could be fixed. This has created difficulties for Moreland who is still thinking in terms of valuation. He ignores the basic fact that a correct valuation depends upon an accurate assessment of state demand and a reliable record of land brought under cultivation. Ignoring this fact Moreland creates difficulties for himself. One factor which has misled him is that he thinks that the word maḥṣūl in the 15th sentence means revenue. If he had referred to the Ā'īn regarding the classification of land, he would have seen that maḥṣūl has been technically defined as the medium produce. By thinking that maḥṣūl has been used in the sense of revenue, Moreland holds that an average of 10 years' revenue receipts would give a new valuation and not a demand rate and, therefore, it is obvious that if maḥṣūl were to mean revenue receipts and not medium produce, the process mentioned in the sentences 15 and 16 would yield only a valuation.

This interpretation, however, leads Moreland into an illogical position. The first difficulty in that position, as he himself recognises, is that this could not be the remedy of the evil mentioned in the beginning, *i.e.*, the breakdown in the method of commutation and the second difficulty which is even more baffling is that the tables following the Ā'īn do not give valuation but demand rates. It would be a very strange situation indeed if in the description of the method of finding a new valuation Abū-'l-Faḍl should start by narrating the difficulties in commuting the state demand into cash and end by giving absolutely irrelevant tables instead of the valuation of the various areas. Moreland tries to get over this difficulty by saying that the text of the Ā'īn must be corrupt. This is by no means a happy position.

Moreland discusses the possibility of the jam'-i-dahsālah meaning the whole process of finding a new valuation by fixing the new demand rate. But he dismisses it for the following reasons:—

(1) New schedules of demand rates were introduced at this time and are on the record in the Ā'īn;

(2) A new valuation was required at this time;

(3) The process described would not give the demand rates on record.

(1) and (3) go together. The calculation of a proper valuation is not ruled out if the process includes the fixation of a new demand rate. As a matter of fact, as I have said before, it was necessary to have a scientific method of fixing the demand rate for the purpose of calculating a new valuation. The only relevant question, therefore, is whether the process described would give the demands on record

Now if it is taken for granted that the rates in the 19 years' Ā'īn and in the 10 years' Ā'in are those of the state demand, the figures given in the Ā'in-i-dahsālah would naturally be different; firstly, because of the diversity of rates mentioned in the 19 years' Ā'īn, it would be difficult to find figures for every area and, secondly, the fact that the rates are based upon calculations arrived at before the Ā'īn-i-dahsālah came into existence. If this were not so, there would have been no need to bring about the new reform. The cash rates, therefore, in the 19 years' Ā'īn must have been revised. Therefore, the figures in the Ā'īn-i-dahsālah should not necessarily be based upon the figures in the 19 years' Ā'īn.

If the word mahsūl is translated as medium produce, the following system seems to be evolved in the new Ā'īn. The figures of the medium produce for ten years would be added and a tenth of the total would be treated as the average yield. The average produce would give the state demand for the year. It could then be converted into cash rates. On the basis of these figures a new valuation would be drawn up. For the purpose of preventing the demand rate from becoming fictitious it would be necessary to base it on the actual data of previous years and to make it progressive. Hence a double process is indicated. The average demand would be found out for the current year and the actual produce as well as the actual level of prices must be ascertained for the purpose of finding out the new average for the next year. This is the only probable method and this is the only conclusion that can be drawn from a correct reading of the Ā'in. To describe this method a little more fully an interpretation of the last 5 sentences of the translation is necessary. The medium produce for 10 years was added up and 1/10th of this total was declared to be the average produce for the ensuing year. The technical word for this was harsāl or harsālah. The Ministry possessed the correct figures for five years from the 20th to the 24th year and the previous figures were taken from the statements of upright men which I presume refers to the local officers who had maintained their records.

The last two sentences of my translation are exceedingly controversial and they require a word of explanation because I have differed from other translators or interpretors of these sentences. The difficulty is based partly upon a wrong appreciation of the technical terms and partly upon a misreading of the simple text. The Ā'in has the following sentence:

وهر سال جنس کامل اعتبار نمود - سالے که افزوں بود برگرفتند

It would be remembered in this very Ā'in harsālah is used for the average produce of the ten years. In this sentence the word harsāl is only another form of harsālah and refers to the average produce of the last 10 years. Jins-i-kāmil is the full produce which has not been affected by any calamity or loss. Therefore, the first sentence means that in this way the (decennial) average of the full produce was obtained. It is obvious that when the figures for 10 years have been added and divided by 10 they give the average produce of the last 10 years and the full produce implies that the figure obtained would give the rate without making allowances for partial or complete failure of crops. It should here be noted that the state always made deductions for such failures. In case of a complete failure the area was excluded from the assessment and realization of the state demand. A proportionate deduction was made for partial failure. The next sentence means that when the medium produce of the last year was added the figures would then be for more than 10 years. Therefore, every year one figure would become superfluous and that was taken out. In other words, when the figure for the 11th year was added the figure for the first year was taken out. This is the simple and most straight forward interpretation of these two sentences. Authors have unnecessarily created difficulties. They have held without justification that whenever the crops improved, the decennial average was left out and the best crop was only taken into consideration. This is absurd, because there was a different schedule for every kind of crop, and, therefore, the question of taking into consideration the better or the worse crop did not arise. If they refer to a good yield, then if the law of average were to apply in cases of poor yield only and good yield were to be charged differently because that would bring more money to the state, it would result in great injustice to the peasant. It is, however, obvious that it was the decennial average only which formed the basis of the state demand; otherwise the whole system would have broken down. Similarly, the last sentence has been interpreted by some writers to mean precisely the same thing, that is, in a year when there was a higher yield, it was the figure of the higher yield only that was taken into consideration in fixing the state demand. Abū-'l-Faḍl who is the soul of brevity so far as the Ā'īn is concerned, was not so foolish as to repeat himself There seems to be no satisfactory interpretation of these two sentences, other than the one which is offered in this appendix.

Irfan Habib (*The Agrarian System of Mughul India*, pp. 191, 204 etc.) has taken strong exception to some of these conclusions (partly published in the *Journal of Pakistan Historical Society*, Vol. I, Pt. iii). First he questions Moreland's and my identification of taqsīmāt with schedules of state demand depending upon yield.

He begins by demanding proof that Barani's phrase qismāt-i-būd-wa-nābūd refers to schedules of yield and failure of crops. One should have thought that the dictionary meanings of the word leave no room for conjecture or doubt. Qismāt is from qismat, a pait or portion, būd is existence and nābūd is non-existence. These are, however, primary meanings, though strongly suggestive of the technical significance of the terms. Taqsīm, any elementary Arabic dictionary would show, is, with reference to revenue administration, the assessment of the state demand on agricultural produce (*e.g.* Steingass; *Al-mu'jam-u'l-ā'ẓam*, Karachi, n.d. etc.). Similarly qismāt, in the same context means a portion of agricultural produce; būd in the context of agriculture is produce and nābūd, lack of it or failure of crops. For būd Irfan Habib could refer to his own book (p. 198, f.u. 10 where he quotes B.M. ms. Additional 6603, f. 849 to define hast-wa-būd as "what is being currently cultivated and grown." Is this not crops? Similarly he uses nābūd (*ibid*, p. 199, f.n. 14) in the sense of lack of crops. This would naturally include lack of cultivation as well as total or partial failure of crops in case of cultivation. Qismāt-i-būd-wa-nābūd, could therefore, be only statements regarding crops grown, yields and failure of crops. I have cited Moreland not "as the only proof" (as Irfan Habib thinks), but just to mention that he agrees with my conclusions.

Now let us turn to taqsimāt. I have referred in the preceding paragraphs to the dictionary meaning of taqsīm, as assessment, taqsīmāt is therefore, statements of state demand which would incorporate yield. Irfan Habib rightly holds that taqsīmāt came to be called mawāzinah in the 17th Century (p. 203 f.n. 35). The mawāzinah, he continues, contained "particulars of the land revenue and other taxes (mal-o-s'air), details of the number of villages in the pargana; and, finally area statistics". He then adds on the authority of the *Hidāyat-u'l-qawā'id* (a ms. in Muslim University Library Aligarh) that "revenue and area" were the main items that the taqsīm or mawāzinah-i-dahsālah contained. From this he argues that taqsīmāt could not be schedules of yield. A perusal of the evidence produced by him would show that the mawāzinah was concerned with the assessment of the state demand and, as a corollary with valuation, the basis of both being schedules of yield. The subsidiary information regarding area and other taxes was obviously included for finding out the total income from the area. It has been already said, as is obvious from the text that the determination of the state demand and valuation were the dual purposes of the Ā'īn-i-dahsālah. The Ā'īn also, when it gives tables after the text of the Ā'īn-i-dahsālah, gives information regarding parganahs, maḥāls, dastūrs etc. Chhatar Mal's *Dīwān Pasand* (B.M. or 2011) says that the 'āmil took mawāzinah-i-dahsālah from the qānūngūs for the purpose of correct assessment of the villages" and that the mawāzinah-i-dahsālah was also called dawl. Khwājah Yāsīn mentions the term dawl-i-ta<u>shkh</u>īṣ, in which the names of villages and parganahs with jam' were written. The jam' was made peasant-wise and was added up to form the assessment for the entire village and then the parganah for the purpose of valuation and accounting. The main purpose of the taqsīmāt, mawāzinah-i-dahsālah or dawl-i-ta<u>shkh</u>īṣ was proper assessment, which could be based only on crop sharing or schedules of produce. The term dawl-i-ta<u>shkh</u>īṣ itself is significant because ta<u>shkh</u>īṣ is assessment, the dictionary meaning being to fix or identify, hence to assess, to diagnose. It is obvious that mawāzinah-i-dahsālah came into use after the reforms mentioned in the Ā'īn-i-dahsālah and earlier taqsīmāt was the only term in use. They must have given the data of the yield and the partial or full failure of crops, hence their identity with qismāt-i-būd-wa-nābūd. Supplementary information regarding area under different crops was included to complete the data.

Now let us take up the question of the determination of the text in sentences 17 and 18. The following are the readings:

Blochhmann—Wa harsāl-i-jins-i-kāmil-i'tibār numūd. Sāle ki afzūn būd bar giriftand.

(وهر سال جنس کامل اعتبار نمود - سالے که افزون بود بر گرفتند)

R A S 116, I.O. 266, 267, 268, 270—Wa harsāl jins-i-kāmil afzūn būd. (و هر سال جنس کامل افزون بود)

I.O. 264, BM. Addl. 6546, 7652—wa har māl-i-jins-i-kāmil i'tibār numūd wa sāle ki afzūn būd bar giriftand.

(وهر سال جنس کامل اعتبار نمود - سالے کہ افزوں بود بر گرفتند)

I.O. 265 has partāl (پرتال) instead of harsāl (هرسال)

BM. Addl. 5645 has har sāl bar māl (هرسال بر مال) instead of harsāl (هرسال)

BM. Addl. 5609 has tarsāl (ترسال) instead of harsāl (هرسال)

Cambridge has harḥāl (هرحال) instead of harsāl (هرسال)

BM or 2169, Add 6552 has nīzmāl (نیزمال) instead of harsāl (هر سال)

Moreland and Irfan Habib are inclined to accept the reading nīz māl, because they think that B.M. Or. 2169 is the earliest of the manuscripts and because it seems to yield an interpretation that is more satisfactory to them. Moreland thinks that this reading "gives a technical sense, much better than anything that can be read into the remainder" (*The Agrarian System of Moslem India*, Allahabad, n.d., p. 250). Moreland translates the sentence as follows:

"And also taking into account the figures known as māl-i-jins-i-kāmil, "they" took the year which was greatest, as the table shows."

Moreland argues that the figures which were averaged were those of demand and not demand rates, that māl-i-jins-i-kāmil is demand on high crops, for which the highest and not the average produce was considered as the basis. For an up to date valuation, in his opinion, it was proper that the demand of the last ten years be averaged except in case of high grade crops, because being the result of improvements provided by the state, the cultivation of such crops should bring the maximum benefit to the state. After having argued all this, Moreland is confronted with the fact that the Ā'īn does not give figures of valuation, but a schedule of demand rates. Surely an interpretation that leads the author into such a gross contradiction cannot be considered satisfactory.

Irfan Habib (p. 207-209) offers the following translation:

> "And the revenue on the high grade (or cash) crops was also fixed (or assumed); they took the year when it was greater. It is accordingly shown in the table."

In the case of perishable commodities an early assessment before they could be marketed was an administrative necessity. He thinks that for certain crops, like indigo, poppy, pān, turmeric, hemp and paundā sugar cane under this category, no crop rate could be fixed that could be of any use, their price being liable to fluctuations every harvest. Unfortunately no evidence has been adduced to substantiate this view. It is unlikely that the price fluctuations were too great in the economy of the period. Besides, was assessme nt made when the crops had already been sold? This also would be against the general pattern of assessment, which was made when crops were harvested in case of sharing and much earlier in case of appraisement, measurement or ḍabṭ. And then the schedule which follows gives rates of demand for these products. It may be argued that these are not based on an average of ten years, but on the figures of "the best" year. What could be the point in this? If the rates for the ten years were not available, then the average of the years for which they were available would have been taken. Supposing for the sake of argument that for some mysterious reason, the averages were considered impracticable, then the figure for the last year was more likely to be included in the table given in the Ā'īn. Thus there arise major contradictions in accepting this interpretation as well.

Let us turn for a moment to the meanings of the terms.

Is it correct to assume that jins-i-kāmil means better grade or cash crops? Irfan Habib refers for instance to *Ā'īn-i-Akbarī*, i, p. 286 where the sentence is

"دریں زمین اگر جنس کامل بکارند در سال اول چهارم حصه از دستورکم
ستاند و در ضبطی اگر از سال گذشته گزیر جنس زیاده و زمین کم آید و جمع
موافق ازیں کاستگی بر نجوشد و درنیاویزد"

"In these lands if they cultivate jins-i-kāmil, a fourth of the rate should be remitted in the first year, and in dabṭī if better jins is more and the area is less and the jam' is the same (compared to the last year) he (the 'āmil) should not be annoyed nor should he enter into an argument".

"These lands" refers in the context of the earlier sentence, to crops sharing holdings which were encouraged to pay revenue in cash on the basis of bazar rates.

The point to note is that Abū-'l-Faḍl uses jins-i-kāmil in one place and jins-i-guzīn in the other. Is it not possible that the concession of a reduction of a fourth was for growing crops to the desired level of production which was considered standard?

Is it logical to rule out that jins-i-kāmil and jins-i-guzīn are not identical in their meaning? If jins-i-kāmil means standard yield, it is obvious that the repetition of jins-i-kāmil in the second instance would be totally inappropriate. Why should the concession be limited to crops sharing lands, if inferior crops were replaced by superior ones? On the other hand if a crops sharing holding was not producing the standard yield, it was first encouraged to accept a cash assessment based on the yield and the current market prices and then to come under the ḍabṭī system by raising its productivity to the desired level. As a concession for its effort a concession of 25 per cent in the standard demand was offered. If on the other hand the holding continued to be crops sharing and produced high grade crops, the state and the peasant would proportionately share the benefit and the standard rate not being applicable to him the question of any reduction in it would not arise. Even if the superior crops were perishable the share of the state would be based on the yield though worked out in cash. A concession of 25 per cent is possible only on 'standard rates' applicable to standard crops. (Here the term 'standard rate' has been used for a demand rate arrived at by working out a decennial average based on medium produce as prescribed in the Ā'īn-i-dahsālah.).

The dictionary defines kāmil as "full" or "complete". To translate it as "superior" is to distort the meaning grossly. It is used as an antonym of nāqiṣ, incomplete. That is the reason why *Akbarnāmah* (iii, p. 458) says "agar jinse nuqṣān pizirad", if there is a partial failure of crops. That jins is often used for crops in the context of revenue administration is borne out by Chhatar Mal in *Dīwān Pasand* (ff 9b, 10a) where it says that the khasrah should show ārāḍī-i-nābūd wa ārāḍī-i-jins, lands without crops and with crops. On f. 5 it says that so far as possible jins-i-kāmil should be cultivated so that jam'-i-kāmil be realised. It is obvious that full cultivation would yield full revenue. Irfan Habib is therefore hasty in saying that jins-i-kāmil invariably refers to better or cash crops and never to crops bearing full or complete yields.

The word i'tibār occurs, as Irfan Habib points out, in the *Āī'n-i-Akbarī* (v. 1, p. 26) in connection with the standard proportion of dāms to rupees:

از چهل دام اگر چه نرخ افزون و کم شود، لیکن درمواجب این قیمت اعتبار رود

Translation: Though the price (of the rupees) fluctuates between more and less than forty dāms, yet this price is the standard for salaries.

Irfan Habib translates i'tibār rawad as adopted (p. 204). His translation conveys the general sense in the context of this passage, but it is not accurate.

I'tibār, say *Ghiyāth-u'l-lughāt* and *Muntakhab*, means to consider something good.

The Arabic *Al-mu'jam-u'l-ā'ẓam* translates i'tibār as respect, esteem. Faiḍi (a contemporary) says

گذشت آنکه زغم خواری سگان درت
میان اهل وفا اعتبار داشتمے

Another poet says
همت بلند دارکه نزد خدا وخلق
باشد بقدرهمت تو اعتبار تو

In the subcontinent i'tibār came to mean trust, confidence. Ghālib says

ترے وعدہ پر جئے هم تو یه جان جهوٹ جانا
که خوشی سے مر نه جاتے اگر اعتبار هوتا

Now it stands to reason that i'tibār numūdan, i'tibār raftan have been used by Abū-'l-Faḍl in the sense of being worthy of esteem, hence acceptable, and therefore standard. The subsequent meaning of i'tibār as trust, confidence must have, historically speaking, grown from it.

Then there is the phrase harsāl. In this very Ā'īn the term harsālah has been defined as the average produce. It is by no means far fetched to think that harsāl is another form of the same term, especially if it can yield a meaning that would give a rational interpretation of the text.

Let us now turn to the various texts:

1. (Harsāl jins-i-kāmil afzūn būd) Every year jins-i-kāmil increased or the annual figure of the yield of full crops increased.

This reading does not fit into the context. Even as a general remark it comes abruptly and is a logical non sequitor.

2. Har māl-i-kāmil i'tibār numūd: Every full revenue [that is revenue without deductions] was standardized.

3. Partāl, harsāl, barmāl, tarsāl, har ḥāl: The last three may be dismissed as yielding little sense. Only partāl may be considered. It is a Hindi word and means appraisal. The meaning would be "Appraisal of full crops were standardized".

4. nīz māl-i-jins-i-kāmil i'tibār numūd, "and the revenue from full crop was standardized."

5. The harsāl of full crops was also standardized. Except for (1) which omits the phrase اعتبار نمود all readings yield one of two meanings: The decennial average of full crops was standardized or the revenue figures of full crops were standardized. It is interesting to see that in spite of the obvious difficulties, the copyists tried to convey almost the same sense. Some of them seem to have wandered into har māl and nīz māl because of their failure to grasp the technical nature of the phrase harsāl.

Now let us take to the sentence no. 18. sāle ki afzūn būd bar giriftand, سالے که افزوں بود بر گرفتند . Once again let us turn to the dictionary, Bar giriftan means to pick up. It has the contradictory meanings of taking up and taking out. There are examples of the former in this Ā'īn itself. For the second: see Ḥāfiẓ who says

ساقی بیا که یار ز رخ پرده بر گرفت
کار چراغ خلوتیاں باز در گرفت

or again

بار غمے که خاطر ما خسته کرده بود
عیسیٰ دمے خدا بفرستاد و بر گرفت

In both of these couplets bar girift cannot mean anything except discarding or lifting out. Afzūn is excessive, also extra or superfluous. But then Irfan Habib challenges this on the basis of facts. He argues that "It is implicit, rather than explicit, in Abul Fazl's account and the nature of the tables, that the final dastūrs were permanent" (p. 210). Simultaneously he concedes that "revisions took place from time to time" (*ibid*). There is evidence to show that Irfan Habib's assumption that the schedules were permanent is not correct. On the other hand the evidence in support of my interpretation is considerable. The Ā'īn was promulgated in the 25th year of Akbar's reign (*i.e.*, 1581-82). Irfan Habib is of the opinion that the schedule given in the Ā'īn was revised and represents the figures of the 40th year rather than the 24th. If that opinion is correct, than surely, whatever the reasons, and I do not agree with Irfan Habib's arguments, it stands to reasons that a schedule proclaimed in 1581-82 could not have lasted until 1707. Is there a record of another promulgation of an entirely new schedule during this period? There are ample references to new measures that were adopted in the subsequent reigns in connection with agrarian administration, but I have not come across (nor for that matter Irfan Habib mentions) the promulgation of new schedules. The reason is obvious. So long as administrative efficiency lasted, the built in device of constant revision of the schedules by adding the "medium" produce of the latest year and taking out the eleventh year (working backwards) was used to bring the demand rates up to date.

But the case for my interpretation does not depend upon historical probability alone. The term mawāzinah-i-dahsālah does not occur before the promulgation of the Ā'īn-i-dahsālah, but it is found in constant use afterwards. That is not all. We have two sets of figures. The first is jam'-i-sanwāt, "the revenue figures for years". Those were to be consulted in cases of assessment. (*Kaifiyat-i-sūbajāt-i-mumālik-i-maḥrūsah-i-Hindustān*, f 229a). The same authority says that the kaifiyat (report on assessment) should have columns on jam'-i-dāmī (cash assessment), ḥāṣil-i-kāmil (full produce, *i.e.*, standard full produce without allowing for partial failure in certain holdings) and jam'-i-sanwāt, that is the assessment of years. Irfan Habib himself has a note (pp. 203-204. f.n. 35) based on several authorities, which mention taqsim-i-sanwāt as well as taqsīm-i-yaksālah. Then he also concedes that taqsim-i-sanwāt is identical with mawāzinah-i-dah sālah. Now taqsīm-i-yaksālah gave figures for one year and as taqsim-i-sanwāt is the same as mawāzinah-i-dahsālah, it must have given, as the latter name shows, figures for ten years. The question is: which ten years? The 15th to 24th years of Akbar's reign, for assessment of revenue in the reigns of Jahāngīr, Shāh Jahān and 'Alamgīr I? Could anything more improbable be imagined? Specially when ḥāl ḥāṣil (actual yield) figures were demanded every year even from jāgīrdārs (Irfan Habib, p. 263). Even here we need not depend upon historical probability alone because a *Dastūr-u'l-'amal* (BM Or 2026) which Irfan Habib identifies as belonging to the reign of 'Ālamgīr I, says definitely in two places (f. 20 a and f. 22 b) that these mawāzinahs were maintained "from the beginning of the reign". As the author is concerned with his own period, he does not go back further. It is, however, certain from this statement that the method of decennial average worked in the reign of 'Ālamgīr I since his accession. And this is not mentioned as an innovation. Therefore it can be safely presumed that it worked all the time since the promulgation of the Ā'īn-i-dahsālah. Therefore the figures of ten years in the mawāzinah-i-dahsālah were not dead and ancient records, but very much needed for striking decennial averages. Mawāzinah itself comes from wazn, weighing, and implies comparison, indeed mawāzinah means comparison as well, and the process implied in the name māwazinah-i-dahsālah is one of arriving at a figure after weighing or comparing the figures of ten years, namely by striking an average.

In my article 'Akbar's Revenue Reforms' published in the *Journal of Pakistan Historical Society* (Volume I Part iii) referred to above, I mentioned on p. 214 that *Farhang-i-kārdānī* 'by Jagat Rā'i Shujā'ī ('Abd-u's-Salām ms. 85/315, Muslim University Library, Aligarh) mentions that the process of assessment based on figures of ten years was continuous and did not come to an end after the first assessment or valuation. Irfan Habib says that the manuscript refers to "the assessment of the jam' under nasaq, while Dr. Qureshi has in mind (one presumes) the rate of revenue under zabt" (p. 209 f.n. 50). No evidence has been adduced to support the thesis that the *Farhang-i-kārdānī* refers to nasaq and not to assessment under the ḍabṭī system. In a model appointment letter for a local amīn, (f. 29 a), it is laid down that he should make the assessment in time after examining the crops and completing the record of mawāzinah-i-dahsālah and the contiguous past year (sāl-i-guzashtah wa paiwastah). This embodies three processes:—(i) the maintenance of decennial figures (mawāzinah-i-dahsālah,) (ii) the incorporation of the figures of the immediately preceding year and (iii) the assessment *on the basis of these figures* for the year concerned. This is clearly ḍabṭ and not nasaq, because the *Ā'īn-i-dahsālah* relates to ḍabṭ, the rates wherein were calculated on decennial averages of mean produce.

In yet another manuscript (also listed by Irfan Habib) Ude Chand's *Dastūr-u'l-'amal-i-sarishtahjāt* (Edinburgh Oriental 83) there is information that confirms these points. This author has a description of the duties of the amīn which narrates the various aspects of his work. From our point of view the most important point is that the amīn has to base his assessment on the figures of twelve years including the mawāzinah-i-dahsālah, the preceding contiguous year (sāl-i-guzashtah wa paiwastah) and naturally the year for which the assessment is being made. [I have consulted the microfilm copy in Karachi University Library which does not show the folio numbers. On my counting from the microfilm reader the folio is in all probability 35.] This is the basis of the next step, *ḍabṭī*, where the rates arrived at by the process described above are applied to the land brought under cultivation by the peasant (*ibid.*).

From the above it can be concluded that (i) jins-i-kāmil refers to yield that has not suffered a total or partial failure (ii) 'i'tibār nūmūd' means 'was recognized or adopted as the standard' (iii) harsāl and harsālah alike mean the decennial average of maḥṣūl (medium produce), (iv) the Ā'īn-i-dahsālah provided a mechanism for the assessment of state demand as well as valuation on the basis of harsālah (v) that harsālah provided the standard rate, therefore partial or total failures were taken into consideration at the time of assessment, for which there is ample evidence in the historical literature of the period, (vi) that the method provided by the Ā'īn was the addition of the maḥṣūl (medium produce) for the latest year (preceding the year of assessment) and dropping the figures for the eleventh year counting backwards, (vii) that figures of actual yield were collected every year for keeping the mechanism alive and (viii) that this method worked at least upto the end of the reign of 'Ālamgīr I.

It seems to me that thesc conclusions, based upon evidence that has been adduced above, provide the cogent "technical sense" that Moreland was trying to find and that Irfan Habib has not been able to offer an alternative interpretation that would explain the working of the system in a rational manner.

APPENDIX B

The Ownership of Agricultural Holdings

THE problem of the ownership of agricultural land during the Muslim rule in India has not received the attention which it deserves. Writers on Indian Muslim History generally assume that the Hindu antecedents and the position of the Indian peasant under British rule are sufficient indications of the rights enjoyed by peasants in Muslim India. This uncritical assumption has resulted in perpetuating our ignorance of the true position and lack of interest in positive evidence on this point, and when some writers have stumbled across certain data conflicting with their preconceived notions, they have tried to minimize the importance of the facts which have forced themselves on their attention. A critical examination, therefore, of the available information is necessary to clear our minds of certain prevailing misconceptions.

But, before such an examination is undertaken, it would be useful to define ownership. Austin defines the right of ownership as "right indefinite in point of use, unrestricted in point of disposition and unlimited in point of duration over a determinate thing."[1] John W. Salmond writes: "We may define the right of ownership in a material thing as the general, permanent and inheritable right to the uses of that thing."[2] A foot note adds that "the full power of alienation and disposition is an almost invariable element in the right of ownership, but cannot be regarded as essential, or included in the definition of it." Without going into a discussion of legal niceties, it would be safe to assert that if a peasant could use his holding without any restrictions for the purposes of cultivation; if he could change its nature by planting a garden or building a house, if he had a permanent right of using this holding, if he could sell, transfer or alienate it permanently or for a fixed period, if he could pass it on to his heirs, he should be considered to be the owner of his holding. We should now try to see if he could be called the owner in this sense of the term.

It would help us in understanding the position of the peasant under Muslim rule if we find out his position during the British period. The peasant's status then varied from province to province. Where he was a tenant of a landlord, the question of ownership did not arise; where he was in direct relationship with the state, he was considered to be the conditional owner of his land so long as he paid the rent. Vincent Smith who was an Indian Civil Servant says: "Even the English laws, which contrary to general ancient custom, recognize private property in cultivable land, insist that the land revenue is the first charge on the soil and permit the enforcement of the charge by sale of land free of all incumbrances, in the event of default."[3] The actual position was that where the peasant was concerned, he was in possession of his holding only so long as the lessor, which was the state, did not assert its ownership; the peasant was more like a lessee, who had acquired a perpetual lease which came to an end when he failed to pay the rent. At best this can be called conditional ownership.

[1] Austin, ii, p. 790.

[2] Salmond, p. 395.

[3] Smith, *Early History of India*, p. 138.

Precisely the same seems to be the condition in Hindu India. To understand the real position we have to take into consideration the arguments advanced by different writers on this subject. On the one hand is the view of Vincent Smith who asserts that "the native law of India has ordinarily recognized agricultural land as being crown property."[4] On the opposite extreme is the opinion of Jayaswal who says about this theory, "Some of these writers have confidently asserted that property in the soil, according to the Hindu view, always vested in the Hindu sovereign. The fact, on the other hand, is that it is exactly the reverse of the Hindu theory on the subject."[5] Jayaswal is supported by P. N. Banerjee who asserts that "the king was never regarded as the owner of the land."[6] F. W. Thomas holds a third view; he says; "Apart from the royal domains, which must have been considerable, the ultimate property in the land appertained, in the sense which has since prevailed, to the king; that is to say, the king was entitled to his revenue therefrom, and in default could replace the cultivator in his holding."[7]

This controversy regarding the position of the peasant during the Hindu period is the result of the conflicting interpretations of controversial evidence contained in Megasthenes, the *Arthashāstra* and its commentary. This is not the place to discuss the evidence in detail; suffice it to say that the *Arthashāstra* has evidence of the cultivator being able to sell and alienate his land.[8] But it also speaks of the right of the king to replace him in his holding if he fails to pay the rent.[9] M. H. Gopal calls this a double ownership; the peasant owned the land so long as he paid the rent; the state became the owner when the peasant defaulted.[10] This is not different from the position of the peasant under British rule so far as his right of ownership is concerned.

[4] *Ibid.*, p. 139.

[5] Jayaswal, Pt. II, p. 174.

[6] Banerjee, p. 179.

[7] *Cambridge History of India*, I, p. 475.

[8] Kautilliya, iii, Chapters IX, X.

[9] *Ibid.*, ii, Chapter I.

[10] Gopal, p. 62.

It is hard to blame scholars who have been tempted to jump to the conclusion that there has been no change during the long interval.

The controversial nature of the evidence shows that it is by no means easy to determine the status of the peasant under Hindu rule. To the Muslim ruler, the problem would be even more difficult to disentangle. Besides, it is but human nature that the conqueror should try to find parallels in the institutions of the conquered people to his own usage. The fine shades of legal differences generally get ignored in the haste to set up a system after a conquest. The conqueror would more naturally be guided by his instincts and traditions, and where he finds himself in difficulties, he would turn to the writings of his own experts. The Turks had such an expert in Al-Bīrūnī. Let us turn to him to see what guidance he would give them. Al-Bīrūnī writes: "With regard to what he earns by the crops or from the cattle, he is bound first to pay to the ruler of the country the tax which attaches to the soil or the pasture ground. Further he pays him one-sixth of the income in recognition of the protection which he affords to the subjects, their properties and their families. The same obligation rests also on the common people, but they will always lie and cheat in the declarations about their property. Further, trading businesses, too, pay a tribute for the same reason."[11] In this passage there is a reference to the state share being the first charge on the land, but it is very much in the background. The greater emphasis is on the statement that landed property was like all other property which paid a tax in return for the protection which was given by the state. The king's right to levy a tax was justified by the fact that he gave his subjects protection: there is no suggestion here of the king's right to eject the peasant from his holding; the peasant's right to possess his holding is based practically on the same basis as the merchant's right to his merchandise; as the payment of a tax did not interfere with the proprietary rights of the merchant, similarly the peasant did not lose his right over his holding because he paid a tax. In this passage there is no question

[11] AlBīrūnī, ii, p. 149.

of conditional ownership: if the king possessed the right of ejectment it does not find a clear mention. Al-Bīrūnī's statement would mean only one thing to his contemporary Muslim reader and that would be that the peasant had the right of unconditional, absolute and complete ownership over his holding.

This position the Muslims were certainly inclined to accept as the natural corollary of agriculture: because their own legal system recognized that the peasant was the owner of the land. From the very beginning of Islam the cultivator was looked upon as the owner of the land he cultivated. [2] Yaḥya bin Ādam al-Qurashī has compiled in his *Kitāb-u'l-kharāj* the earliest traditions on kharāj and 'ushr.[13] He has an entire chapter on the problem of buying and selling of kharāji land.[14] He has a similar chapter on "the bringing to life of dead lands" which is a well-known Islamic technicality, for bringing uncultivated and waste land under cultivation.[15] The Prophet unambiguously laid it down that the reviver of dead land is its owner, provided it does not belong to some other owner.[16] This rule applies equally to Muslims and non-Muslims, to those who pay 'ushr and to those who pay kharāj.[17] The *Nūr-u'l-Hidāyah*, a well-known book on Muslim jurisprudence says, "If the owner of kharāji land ... turns a Muslim, he will still have to pay kharāj".[18] This shows not only that the owner of kharāji land had the right to sell and alienate his holding but also that he was looked upon as its owner. Almost any book of Muslim law would contain the same ruling on kharāji land; indeed it sounds superfluous to quote any authorities. The ownership of the land by the peasant has been such an established principle of Muslim law that hitherto it has never been doubted and all law books take it for granted.

12 Abū Yūsuf, pp. 35-38.

13 Yaḥyā bin Ādam al-Qurashī.

14 *Ibid.*, pp. 54 ff. Kharāj and 'ushr are in this context state demand on agricultural produce. For a fuller discussion of the seterms vide I.H. Qureshi, *The Administration of the Sultanate of Dehli*, Chapter VI. Also *Supra*.

15 Yaḥyā bin Ādam al-Qurashī pp. 84 ff.

16 The tradition is in Musnad Imām Aḥmad and Bukhāri.

17 *Nūr-ū'l-Hidāyah*, ii, p.353.

18 *Ibid*.

The Muslim conquerors of India, therefore, would be guided by their law and tradition in laying down the conditions on which agricultural land was to be held by the peasant. In the view of their law, the land belonged to the peasant. Al-Bīrūnī, who may have read his own ideas in discerning the position of the peasant which was not so well defined under the Hindus, led them to believe that the peasant was the owner. Their own tradition is crystallized by Imām Māwardī, the great jurist whose outlook was moulded by practical considerations and who based his discussions on the facts of his environment. He divides kharājī land into two categories: the first is the land acquired by the Muslim state from a combatant population on the terms that the land would belong to the state and the peasant in such land would be a mere tenant who would earn his share of the produce as the wages of his labour; and the second is the land where the conquered population is left in the ownership of the soil. In the second kind of land the peasant has proprietary rights; he is the owner of the holding. The Imām, also, points out the features which distinguish one kind of land from the other. In the land owned by the state, the peasant has no right to sell or alienate his holdings; where the peasant is the owner he can do so.[19] There are instances of state-owned land in the world of Islam; one example is the arḍ-i-mumlikat in Turkey.[20] In India, there is no mention or instance of arḍ-i-mumlikat. The discussion up to this point, it is hoped, has made it clear that the Muslim conquerors could not but look upon the peasant as the proprietor of the land, circumstanced as they were in the matters of their law, their traditions, and their knowledge of the conquered population. The only other possibility for them would have been of declaring their newly conquered territories to be arḍ-i-mumlikat.

The fact that the Muslims did not look upon the land in India as arḍ-i-mumlikat is beyond the pale of controversy. There is not a single occasion in the course of the entire historical literature of the subcontinent where this kind of land has been mentioned

19 Māwardī, (Urdu Tr.) p. 243.

20 Aghnides, p. 376.

On the contrary, Kirāmi (*Fiqh-i-Firūz Shāhī*) mentions the rulings regarding the sale and transfer of kharāji lands by Muslims and dhimmis.[21] This would show that Muslim rulers and jurists regarded the peasant to be the owner of his holding; because if they permitted the sale and transfer of his land by the peasant, they could not have regarded the land to be arḍ-i-mumlikat, and if it is kharāji (and is not arḍ-i-mumlikat), it belongs to the peasant. It should, also, be remembered that the state having once established its ownership over agricultural land was not likely to forego it in a moment of generosity, because the ownership of the peasant's holding gives great power to the state over the cultivator. If we find that the Muslim state in the Indo-Pakistan subcontinent considered the peasant to be the owner of his land, it would not be unreasonable to assume, particularly when there is so much independent evidence as well, that the state never attempted to assert its ownership.

We find in Akbar's reign that the state demand on agricultural produce was not regarded as "rent". On the contrary the *Ā'in-i-Akbarī*—that compendium of administrative regulations and methods, which also has the advantage of being almost an official document—uses phrases like "the wages of guarding", "the emoluments for ruling", "the wages of sovereignty", "the emoluments of sovereignty" for the state demand on agricultural produce.[22] We find in these phrases an echo of Al-Birūnī's theory that the tax charged by the Hindu rulers from their peasant subjects was "the price of protection." The continuity in the tradition of legal ideas seems to be uninterrupted as, indeed, it was. Abū-'l-Faḍl, in the Ā'in relating to the treasurer, discusses under the sub-heading of the means of subsistence, the whole theory of the state demand and calls it the price paid by the subject for the protection afforded by the monarch. The position of the cultivator would become clear from the following statement which Abū-'l-Faḍl makes: "It is evident that in all cultivated areas, the possessors of property are numerous, and they hold their lands by ancestral descent, but

[21] *Fiqh-i-Fīrūzshāhī*, f. 410b-414b.

[22] Abū-'l-Faḍl, *Āin-i-Akbāri*. pp. 291, 292, 297, 298, 300, etc.

through malevolence and spite, their titles become obscured by the dust of uncertainty and the hand of firmness is no longer stretched over them. If a cultivator holds in awe the power of the adorner of the universe and the elixir of the living, and the merchant turn back from evil designing and reflect in his heart on the favour of the lord of the world, the depository of divine grace, his possessions would assuredly be approved of wisdom".[23] This is an unambiguous statement, making it abundantly clear that the author took it for granted that the peasant was as absolute in his ownership of his holding as the merchant in the ownership of his merchandise. This is no conditional ownership; it is absolute, intrinsic and complete. It should be remembered that Abū-'l-Faḍl is a panegyrist of Akbar; he loses no opportunity of exaggerating the rights and powers of the crown. If he abstains from calling the Emperor the owner of the land and his share in the produce of agricultural land the rent accruing to the sovereign from the property, it is a strong proof that the idea of the state ownership of agricultural holdings was repugnant to the legal theory of the day as well as previous tradition which could not have been unknown to a learned writer like our author.

Even more positive evidence is contained in a farmān of 'Ālamgīr I addressed to Muḥammad Hāshim. A translation of this farmān has been published by Sir Jadu Nath Sarkar in his '*Studies in Mughul India*'.[24] The text of this farman has also been incorporated by 'Alī Muḥammad Khān, in the *Mir'at-i-Aḥmadi*. In the lithograph edition of Bombay (1307 A.D.) the text has been badly mutilated. The text printed in the Gaekwad Oriental Series is better, but unfortunately not free from errors.[25] Here is a literal translation of the important passage:—

'When kharāj-i-muwaẓẓaf has been fixed, if the owner of the land is unable to provide the means for cultivation or if he runs away leaving the land uncultivated, give that land on lease or for cultivation to some other person and recover the kharāj from the

[23] *Ibid.*, (Eng. Tr.), ii, p. 52.

[24] Sarkar, *Studies in Mughul India*, pp. 169-187.

[25] 'Alī Muḥammad Khān, i, pp. 268-278.

amount realized from the lease or, if the land has been given to another person for cultivation, realize the kharāj from the share of the owner of the land. If there is any surplus left, pay it to the owner. The land may also be given to some person who is appointed to take the place of the owner so that he may pay the kharāj and utilize the surplus himself. Whenever the owner is able to provide the means of cultivation, the land should be returned to him".[26]

This passage requires a little explanation. Three methods are prescribed here for getting cultivable land cultivated in case the owner is unable to undertake cultivation or he runs away for some reason:—

(i) The state should give the land on lease to some other person and realize the kharāj out of the lease money. It is obvious that the remainder of the income would be paid to the owner.

(ii) The state might employ some man to cultivate the land who would be given a fixed portion of the yield or even a sum of money as his wages. In this case the kharāj would naturally be recovered from the share of the owner, because the man employed to cultivate the land is a mere labourer.

(iii) The state might ask someone tor epresent the owner, he would enjoy the rights of the owner during the time he cultivates the land. It is obvious from the context that this method would be adopted when the owner is absconding. If the owner leaves an heir behind, he would be the most natural person to be appointed his representative.

The peasant has been clearly defined as the owner and an elaborate machinery has been provided to keep up the production and also to safeguard the rights of ownership which is not conditional because it does not depend on the payment of the state demand, but is absolute and complete.

Another passage is worth quoting:– "(If a waste) land is the property of someone and the owner is present and is able to cultivate it, he should be asked to bring it under cultivation; and if such land is not owned by any one, or if its owner is not known,

[26] *Ibid.*, p. 269.

it should be given to some one who has the means of bringing it back to life so that he does so."[27]

In a third passage the farmān speaks of the rule that he who brings unowned waste land 'to life' is its owner, irrespective of his being a Muslim or a non-Muslim. Such land, the farmān lays it down, cannot be taken away from him. The farmān has also rules regarding the realization of the state demand from holdings which have been leased, mortgaged or sold by their owners.[28] This makes it clear that the peasant had all the rights of sale and transfer granted to him by the state.

The text of the farmān is so clear that it should set all controversy at rest, because it not only calls the peasant the owner of the land unambiguously but also enumerates the various accidents which lawyers associate with ownership and provides methods to safeguard those rights even when the state, in its endeavour to maintain the prosperity and productivity of the empire takes steps to keep his holdings under cultivation.

But the evidence contained in the farmān has been challenged. The first ground for this challenge is that a manuscript of the farmān in the Berlin Royal Library has an interleaved commentary in Persian by an unknown author who tries to explain away the term 'the owner of the land' by saying that it could mean only 'the owner of the crops,' for the owner of the land is the sovereign. The only reason advanced for this statement is that the owner of the land would not run away leaving his land and would discharge his obligations to the state by selling it.[29] But surely the reason for running away need not be necessarily the lack of the means of cultivation; it might be the fear of punishment for some crime or some other cause entirely unconnected with the cultivation of the holding. Actually the state was willing to help the cultivator to an extent that running away was not necessary. The text says that the owner might be too poor to undertake cultivation or might run away, and the use of the word 'or' shows

[27] *Ibid.*, p. 289.

[28] *Ibid.*

[29] Sarkar, *Studies in Mughul India*, pp. 172.

that the two contingencies might not be connected. In one of the passages quoted above the farmān mentions 'the owner of desert or waste land': how could the owner of a desert or waste land be 'the owner of the crops' of a cropless holding? Similarly the man who has mortgaged or leased his land to another man for cultivation can, by no stretch of imagination, be called the owner of the crops. Actually the commentary contradicts itself at so many places that it cannot be taken seriously by any student of history and therefore its objections can be dismissed.

The other objections come from Moreland, who holds the view that the farmān deals with matters which have no reference to facts of agrarian administration in India.[30] It would be better to bear in mind the fact that this farmān is not a theoretical enunciation of legal principles in a text-book, but a document of instructions sent by the Emperor to an official of the state. However, let us examine Moreland's reasons:—

(i) "The anonymous commentator whose observations are included in Professor Sarkar's translation of the farman was obviously puzzled by the unfamiliar term (that is, 'the owner')."

The reply to that objection is that the commentator has not been proved to be a contemporary; a man living during the days of post-'Ālamgīr anarchy or later would naturally be puzzled because a new theory was coming into existence which resulted in the establishment of the zamindari system.

(ii) "The force of parts of the farmān is distorted by the conception of land devoted permanently to a particular crop."

I have not been able to discover any such passage.

(iii) "We are given detailed rules for lands under dates and almonds, which were almost, irrelevant in India, but we find nothing about the particular difficulties connected with characteristic Indian crops such as sugarcane."

Dates are not mentioned; probably Moreland is referring to grapes and almonds. The passage occurs in connection with gardens and not with agricultural crops. Certain general rules regarding gardens have been mentioned; grapes and almonds, on

[30] Moreland, pp. 139, 140.

account of their different nature, have been exempted from these rules. This passage has a relevance, because the Empire included Kashmir as well as parts of Baluchistan, the North West Frontier and modern Afghanistan and these areas are well known for the cultivation of these crops. The cultivation of grapes was not unknown in India proper as well. The farmān is not referring to any difficulties in growing these crops, it only is referring to the rate of assessment of state demand. In connection with sugarcane and other characteristically Indian crops, the farman takes schedules of the demand rate for granted.

(iv) "The farman stresses the distinction between tithe land and tribute land . . . but I have failed so far to find a single case of tithe land existing in India . . ."

One can only say that Moreland has overlooked important evidence contained in *Chachnāmah*, *Tārīkh-i-Fakhr-u'd-dīn Mubārakshāh*, *Futūḥāt-i-Fīrūzshāhī* and *Fiqh-i-Fīrūzshāhī*.[31]

Hence the items which Moreland considers to be irrelevant were part of the agrarian administration of India; and, therefore, the farmān and the evidence which it contains cannot be dismissed so easily. The farmān should not be looked upon as a complete manual of instructions; it only brings to the notice of the officers concerned certain definite needs felt at the time. The main thing is that it does not contain a new instruction to look upon the peasant as the owner of the land but takes his ownership for granted.

A number of modern writers have suggested that the peasant's holding was confiscated in case of rebellion and, therefore, ownership could not be complete. The punishment for high treason and rebellion could extend to the confiscation of property; this applied to movable as well as immovable property. This confiscation, however, was only punishment; it falls under a different legal category; it was not the resumption of its own property by the state. Such confiscation is, therefore, entirely irrelevant in considering the legal rights of the peasant. It should, however, be remembered that the confiscation of agricultural holdings would be

[31] I.H. Qureshi, *The Administration of the Sultanate of Dehlī*, pp. 101, 102.

a very rare phenomenon because the state would gain nothing. An empty holding is no asset, and there was but little competition for land in those days for there was still plenty of land awaiting development. Besides an unemployed desperate peasant without any stake would be a source of greater danger, and in those days of deep forests it would be well nigh impossible to punish him. Muḥammad bin Tughluq made the mistake of alienating the peasantry of the Doab and we all know the results. Indeed it was the consistent policy of the state to increase production and because there was a great deal of uncultivated land and the pressure on land, owing to the smallness of population and the wider opportunities of alternative employment, was much weaker, a peasant was a cherished asset. The entire historical literature of the period lays emphasis on the fact that the peasant was the foundation of the property and wealth of the state.[32] It is generally not realized that one of the causes of the stability and progress of the Muslim dominion in India was the instinctive alliance between the state and the peasantry who were protected from the exactions and tyranny of the hereditary chiefs.[33] It is significant that Baranī uses the word 'Hindū' for the chieftains and the men of upper classes, the peasantry are always thought of as a separate class and the mainstay of Muslim empire in India.[34]

It has been suggested that the relations between the state and the peasantry were governed by the conception of duty so far as the peasants were concerned and not by the determination of rights. An elementary knowledge of Muslim law would convince the inquirer that the Shar' takes cognizance both of rights and duties. We have already noticed how the right of ownership was guaranteed and respected. We hear of the duty of the peasant to cultivate his holding under 'Ālamgīr I, but this duty did not make the peasant's ownership partial or conditional.[35] He still remained the owner whether he cultivated his soil or not; even when the

[32] *Ibid.*, p. 206.

[33] Baranī, p. 432.

[34] *Ibid.*, pp. 287, 288.

[35] Just as the state may billet soldiers in private houses, but this does not take away the proprietary rights of the owner of the house.

state cultivated the holding for him, it respected his right of ownership. The duty to cultivate the land was a public duty; its purpose was to keep up the level of production; it nowhere interfered with the peasant's right to ownership.

'Ālamgīr I's farmān as well as the law-books give the right to the peasant to build a house on his holdings, to convert it into a garden or endow it for charitable purposes. Thus all the incidents of property which were mentioned in the beginning of this discussion are found to be included in the rights of the peasants. An eighteenth century writer, who was not too far removed from the period, reaches the same conclusion regarding the ownership of land. He bases his arguments mostly on Islamic law.[36] Actually the proprietary rights of the peasant in his holding are so manifest that it is surprising that any contrary opinion should have been held at any time.

[36] Ameer Hyder Belgramy, Chapter II, pp. 73, 75.

APPENDIX C

The Mughul Emperors

A.H.		A.C.
932	Bābur, Ẓahīr-u'd-dīn Muḥammad	1526
937	Humāyūn, Naṣīr-u'd-dīn Muḥammad	1530
(945	(Sher Shāh Sūr)	1538)
962	Humāyūn (restored)	1555
963	Akbar Jalāl-u'd-dīn Muḥammad	1556
1014	Jahāngīr, Nūr-u'd-dīn Muḥammad	1605
1037	Dāwar Bakhsh	1627
1037	Shāh Jahān, Shihāb-u'd-dīn Muḥammad	1628
1068	Murād Bakhsh	1657
1068	Shāh Shūjā'	1657
1068	'Ālamgīr, Muḥiy-i'd-dīn Muḥammad Awrangzīb	1658
1118	A'ẓam Shāh'	1707
1119	Kām Bakhsh	1707

A.H.		A.C.
1119	Shāh ‘Ālam Bahādur, Quṭb-u’d-dīn Muḥammad	1707
1124	‘Aẓīm-u’sh-Shān	1712
1124	Jahāndār Shāh, Mu‘izz-u’d-dīn	1712
1124	Farrukh-siyar, Mu‘in-u’d-dīn Muḥammad	1713
1131	Rafī‘-u’d-Darajāt, Shams-u’d-dīn Muḥammad Abū-’l-Barakat	1719
1131	Shāh Jahān II, Shams-u’d-dīn Muḥammad Rafī‘-u’d-Dawlah	1719
1131	Muḥammad Shāh, Nāṣir-u’d-dīn	1719
(1132	Ibrāhīm, Muḥammad	1720)
1161	Aḥmad Shāh Bahādur, Mujāhid-u’d-dīn	1748
1167	‘Ālamgīr II, ‘Azīz-u’d-dīn Muḥammad	1754
1173	Shāh Jahān III	1759
1173	Shāh ‘Ālam II, Jalāl-u’d-dīn Muhammad	1759
(1202	Bīdār Bakht	1788)
1221	Akbar II, Mu‘īn-u’d-dīn Muḥammad	1806
1253	Bahādur Shāh II, Sirāj-u’d-dīn Muḥammad	1837

A Select Bibliography

(Books on the Islamic and Hindu background have not been listed unless there are references to them. For these the reader is referred to a fairly detailed bibliography in I. H. Qureshi, *The Administration of the Sultanate of Dehli.*

It has been impossible to be fully logical in the alphabetical arrangement of the names of the Muslim and Hindu authors of the period. Normally the better known part of the name has been selected for guidance. References are by the part of the name selected. The method of using surnames only was fraught with difficulties because of their occasional multiplicity).

B.M. = British Museum, London.
I.O. = India Office Library, London.
Bod. = Bodleian Library, Oxford.
Bib. Nat. = Bibliotheque National, Paris.
Bib. Ind. = Bibliotheca Indica.

All Ethe' numbers are in I.O.L.

Abdul Aziz, *The Mansabdari System and the Mughul Army*, Lahore, 1942.

Abdul Aziz, *Thrones, tents and their furniture used by the Indian Mughuls*, Lahore, n.d.

'Abd-u'l-Ḥamīd Lāhūrī, *Pādshāhnāmah*, Bib. Ind., Calcutta, 1866-72.

'Abd-u'l-Ḥayy, *Kitāb-u't-tarātīb-u'l-idāriyah*, Rabat, 1346 A.H.

'Abd-u'llah, *Tārīkh-i-Dāūdī*, ed. S.A. Rashid, Aligarh, 1954. also B.M. Or 197.

'Abd-u'r-Razzāq, *Maṭla'-u's-sa'dain*, Volume ii, Ethe' 193.

'Abd-u'ṣ-Ṣamad, *Inshā'-i-Abū-'l-Faḍl*, Kānpūr, 1872.

Abū-'l-Faḍl, *Ā'īn-i-Akbarī*, Ed. Blochmann, Bib. Ind., Calcutta, 1867-77; English Translation by Blochmann and Jarret, Bib. Ind., Calcutta, 1894.

Abū-'l-Faḍl, *Akbarnāmah*, Bib. Ind., Calcutta, 1873-87.

Imām Abū Yūsuf, *Kitāb-u'l-kharāj*, Cairo, 1302 A.H.

Shams-i-Sirāj 'Afif, *Tārīkh-i-Fīrūz Shāhī*, Bib. Ind., Calcutta, 1891.

Nicholas P. Aghnides, *Muhammadan Theories of Finance*, New York, 1916.

M.B. Ahmad, *The Administration of Justice in Medieval India* Karachi, 1951.

Shaikh Aḥmad Sarhindī, *Maktūbāt-i-Imām-i-Rabbānī*, Lucknow, 1913.

C. Aitchison, *A Collection of Treaties, Engagements and Sanads*, Calcutta, 1909.

Akhbārāt-i-Dārbār-i-Mu'allā, News-letters from the Imperial Court, 'Ālamgīr's reign, 9 volumes in Case 47 at the R.A.S.

Al-Bīrūnī, *Kitāb-u'l-Hind*, Eng. Tr. by Sachau, London, 1910.

'Alī Muḥammad Khān, *Mir'at-i-Aḥmadī*, Ed. Nawab Ali, 2 Vols. and *Supplement*; Baroda, 1927-28, 1930.

Sir Thomas W. Arnold, *The Caliphate*, London, 1884.

Muḥammad Ṭāhir Āshnā, *Shāhjahānnāmah*, Ethe' 331.

Saiyid Ashraf Khān Mīr Muḥammad al-Ḥusainī, *Raqā'im-i-karā'im*, Ethe' 375.

John Austin, *Lectures on Jurisprudence*, London, 1911.

Mīr Āzād Bilgrāmī, *Ma'āthir-u'l-kirām*, Lahore, 1913.

Ẓahīr-u'd-dīn Muḥammad Bābur, *Bāburnāmah:* Turki text, Hyderabad Codex, Facsimile reproduction, ed. A.S. Beveridge, Leiden & London, 1905; Persian tr. by 'Abd-u'r-Raḥīm Khān Khānān, Bombay 1308 A.H; English tr. by A.S. Beveridge, London, 1921.

'Abd-u'l-Qādir Badā'ūnī, *Muntakhab-u't-tawārīkh*, ed. Ali Ahmad and Lees, Bib. Ind., Calcutta, 1864-69.

Muḥammad Bakhtāwar Khān, *Mir'at-u'l-'ālam*, B.M. Add. 7657.

P.N. Banerjee, *Public Administration in Ancient India*, London, 1916.

Ḍiyā-u'd-dīn Baranī, *Tārīkh-i-Fīrūz Shāhī*, Bib. Ind., Calcutta, 1862.

Duarte Barbosa, *The Book of Duarte Barbosa*, tr. & ed. by M.L. Dames, London, 1918.

Bāyazīd Bayāt, *Tadhkirah-i-Humāyūn wa Akbar*, ed. M. Hidāyat Ḥusain, Bib. Ind., Calcutta, 1941.

Ameer Hyder Belgramy, " Dissertation concerning the revenue of government and of land tenures according to the Muhammadan Law", *Oriental Miscellany, Vol I*, Calcutta, 1798.

Francois Bernier, *Travels in the Mogul Empire*, tr. A. Constable, 2nd edition, revised by V.A. Smith, London, 1916.

Munshī Bhāg Chand, *Jāmi'-u'l-inshā'*, B.M. Or. 1702.

Rā'i Bindrāban, *Lubb-u't-tawārīkh-u'l-Hind*, Ethe' 358.

E.L. Bogart and D.L. Kemmerer, *Economic History of the American People*, New York, 1947.

Thomas Bowrey, *A Geographical Account of Countries Round the Bay of Bengal*, ed. R.C. Temple, Cambridge, 1905.

Rā'i Chandra Bhān Brahman, *Chahār Chaman-i-Brahman*, B.M. Addl 16,863.

Rā'i Chandra Bhān Brahman, *Qawā'id-i-Salṭanat-i-Shāh Jahān*, forming part of Francis Gladwin, *The Persian Munshi*, Calcutta 1795.

Percy Brown, *Indian Painting under the Mughals*, Oxford, 1924.

Cambridge History of India, IV, Cambridge, 1928.

Rā'i Chatur Man Saksena, *Chahār Gulshan yā Akhbār-i-nawādir*, Bodl. Elliot 366.

Makhan Lal Roy Chaudhury, *Dīn-i-Ilāhī*, Calcutta, 1941.

Chhatar Mal, *Dīwānpasand*, B.M. Or. 2011.

Daftar-i-dīwānī wa māl wa mulkī-i-Sarkār-i-A'lā, Hyderabad, 1939.

Dastūr-u'l-'amal. B.M. Or. 2026.

Dastūr-u'l-'amal, Ethe' 432.

Dastūr-u'l-'amal, Bodleian, Fraser 86.

Dastūr-u'l-'amal, B.M. Addl. 6588.

Dastūr-u'l-'amal, B.M. Or. 1690.

Dastūr-u'l-'amal, Ethe' 415.

Dastūr-u'l-'amal, (collected at the request of Rā'i Ayā Mal) Ethe' 380.

Dastūr-u'l-'amal-i-Awrangzīb 'Ālamgīr Pādshāh Ghāzī, B.M. Addl. 6598.

Dastūr-u'l-'amal-i-'ilm-i-nawīsindagī, B.M. Addl. 6599.

Dastūr-u'l-'amal-i-khāliṣah-i-shārīfah, Edinburgh 230.

Dastūr-u'l-'amal-i-nawīsindagī, B.M. Add. 6641.

Ḍawābiṭ-i-'Ālamgīrī. B.M. Or. 1641.

Elliot & Dowson, *History of India as told by its own Historians*, 8 volumes, London, 1867.

Sir Henry Elliot, *Bibliographical Index to Historians of Mohammadan India*, London, 1849.

Manuel Godinho de Eredia, "*Description of Indostan and Guzarate*" ed. and tr. H. Hosten, JASB, Letters, IV, 1938.

W.A. Erskine, *A History of India under the First two Sovereigns of the House of Taimūr*, London, 1854.

Faḍl bin Rūzbahān al-Iṣfahānī, *Sulūk-u'l-mulūk*, B.M. ms. Or. 253

Ilah Dād Faiḍī Sarhindī, *Akbarnāmah*, B.M. Or. 169.

Muḥammad bin Manṣūr Quraishī alias Fakhr-i-mudabbir, *Ādāb-u'l-mulūk wa kifāyat-u'l-mamlūk*, I.O.L. ms. 647.

'Abd-u'l-Wahhāb Fanā'i, *Gulshan-i-balāghat*, Ethe' 288.

Muḥsin Fānī, *Dabistān-i-madhāhib*, Kanpur, 1904.

Muḥammad ibn-u'l-Ḥusain al-Farrā, *al-Aḥkām-u's-sulṭaniyah*, Cairo, 1938.

Muḥammad Qāsim Firishtah, *Gulshan-i-Ibrāhīmī*, Lucknow, 1865.

Ralph Fitch, *Narrative*, ed. by J.H. Ryley as *Ralph Fitch, England's*

Pioneer in India and Burma, London, 1899.

Peter Floris, *His Voyage to the East Indies in the 'Globe'*, 1611-15, ed. by W.H. Moreland, Hakluyt Society, 2nd Series, LXXIV, London, 1934.

Caesar Frederick (Caesar de Frederici), "Extracts of his eighteen years' Indian Observations", *Purchas his Pilgrims*, Glasgow, 1905.

John Fryer, *A New Account of East India and Persia being Nine Years' Travels*, ed. by W. Crooke, 3 vols., Hakluyt Society, London, 1909, 1912 & 1915.

Futūḥāt-i-Fīrūzshāhī, B.M. Or. 2039.

Ghulām Ḥusain Salīm Zaidpūrī, *Riyāḍ-u's-salāṭīn*, Bib. Ind., Calcutta, 1890.

M.H. Gopal, *Mauryan Public Finance*, London, 1935.

James Grant, *Fihrist-i-ṣubajāt-i-Hindustān*, Ethe, 433.

B.R. Grover, *Nature of Land Rights in Mughal India*, cyclostyled, Delhi, 1961.

Fernao Guerreiro, *Relations*. (Parts) tr. by C.H. Payne as *Jahangir and the Jesuits*, London, 1930.

Gulbadan Begam, *Humāyūnnāmah*, London, 1902.

Irfan Habib, *The Agrarian System of Mughal India*, Bombay, 1963.

Mirzā Ḥaider Dughlat, *Tārīkh-i-Rashīdī*, Eng. tr. by Sir E. Denison Ross, London, 1893.

Har Karan, *Inshā'-i-Har Karan*, ed. & tr. into English by Francis Balfour, Calcutta, 1781.

Ḥasan 'Ali Khān, *Tawārīkh-i-dawlat-i-Sher Shāhī*. Fragment of text and R.P. Tripathi's translation published by S.A. Rashid in *Medieval India Quarterly, Vol. I No. 1.* (1950).

Bikramjit Ḥasrat, *Dārā Shikūh, Life and Works*, Calcutta, 1953.

Muḥammad bin Khalaf bin Ḥayyān, *Akhbārāt-u'l-quḍāt*, Cairo 1947.

S.H. Hodivala, *Historical Studies in Mughal Numismatics*, Bombay, 1938.

S.H. Hodivala, *Studies in Parsi History*, Bombay, 1920.

S.A.Q. Husaini, *Administration under the Mughuls*, Dacca 1952.

S.A.Q. Husaini, *Arab Administration*, Madras, 1949.

S.A.Q. Husaini, *Constitution of the Arab Empire*, Lahore, 1954.

Ibn Hasan, *The Central Structure of the Mughal Empire*, London, 1936.

Ibn Khaldūn, *Muqaddimah*. Urdu Translation by Shams-u'l-'ulamā Mawlawi 'Abd-u'r-Raḥmān, Lahore, 1904. English translation by Franz Rosenthal, London, 1958.

Ibn Sa'd, *A'ṭ-Ṭabaqāt-u'l-kubrā*. Beirut 1957.

'Ināyat-u'llah Khān, *Aḥkām-i-'Ālamgirī*, B.M. Addl. 26238.

'Ināyat-u'llah Khān, *Kalimāt-i-ṭaiyibāt*, Ethe' 373.

'Ināyat-u'llah Rāsikh, *'Ināyatnāmāh*, Ethe' 411.

Intikhāb-i-Jahāngīr Shāhī, B.M. Or. 1648.

W. Irvine, *The Army of the Indian Mughals*, London, 1903.

Izad Bakhsh Rasā, *Riyāḍ-u'l-widād*, B.M. Or. 1725.

Jagat Ra'i Shujā'i, *Farhang-i-kārdānī*, 'Abd-u's-Salām ms. 85/315, Muslim University Library, Aligarh.

Jagjīvan Dās, *Jam'-i-kāmil ba-qaid-i-gūshwārah-i-ṣūbajāt*, Ethe,' 434

Jagjīwan Dās Gujrātī, *Muntakhab-u't-tawārīkh*, B.M. Add. 26, 253.

Nūr-u'd-dīn Muḥammad Jahāngīr, *Tūzuk-i-Jahāngīrī*, Ghazipur and Aligarh, 1863-64. English Translation by Rogers and Beveridge, 2 volumes, London, 1909-14.

Jai Singh, *'Arḍdāshts*, 1655-58 & c. R.A.S. Pers. Cat. 173.

Shaikh Ismā'il al-Jarrāḥi, *Kashf-u'l-khifā*, Cairo, 1351 A.H.

Du Jarric's account of the Jesuit missions to the Court of Akbar. tr. by C. H. Payne, *Akbar and the Jesuits*. London, 1926.

Jawhar Āftābchī, *Tadhkirat-u'l-wāqi'āt*, B.M. Add. 16, 711.

S. Jayaswal, *Hindu Polity*, Calcutta, 1924.

K.M. Jhaveri, *Imperial Farmans (A.D. 1677 to A.D. 1805) granted to the ancestors of the Tikayat Maharaj*, Bombay, 1928.

Wollebrand Geleynssen de Jongh, Extracts from, tr. by W.H. Moreland, as "A Dutch Account of Mogul Administrative Methods" JIH, IV, 1925-26.

John Jourdain, *Journal* 1608-17. ed. Foster, Hakluyt Society, 2nd Series, No. XVI, Cambridge, 1905.

Kaifiyat-i-ṣubajāt-i-mumālik-i-maḥrūsah-i-Hindustān, B.M. Or. 1779

Abū-'l-Khaṭṭāb 'Umar bin Shaikh, commonly called Ibn Diḥyah al-Kalabī, *Kitāb-u'n-nibrās fī tārīkh-i-khulafā-i-Banī 'Abbās,*

(edited by 'Abbās-al-'Azawi, Baghdad, 1946.)

Kāmgār Ḥusainī, *Ma'āthir-i-Jahāngīrī*, B.M. Or. 171.

Muḥammad Hādi Kāmwar Khān, *Haft Gulshan*, Ethe' 394.

Muḥammad Hādi Kāmwar Khān, *Tadhkirat-u's-salāṭīn-i-Chaghatā*, Ethe' 395.

Imām 'Alā-u'd-dīn Abī Bakr bin Mas'ud-al-Kāsāni, *Kitābu badā'i'-iṣ-ṣanai'-fī-tartīb-ish-sharai'*, Cairo, 1910.

Kautillya, *Arthashastra*, Eng. Tr. Shama Shastry, Mysore, 1923.

Muḥammad Kāẓim, *'Ālamgirnāmah*, Bib. Ind., Calcutta, 1865-73.

Kewal Rām, *Tadhkirat-u'l-umarā*, B.M. Add. 16703.,

Muṣtafā bin 'Abd-u'llah Khalīfah, *Kashf-u'ẓ-ẓunūn 'an asāmi'l-kutub wa'l-funūn*, Istanbul, 1941.

Khānahzād Khān, *Inshā'-i-Khānahzād Khān*, B.M. Or. 1410.

Shaikh Zain Wafā'i Khawāfī, *Ṭabaqāt-i-Bāburī*, B.M. Or. 1999.

Muḥammad Hāshim Khawāfī Khān, *Muntakhab-u'l-lubāb*. Bib. Ind., Calcutta, 1860-74, 1909-25.

Khuda Bakhsh, *Essays, Indian and Islamic*, London, 1912.

Khulāṣat-u'l-inshā, B.M. Or. 1750.

Amīr Khusraw Dehlawī, *Diwalrānī Khiḍr Khān*, Aligarh, 1917.

Khwāndamīr (Ghiyāth-u'd-dīn), *Ḥabīb-u's-siyar*, Bombay, 1857.

Ya'qūb Muẓaffar Kirāmi, *Fiqh-i-Fīrūzshāhī*, Ethe 2564.

Von Kremer, *Kulturgeschichtliche Streifzuge*, Eng. tr. by Khuda Bakhsh, in *Contributions to the History of Islamic Civilization*, Calcutta, 1929-30.

Lachhmī Narāyan Shafīq Awrangābādī, *Ḥaqīqathā-'i-Hindustān*, B.M. Or. 1710.

Joannes De Laet, *De Imperio Magni Mogolis*, &c., tr. by J. S. Hoyland and annotated by S.N. Banerjee as, *The Empire of the Great Mogol*, Bombay, 1983.

Letters of 'Ālamgīr I to Prince Muḥammad A'ẓam Shāh, Ethe' 383.

J.H. van Linschoten, *The Voyage of John Huyghen van Linschoten to the East Indies*, ed. A.C. Burnell (Vol. I) and P.A. Tiele (Vol. II), Hakluyt Society, Vols. 70-71, London, 1885.

Mirzā Mahdī Khān Ṣafawī, *Majmū'ah-i-Mirzā Mahdī Khānī*, Ethe' 412.

'Ain-u'l-mulk Māhrū, *Inshā'-i-Māhrū*, Bankipore ms.

R.H. Major, *India in the XV Century*, Hakluyt Society, London, 1857.

Malikzādah, *Nigārnāmah-i-Munshī*, Lucknow, 1882.

Fray Sebastien Manrique, *Travels*, tr. C. E. Luard and Hosten, 2 vols., Hakluyt Society, series 2, volumes 59, 61, London, 1927.

Niccolao Manucci, *Storia do Mogor*, 1656-1712, tr. by W. Irvine, 4 vols., London, 1907-8.

John Marshall, *Notes and Observations on East India*, ed. S. A. Khan, *John Marshall in India—Notes and Observations on Bengal*, London, 1927.

Streynsham Master, *The Diaries of Streynsham Master, 1675-80, & Other Contemporary Papers relating thereto*, ed. by R.C. Temple, Indian Records Series, 2 Vols., London 1911.

Muḥammad Ma'ṣūm, *Tārīkh-i-Shāh Shujā'ī*, Ethe' 340.

Mīr Ma'ṣūm, *Tārīkh-i-Sind*, ed. by U. M. Daudpota, Poona, 1938.

Abū-'l-Ḥasan 'Alī al-Māwardī, *al-Aḥkām-u's-sulṭāniyah*, Cairo, 1298 A.H.

Mirzā Maẓhar Jān Jānān Shahid, *Kalimāṭ-i-ṭayyibāt*, Delhi, 1309 A.H.

James Mill, *The History of British India*, 4th Edition, London, 1848.

Mir'at-u'l-ḥaqā'iq, Bodleian, Fraser, 124.

A. Monserrate, *Commentary on his Journey to the Court of Akbar*, tr. by J. S. Hoyland and annotated by S. N. Banerjee, Cuttack, 1922.

A. Monserrate, *Informacion de los X'pianos de S. Thome'*, Portions tr. by H. Hosten, JASB, NS XVIII, 1922.

Radhakumud Mookerji, *History of Indian Shipping*, Bombay, 1957.

W. H. Moreland, *From Akbar to Aurangzīb*, London, 1923.

W. H. Moreland, *India at the Death of Akbar*, London, 1920.

W. H. Moreland, *The Agrarian System of Moslem India*, Cambridge, 1929.

Anand Ram Mukhliṣ, *Safarnāmah-i-Mukhliṣ*, ed. S. Azhar Ali, Rampur, 1946.

Anand Ram Mukhliṣ, *Mir'at-u'l-iṣṭilāḥ*, B.M. Or. 1913.

Peter Mundy, *Travels*, Vol: II: *Travels in Asia*, ed. by Sir R. C.

Temple, Hakluty Society, London, 1914.

Muḥammad Murtaḍā al-Ḥusainī, *Tāj-u'l-'urūs*, Cairo, 1360 A.H.

Rizq-u'llah Mushtāqī, *Wāqi'āt-i-Mushtāqī*, B.M. Or. 1929.

Sāqī Musta'id Khān, *Ma'āthir-i-'Ālamgīrī*, Bib. Ind., Calcutta, 1870-73.

Mu'tamad Khān, *Iqbālnāmah-i-Jahāngīrī*, Bib. Ind., Calcutta, 1865.

Mehta Īsardās Nāgar, *Futūḥāt-i-'Ālamgirī*, B.M. Add. 23, 884.

Najaf 'Alī, *Risālah-i-manāṣib*, B.M. Or. 1906.

Najaf 'Alī Khān, *Sharḥ-i-Ā'īn-i-Akbarī*, B.M. Or. 1667.

Saiyid Najib Ashraf Nadwī, *Ruqqa'āt-i-'Ālamgīr*, Azamgarh, 1930.

'Ārif a'n-Nakdi, *Al-Qaḍā-fi-'l-Islām*, Damascus, 1922.

Nand Rām Shrivāstava, *Siyāqnāmah*, Lucknow, 1879.

Ni'mat Khān 'Ālī, *Waqā'i'*, Lucknow, 1259 A.H.

'Alā-u'd-dīn Ghaibī Iṣfahānī Mirzā Natthan, *Bahāristān-i-ghaibī*, English translation by Borah, 2 Vols., Gauhati, 1936.

'Abd-u'l-Bāqī Nihāwandī, *Ma'āthir-i-Raḥīmi*, Bib. Ind., 3 Vols., Calcutta, 1910-31.

Niẓām-u'd-dīn Aḥmad, *Ṭabaqāt-i-Akbarī*, 3 Vols: Calcutta, 1913, 1927, 1931 & 1935.

Abū 'Alī Ḥasan Ṭūsī Niẓām-u'l-mulk, *Siyāsatnāmah*, edited by Charles Scheffer, Paris, 1897.

Notes and Letters of 'Ālamgīr in reply to letters from Prince Mu'aẓẓam Shāh and Dhū-'l-fiqār Khān, Ethe' 384.

Nūr Muḥammad, *Ruqqa'āt-i-Shaikh Abū-'l-Faḍl*, Ethe' 287.

Nūr-u'l-Ḥaqq al-Mashraqī-a'd-Dehlawī, *Zubdat-u't-tawārikh*, B.M. Addl. 10580.

Nūr-u'l-hidāyah, tr. into Urdu as *Sharḥ-i-wiqāyah*, Kanpur, 1310 A.H.

Shihāb-u'd-dīn Aḥmad bin 'Abd-u'l-Wahhāb a'n-Nuwairī, *Nihāyat-u'l-irab fī funūn-i'l-adab*, Cairo, 1926.

J. Ovington, *A Voyage to Surat in the Year 1689*, ed., by H. G. Rawlinson, London, 1929.

Francisco Pelsaert, *Remonstrantie*, tr. by Moreland and Geyl, as *Jahangir's India*, Cambridge, 1925.

Beni Prasad, *History of Jahāngīr*, Allahabad, 1940.

Ishwari Prasad, *Life and Times of Humayun*, Bombay, 1955.

'Abū-'l-Fatḥ Qābil Khān and Muḥammad Ṣādiq Muṭṭallibī, *Ādāb-i-'Ālamgīrī*, Ethe' 371.

Amīna Qazwīnī, *Pādshāhnāmah*, B.M. Or. 173.

I. H. Qureshi, *The Administration of the Sultanate of Dehli*, 4th Edition, Karachi, 1956.

I. H. Qureshi, *The Muslim Community of the Indo-Pakistan subcontinent*, The Hague, 1962.

Al-Qurṭubī, See 'Umar bin 'Abd-u'llah

T. Raychaudhuri, *Bengal Under Akbar and Jahangir*, Calcutta, 1953.

'Alī Khān Rāzī, *Wāqi'āt-i-'Ālamgīrī*, also called *Ẓafarnāmah-i-'Ālamgīrī*, Ethe' 345.

Amīn Aḥmad Rāzī, *Haft Iqlīm*, B.M. Or. 203.

Relations of Golconda in the Early Seventeenth Century, a collection of the relations of Methwold, Schorer and an anonymous Dutch factor, ed. & tr. by W. H. Moreland, Hakluyt Society, London, 1931.

Thomas Roe, *The Embassy of Sir Thomas Roe*, 1615-19, ed. W. Foster, London, 1926.

Ruqqa'āt-i-'Ālamgīr, Kanpur, 1884.

Sabad Mal, *Ramz wa ishārahāi'i-'Ālamgīrī*, B.M. Add. 26, 240.

Muḥammad Ṣādiq Khān, *Shāhjahānāmah*, B.M. Or. 174.

Ṣāḥib Rā'i Sūrdāj, *Durr-u'l-'ulūm*, Bodl, Walker 104.

Banarsi Prasad Saksena, *History of Shah Jahan of Dihli*, Allahabad, 1932.

Joseph Salbancke, *'Voyage'* Purchas MacLehose III.

Muḥammad Ṣāliḥ Kanbū Lāhūrī *'Amal-i-Ṣāliḥ*, 4 Vols., Bib. Ind., Calcutta, 1912-46.

Muḥammad Ṣāliḥ Kanbū Lāhūrī, *Bahār-i-sukhan* B.M. Or. 178.

John W. Salmond, *Jurisprudence*, London, 1907.

Ṣāmṣām-u'd-dawlah Shah Nawāz Khān, *Ma'āthir-u'l-'umarā*, Bib. Ind., 3 Vols., Calcutta, 1887-94.

P. Saran, *The Provincial Government of the Mughals*, Allahabad, 1941.

Jadunath Sarkar, *Fall of the Mughal Empire*, Calcutta, 1949.

Jadunath Sarkar, *History of Aurangzeb*, Calcutta, 1921.

Jadunath Sarkar, *Mughal Administration*, Calcutta, 1952.

Jadunath Sarkar, *Studies in Mughal India*, Calcutta, n.d.

Shams-u'd-dīn a's-Sarkhasī, *Kitāb-u'l-mabsūṭ*, Cairo (1st edition), n.d.

'Abbās Khān Sarwānī, *Tuḥfah-i-Akbarshāhī*, Ethe' 219.

Girdlamo Seringi, see Vasco da Gama.

Muḥammad Shafī', "Farmans of Babur, Sher Shah and Humayun", *Oriental College Magazine*, Lahore, Vol. IX, No. 3, May 1933.

Imām Shāfi'ī, *Ar-risālah*, Edited by Aḥmad Muḥammad Shākir, Cairo, 1940.

Selected documents of Shah Jahan's Reign, published by the Daftar-i-Diwani, Hyderabad, Deccan, 1950.

Shāh Nawāz Khān, Ṣamṣām-u'd-dawlah, *Ma'āthir-u'l-umarā*, Bib. Ind., 3 Vols. Calcutta, 1887-94.

Shākir Khān, *Tārīkh-i-Shākir-Khānī*, B.M. Addl. 6585.

Muḥammad Sharīf Najafī, *Majālis-u's-salāṭīn*, B.M. Or. 1903.

'Alī Isḥāq Ibrāhīm a'sh-Shīrāzī, *Al-muhadhdhab*, Cairo, 1776 A.H.

Sri Ram Sharma, *Mughal Government and Administration*, Bombay, 1951.

Vincent Smith, *Akbar, the Great Moghul*, Delhi, 1958.

Vincent Smith, *Early History of India*, Oxford, 1924.

Richard Steel and John Crowther, *Journal*, 1615-16, Purchas McLehose, IV.

Sudhari Lal, *Tuḥfah-i-Shāhjahānī*, Ethe' 337.

Sujān Rā'i Bhandārī, *Khulāṣat-u't-tawārīkh*, ed. Zafar Hasan, Delhi, 1918.

Saiyyid Sulaimān Nadwī, *Ḥayāt-i-Shiblī*, Azamgarh, 1943.

Saiyyid Sulaimān Nadwī, *Hindū'on kī ta'līm Musalmānon ke 'ahd men*, Karachi, 1958.

Shihāb-u'd-dīn Ṭālish, *Fatḥiyah-i-'ibriyah*, Bodl, Or. 589.

Syed Ahmed Khan, *Āthār-u'ṣ-ṣanādīd*, Delhi, 1954.

Muḥammad bin Jarīr a'ṭ-Ṭabarī, *Tārīkh-u'l-umam wa-'l-mulūk*, Cairo, n.d.

Tadhkirat-u'l-khulafā fī tawṣiyati-'l-mulūk wa'l-umarā, I.O.L. Delhi Persian Collection No. 910.

Tara Chand, *The Influence of Islam on Indian Culture*, Allahabad, 1946.

Jean-Baptiste Tavernier, *Travels in India*, tr. by V. Ball, 2nd edition revised by W. Crooke, London, 1925.

Edward Terry, *A Voyage to East India*, London 1665.

Thākur La'l, *Dastūr-u'l-'amal-i-Shāhanshāhī*, B.M. Addl. 22831.

Jean de Thevenot, *Relation de l'Indostan*, ed. S. N. Sen in *The Indian Travels of Thevenot and Careri*, New Delhi, 1949.

Edward Thomas, *Revenue Resources of the Mughal Empire in India, from 1593 to 1707*, London, 1871.

Imām Tirmidhī, *Jāmi'-u't-Tirmidhī ma' Sharḥ-i-Tuḥfat-u'l-Aḥwadhī*, Edited by Mawlānā 'Abd-u'r-Rāḥmān Mubārakpūrī, Delhi, 1346-1349 A.H.

Early travels in India (1583-1619), being a collection of the narratives of Fitch, Mildenhall, Hawkins, Finch, Withington, Coryat and Terry. ed. W. Foster, London, 1927.

R. P. Tripathi, *Some Aspects of Muslim Administration*, Allahabad, 1936.

Ibn Ḥazm al-Undulusī, *al-Muḥaṭṭā*, Damascus, 1352 A.H.

John van Twist *'A General Description of India'*, extracts, tr. by W.H. Moreland, JIH, XVI (1937).

Ude Chand, *Dastūr-u'l-'amal-i-sarishtahjāt*, Oriental ms. 83, Edinburgh.

'Umar bin 'Abd-u'llah al-Qurṭubī, *Kitāb-u'l-istī'āb fī ma'rifat-ī'l-aṣḥāb*, Hyderabad, Deccan, 1336 A.H.

Pietro Della Valle, *The Travels of Pietro Della Valle in India*, tr. Edward Grey, Hakluyt Society, 2 Vols. London, 1892.

Viladimirtrov, *Chingiz Khan*, Eng. tr. D. S. Mirsky, New York, 1930.

Muḥammad Wārith, *Tatimmah-i-Pādshāhnāmah*, B.M. Or. 1675.

Vasco da Gama's First Voyage, Hakluyt Society, London, 1898 (contains extracts from Girdlamo Seringi's letters).

J. Xavier, *Letters, 1593-1617*, tr. by Hosten, JASB., NS., XXIII, 1927.

Aḥmad Yādgār, *Tārīkh-i-salāṭīn-i-Afāghinah*, Bib. Ind. Calcutta, 1939.

Yaḥyā bin Ādam al-Qurashī, *Kitāb-u'l-kharāj*, Cairo, 1347 A.H.

Yaḥyā Khān, *Tadhkirat-u'l-mulūk*, Ethe' 409.

Khwājah Yāsīn, *Sharḥ-i-iṣṭilāḥat*, Add. 6603.

Yusuf Husain Khan ed. *Selected Documents of Aurangzeb's Reign, 1659-1706*, Hyderabad, 1958.

Yusuf Husain Khan, *Selected Waqā'i' of the Deccan, 1660-1671*, Hyderabad, 1953.

Yūsuf Mīrak, *Maẓhar-i-Shāhjahānī*, Karachi, 1961.

Jurjī Zaydān, *Tārīkh-u't-tamaddun-u'l-Islāmī*, Cairo, 1902.

PERIODICALS

Bengal Past and Present, Calcutta.

Indian Culture, Calcutta.

Islamic Culture, Hyderabad.

Journal of Indian History, Allahabad, Madras, Trivandrum.

Journal of the Asiatic Society of Bengal, Calcutta.

Journal of the Pakistan Historical Society, Karachi.

Ma'ārif, Azamgarh.

Medieval India Quarterly, Aligarh.

The Oriental College Mazagine, Lahore.

Oriental Miscellany, Calcutta.

Proceedings of the Indian History Congress.

Proceedings of the Pakistan History Conference.

Index